UNMESH R. JADHAV

# C.A.G.E.

*journey from crisis to clarity*

First published by Soul Sereenity Publication 2023



First edition

ISBN: 9789334001310

This book was professionally typeset on Reedsy.
Find out more at reedsy.com

# Contents

III PLAYING THE GAME FOR EXTRAORDINARY LIFE



IV THE RIPPLE EFFECT OF SPIRITUAL LIVING

# Preface

Thank you for your interest in my book. It means a lot to me that you've chosen to spend your precious time reading this book.

What are your first thoughts when you hear the word CAGE? Limitations on liberty, or confinement? However, I have employed CAGE to help us escape the impasse we find ourselves in. This book offers a guide to finding ever lasting happiness by applying four key spiritual principles: managing *Change*, practicing *Acceptance* , cultivating an attitude of *Gratitude* and letting go of *Expectations*.

Like most of you, I've had problems in my personal and professional life. I tried to figure out why my happiness was always tied to things outside of my control. While searching for answers, I was drawn to spirituality by chance rather than choice. I started to read the Bhagavad Gita and other holy texts to learn about spiritual ideas, but my logical mind immediately dismissed them as mere philosophical ideas only useful in books and not in real life. But one of my teachers advised me to try them out for three months with complete devotion. Surprisingly, I discovered that understanding and practicing these spiritual principles had a significant impact on my emotions, relationships, and career.

I'm not a spiritual master, but the idea of sharing these principles came to me two years ago. However not being a professional writer, I assumed that writing a book was not my cup of tea. But the desire to share my learning ultimately overcame my logical mental blockages, and I started penning this book. The journey was not easy; juggling work and passion was challenging, but the desire was stronger than the obstacles, and I was able to finish writing this book with the grace of Lord Krishna.

This book takes you on a roller coaster ride with the main characters as they deal with personal problems and setbacks in their careers. I am convinced that you will relate to these characters as you read through, since I have worked to keep them realistic. I intended to convey these principles in a way that is entertaining, inspirational, and practical for readers.

By writing about my own spiritual journey and the spiritual journeys of others, I hope to encourage people to follow the spiritual path and see how it can change their lives. My intention is that this book will serve as a guide to realize your full potential and living a more fulfilling life. Whether you want to enhance your relationships, find meaning in your profession, or simply live a more joyful life, this book will help you get started.

I urge you to join me on this journey and experience how spirituality can improve your life in ways you never imagined possible. I promise you will not be disappointed since here is an engaging story that will inspire you to follow the path of spirituality and live an incredible life.

**Unmesh Jadhav**
https://soulsereenity.in

# Acknowledgement

I bow down to Lord Krishna for motivating me to put pen to paper. For someone like me, who never ever considered the possibility of publishing a book, nothing would have been conceivable without His divine favor. I dedicate this book to His lotus feet.

I would also like to thank my spiritual mentors, BK Shivani Didi and Sadhguru Jaggi Vasudev, for their guidance and wisdom, which have helped me take baby steps on the path of spirituality. Their teachings have been invaluable to me, and I shall remain forever grateful for their influence on my life. To the authors and content creators whose works have inspired me, thank you for shaping the ideas in this book.

My parents have always been there for me, no matter what, and for that I am eternally grateful. All through my life, they have been there to cheer me on and give me strength. My wife, Rajeshri, has been incredibly supportive and encouraging, and I owe her a great deal for believing in me and sticking by me. Her insightful criticism and helpful ideas have been invaluable in enhancing the quality of this book. My two sons, Shrot and Vivaan, were very supportive and patient while I dedicated my time to working on this book.

I would like to express my appreciation to my editors, illustrators, publishers, and everybody else, who shared their experiences with me and has helped me in various ways to bring this book to fruition.

Lastly, I dedicate this book to my colleagues and fellow working professionals, hoping that it would assist them in beginning their journey toward true happiness.

Thank you all from the bottom of my heart.

# I

# THE BREAKING POINT

# 1

## SIMILAR PROFESSION, CONTRASTING CHARACTERS

As Aman zoomed past in his sleek BMW X1, his neighbors Mr. Patil and Mr. Khare stood with sour expressions on their faces. Their disdain for Aman was palpable, and they wasted no time in engaging in malicious gossip.

Mr. Patil sneered, "If only this man had a shred of empathy, he would understand that there's more to life than just him."

Mr. Khare nodded in agreement, adding, "If he can turn his back on his aging parents, then his life is truly devoid of purpose!"

Little did they know that their words were being overheard by Maya Allahbadia, a brilliant 31-year-old lawyer and Aman's neighbor. In a world where Aman's success, youth, and charm brewed jealousy and hatred in most of the people, Maya stood out as one of the few who held the dashing businessman in high esteem.

Maya suppressed a grin as she listened to the older men's comments. She thought to herself, 'These average folks will never understand what drives successful people like Aman. All they can do is resent what they can't comprehend. I hope he shows up at one of my parties soon.' As a well-known socialite and host of high-profile networking events, Maya was a regular fixture on the Page 3 scene.

Aman had moved into his opulent villa in Panchsheel Enclave, Pune's most affluent neighborhood, only a few months ago, but the ripples of his arrival had already spread far and wide. However, he had no idea that he was the subject of so much curiosity and attention in his new community. His mind was occupied with the impending problem at his company, HealthTech Limited; a problem that he had kept under wraps.

Aman's car squeaked into his villa's parking, and he rushed in. Ignoring his wife Anita and their young son, he proceeded into the home bar. A drink of scotch was Aman's attempt at controlling his frustration so that he could work through his troubles.

It had been obvious to Anita over the past week that Aman was in some trouble. He had been refusing to answer her questions, no matter how many times she asked. She decided to give it another go.

"Aman, what's the matter? You've been upset all week, and despite my constant attempts, you haven't told me anything!"

"What are you going to do even if I tell you, Anita? What business knowledge do you have? Just enjoy your kitty parties!" Aman snarled.

"Aman, show some respect; I am your wife!" She shouted back.

"Just leave me alone!" Aman yelled and slammed the door on Anita as he stormed into his room with a bottle of scotch.

He recalled the intense discussion he had with Murli that

had made him extremely agitated. He had kept the brewing crisis in his company to himself for a week, but as he needed Murli's support to carry out his plans, he was forced to tell Murli everything.

Murli was second in command in Aman's start-up and had a contrasting leadership style compared to Aman. He was just a few years shy of 35 and had been through several ups and downs in his life. He was a deeply spiritual person, and the Bhagavad Gita was his guiding light as he navigated the difficulties of life. Whenever he felt lost or troubled, the words of the ancient text offered him comfort and clarity. Even he was overwhelmed by the challenging circumstances at the company once Aman informed him of the brewing troubles.

Murli's study was his sanctuary, but even in that peaceful space, he wasn't able to shake off the weight of the day's events. The room, with its temple, library, and working desk, offered everything he needed to find solace, but not today. The otherwise calming aroma of jasmine incense sticks burning in the temple failed to ease his troubled mind. It was as if the walls were closing in on him, and the future appeared bleak.

Ruchi, his wife, entered the room. "What's wrong, Murli?" she asked, sensing his distress. "I've never seen you look that stressed before."

"I'm not in the right mindset to discuss it right now, Ruchi," Murli replied, wanting to avoid any further inquiries.

Ruchi placed a hand on his shoulder and said softly, "Take your time, and remember, you always have me and your savior, the Bhagavad Gita, to turn to when you feel lost."

Murli felt a sense of relief wash over him. "Oh, yes, thank you for reminding me," he said, a small smile creeping onto his face.

Ruchi's eyes glowed with love and admiration as she ran her hand across his face. He took her hand and kissed it gently.

"What is she doing now?" he inquired about their daughter, Radha.

"It's 9:30 in the evening. What do you think she must be doing?" Ruchi replied with a grin.

"Sleeping?" Murli guessed.

"Of course! You've instilled in her the wonderful habit of going to bed early. She wakes up on her own and prepares for school. It's quite helpful in the mornings," Ruchi said, beaming with pride.

Murli chuckled to himself, momentarily forgetting his troubles. "We're so lucky to have her," he said.

However, his brief period of respite was interrupted by a ring on his mobile. It was Aman. Murli chose to ignore it, and Ruchi, recognizing Murli's need to be alone, quietly exited the room, closing the door behind her.

Murli grabbed the Bhagavad Gita, his faithful companion for many years, and sank back into his chair. Memories flooded his mind, particularly those of his mother, who had given him the book as a way to distract him from his endless questioning. As he let himself drift into the past, he felt a sense of peace wash over him.

Murli was a curious boy from a small village near Coimbatore. His family had deep religious and cultural roots. However, from a young age itself, he challenged the customs and rituals that his family followed. But every time he did so, he met with warnings about angering the gods. Murli couldn't help but wonder why the all-powerful gods would waste their time being angry with humans. His questions were met with silence, and nobody seemed to have any answers.

One day, when Murli was 12 years old, his mother had enough of his questions. She thrust the Bhagavad Gita into his hands and told him to find his own answers. But when Murli asked if anyone had read it, his mother simply replied that they believed in God and didn't question Him like he did. With a dismissive wave of her hand, she left for work, leaving Murli to figure it out on his own.

The massive book lay untouched by Murli's side for several days. Its size intimidated him, and he didn't know where to start. But one day, while his family was busy with a holiday ritual, Murli's attention was drawn to it, the Bhagavad Gita. He picked it up and started reading.

Intrigued by the battles and the conversations between Arjuna and Lord Krishna, Murli found himself drawn into the story, imagining himself in Arjuna's shoes. But the messages presented by Lord Krishna didn't make sense to his young mind. Nevertheless, he read it through and then kept reading it again and again, determined to uncover the answers he was looking for. Murli's journey of self-discovery had only just begun, and he knew that the Bhagavad Gita would be his guide.

It wasn't until he went to Pune to complete his studies in engineering and met his guru, Dr Ram, that he was able to relate to the teachings of the Bhagavad Gita, which ultimately led to a complete transformation of his life from inside out. He has been grateful to his mother and guru for this gift from God.

Another phone call from Aman jolted him back into the present. He opted to ignore one more time. His thoughts were still running wild.

Murli thought to himself, 'What exactly am I doing? Do I need to work for a person like Aman? Perhaps I should just quit!'

He couldn't get out of the discussion he had with Aman in the office earlier that day. His mind was racing with a flurry of different thoughts. As he was getting ready to write an email to Aman, he recalled a passage from the Bhagavad Gita that his Guru had taught him: *Avoid making decisions when you are overly happy or sad, as such emotions can cloud your judgment and prevent sound decision-making.*

Turning to his savior, the Bhagavad Gita, he took a few moments to compose himself by closing his eyes and focusing inward. No matter how many times he read it, the Bhagavad Gita never failed to provide him with answers to the challenges he faced at any point of time.

Murli discovered that he could relate to Arjuna's dilemma in the first chapter of the Bhagavad Gita, titled 'Arjuna VishadYog.' Just like Arjuna during the battle of Kurukshetra, Murli was struggling with conflicting thoughts about his purpose and duty. Arjuna didn't want to fight and kill his own family, friends, and guru, and Murli was faced with questions about his own beliefs and customs. Despite being a warrior on the battlefield to vanquish evil, Arjuna's logical mind found it difficult to come to terms with the notion that he had to murder his own people, and he wanted to run away from the battleground to avoid the war.

*As Chapter one came to a close, Murli had this notion for himself. Isn't it true that I'm doing the same thing to avoid challenges at the office?*

In his reading of the Bhagavad Gita, Murli had come to the realization that the root cause of human suffering is often the result of our inability to confront and effectively manage the challenges that life presents us. He learned that avoiding a problem by running away from it is not a viable solution. *Because doing nothing is itself a decision with potential negative consequences, facing the problem head-on is necessary if you want to improve your chances of succeeding.*

As Murli's thoughts began to quiet, he prayed to Lord Krishna and began taking slow, deep breaths. He was now at ease. He reasoned that perhaps Aman was correct in his position and that he was doing what was good for the company, despite the fact that it was completely unjust from Murli's perspective; however, he acknowledged that it is everyone's right to have their own opinion and that everyone is entitled to their own point of view.

*Then he recalled something that his Guru, Dr Ram had told him recently: Nobody is right or wrong; they just do things that are right from their point of view. When I disagree with someone's viewpoint, I label that person as wrong.*

After that, Murli made up his mind to stop pointing fingers at others and instead focus on helping his team through the difficult times ahead. He desired to save them from the perilous waters.

In the meantime, Aman called Murli again. This time Murli picked up the call.

"I apologize, Murli, for all that occurred this morning." Aman was trying to defend his outburst at the office. "You know we are looking towards a big tragedy, and it can strike any time."

"It's all good, Aman. Let's talk about it at the office tomorrow."

"Yes, let's do that," Aman said as he ended the call and finished his glass of scotch. He was furious that he had to apologize to Murli, but he had no choice but to get help from

Murli if he wanted to save his company from the impending disaster.

He depended heavily on Murli as a key contributor. He was in charge of developing Aman's dream product, 'Unified Healthcare Platform.' Aman had high hopes for this product, as it could change his fortunes.

Murli was a tech-savvy project manager with vast experience managing a number of different technical healthcare projects. Because of his simple and down-to-earth attitude, as well as the fact that he cared genuinely about his team, the entire team was fond of Murli. He had a lot of compassion and paid close attention to what the team had to say in order to fully get their perspective.

'Without him, I won't be able to carry out my plan. Yes, we have different styles of working, but Murli gets work done by the team.' Aman kept thinking to himself about the vicious plan he was about to unleash.

# 2

# A RIVALRY TAKES ROOT

It was business as usual at HealthTech the next morning, with no one aware of the impending storm that would knock everyone off their feet.

Aman and his team had recently celebrated the first anniversary of HealthTech. Located at the heart of the happening IT park in Pune, this 80-seat office space had sleek design on modern lines, with cutting-edge technology, reflecting a dynamic and successful next-generation start-up. The walls were painted in bold, playful colors, and there was an eclectic mix of seating options, from sleek, modern chairs to cozy couches and bean bag chairs for the comfort of employees. In the corner of the office, beside the glass facade, was a large communal table where the team gathered to chat, brainstorm, and enjoy leisure time together. The table was often littered with papers, laptops, and other work materials, evidence of the team's boundless energy and dedication to their work.

The cafeteria, in particular, was a hub of activity and youthful energy. The space was bright and airy, with large windows and plenty of natural light. Despite the high-tech gadgets and cutting-edge software on display, there was a sense of humanity and connection in the cafeteria. The team was friendly and approachable, always eager to collaborate and learn from one another. There was a palpable sense of excitement and possibility in the air as the team worked together to change the world through their innovative technology.

Aman Rajput's HealthTech office, in general, was a vibrant and exciting place, befitting his ambitious plans and vision. This being Aman's first venture into entrepreneurship, he had dived headfirst into every aspect, from conceptualizing the company's name to designing the interiors of the office.

Aman had an amazingly talented team working for him at his start-up. Parth and Karan were team leads at HealthTech, the absolute best, and it was Aman who got them on board.

Parth looked over at his counterpart, Karan, who was working on a separate module of the same product. Karan had been at HealthTech only for a week. His main role was to take over some parts of the Unified Healthcare Platform project from Parth, who had been stressed out for several months due to a busy schedule. While Parth was relieved that his workload would now be reduced, he also harbored resentment towards Karan. He couldn't help but feel uncomfortable and insecure. Although he had greeted Karan with a welcoming smile, inside he was having an outburst of emotions. Parth had always been the most dependable and indispensable member in the organization, and he was well aware that now Karan was a competition.

Within a week, Parth realized that he needed to get along with Karan because they would be working on the same project in future. He went up to Karan and asked if he would like to have a cup of tea with him in the cafeteria, and Karan agreed right away.

Seeing them together made Nidhi anxious, as it was not in her best interest.

"How long have you been working for HealthTech, and how did you join this fantastic company?" Karan inquired of Parth.

Parth saw this as an opportunity to brag about himself. "Well, it's been almost 11 months." He began to recount his journey to HealthTech.

"I am from Pune itself, and I met Aman while I was attending a networking event in one of the 5-star hotels here in Pune. I was captivated by the vivid thoughts of a young and brilliant entrepreneur like him. He was talking about how technology was evolving and taking over the healthcare industry.

"I was blown away by his very inspirational speech, in which he discussed how HealthTech is at the vanguard of the healthcare industry's revolution and how the initial version of their product had made waves in the healthcare industry in just a few months. His vision of establishing new global norms and standards while building solid healthcare systems around the world swept me off my feet.

"My heart moved with Aman as I heard him speak. I was determined to connect with him and share my ideas. I strongly desired to work with him, and I was confident that, looking at my experience and knowledge, he would be keen on hiring me.

"Despite drawing a hefty package from my employer at that time, I was keen on working with Aman. It was not money that motivated me to join hands with him. I yearned to be a part of the change that he was bringing to the industry, to witness the revolution firsthand, and also to benefit from HealthTech's growth story. I knew that my experience and knowledge would make me a valuable asset to HealthTech, and I was determined to be a part of this transformative journey.

"With my heart pounding, I finally worked up the courage to approach Aman at the networking dinner. As I walked up to him, while he was surrounded by important people, I praised his ideas and told him how much I admired him, the young business owner. Aman chuckled at the overwhelming praise, but something about me caught his attention, my jacket which bore the emblem of my established healthcare organization employer, the same industry that he was revolutionizing. Intrigued, he invited me to join him at his table, where I saw an opportunity to properly introduce myself and make my ambitions known.

"After getting to know me, he was actually able to see through me. He gave me an offer to join HealthTech that I couldn't refuse."

"That's impressive, Parth; you seem to be a go-getter!" Karan responded with a genuine sense of appreciation.

Parth smiled as he welcomed Karan's compliment. "And what about you, Karan?"

"As you know, I am from Bangalore. In my previous organization, I had earned myself a promotion and a considerable raise each year for three years running, so I was happy working there. Aman visited my company a few months ago to purchase billing software from our company. I was in charge of customizing our software to meet HealthTech's requirements. In those two days, I handled all of Aman's queries, leaving him no choice but to sign a contract with our company.

"He was about to leave for Pune, so we went for coffee to have some casual talks. He appreciated my work and said lots of good things about me. With respect and admiration for Aman, I couldn't help but feel a sense of pride when I heard the words coming from such a successful entrepreneur's mouth. I thanked him from the bottom of my heart for those kind words.

"But it seems that he wasn't just offering empty compliments. With a glint in his eye, he told me that talent like mine needed a more dynamic platform to thrive and that I was at the wrong place. I knew where this was headed. I told him that I was happy with my work, and the company had given me exceptional promotions for consecutive three years. I was hoping to deflect Aman's overtures, but he was persistent. He offered me to join HealthTech and promised to change my definition of exceptional promotion.

"I was stunned. I had expected some sort of offer, but I didn't know it would be that good. My mind was racing. I knew I wanted to take the offer, but I also knew that I couldn't just jump at it without thinking things through, so I requested time until the evening to think about the offer and share my response, and I tried to buy some time. The way Aman responded, I got the impression that he had been taken aback by my cold shouldering; and it appeared that he is not used to hearing 'no' or 'maybe' from anyone.

"On the same day, I sent him a message that said, 'Aman, I admire your accomplishments and respect you as a person, but at this time in my career, I don't want to make a move. I need a few more years to mature here before I commit to joining you for the long term.'

"I didn't receive a response from him on my message, and to be honest, I wasn't expecting one. I had heard of his tough reputation, and I was not used to working with such methods; therefore, I had no desire to join HealthTech."

"That's interesting! Then how did you land here?" Parth

was curious to know.

Karan continued with his story. "Surprisingly, Murli called me a few days later. He told me that Aman was eager to have me at HealthTech and wasn't going to take 'No' for an answer. He promised that if I joined them, I would be part of the top team in the healthcare sector and would be capable of demanding any package. It was a 30-minute call, and Murli's honesty and passion for his team obviously astounded me.

"I modestly told Murli that the aspect that touched me the most from all that he stated was that he takes care of his team. I am also more of a people person than someone who is motivated to make decisions based on monetary gains alone. I was transparent with Murli and told him that I hadn't heard great things about Aman's treatment of his employees but talking to him had made me feel better. I promised him that I would seriously consider his offer and notify him of my decision by the evening.

"Later that evening, I called Murli and told him that I trusted him and HealthTech's mission and that I was ready to take on this challenge and become a member of his team. Murli assured me that I would not be sorry and that HealthTech was committed to their employees' development. That's how I landed here, Parth."

While Parth acknowledged Karan's narrative with a smile, he realized that Aman and Murli had personally followed up to get Karan on board and these revelations made him even more nervous. He had invited Karan for tea to break the ice, but now he was feeling even more resentment towards him.

As they were walking back to their desks, they noticed Murli strolling into the office.

Karan and Parth greeted him "Good morning, Murli!"

Murli greeted them back in a flat voice avoiding eye contact and just went into his cabin.

This was surprising for both Parth and Karan, as Murli was the most humble and loving manager they had ever seen. Much about Murli could be understood from how he had set up his office.  As one stepped into Murli's office cabin, one could immediately notice how different it was from other high-powered corporate spaces. The cabin was furnished simply, with a comfortable desk, a small seating area for guests, and a few bookshelves filled with volumes on IT and philosophy. There was a small statue of Lord Krishna occupied a prominent place on his desk, a symbol of his devotion to the teachings of the Bhagavad Gita.

Despite lack of flash and glamour, there was an aroma of peace and contentment in the space. Murli's work ethics and devotion to his craft were evident in every detail, from the carefully arranged notes and documents on his desk to the way he greeted each visitor with a warm smile and genuine interest.

Perhaps most striking was the sense of approachability that permeated the space. Unlike the imposing and formal offices of many high-powered executives, Murli's cabin felt like a safe haven, a place where colleagues and clients alike could come to discuss business or simply chat over a cup of tea. In a world that often values wealth and power above everything else, Murli's office cabin was a refreshing reminder of the importance of humility, principles, and dedication to one's craft.

Murli was interrupted from his thoughts by a knock on the door.  The peon informed him that Aman had urgently requested a meeting with him in his cabin. Murli felt his heart skip a beat!

3

# WOOING AN OPPORTUNIST HEART

Aman's cabin radiated with a lively spirit that could be felt by anybody who entered. The room was ultra-contemporary, with the latest design and an open floor plan that emphasized collaboration and creativity.

The walls were adorned with abstract artwork and motivational quotes, inspiring Aman and his team to push beyond their limits and achieve their goals. The furniture was sleek and minimalist, with a mix of comfortable lounge chairs and ergonomic workstations designed to promote productivity and comfort.

The office was flooded with natural light, thanks to the floor-to-ceiling windows that offer sweeping views of the city below. On clear days, you could see for miles, and Aman often took a moment to gaze out at the skyline, gathering his thoughts and seeking inspiration. But what truly set Aman's office apart was the attention to detail. From the carefully curated bookshelves filled with titles on business, entrepreneurship, and innovation to the high-tech gadgets and gizmos that line his desk, everything in the space was designed to foster creativity and inspire greatness.

As you move through the space, you can't help but feel that anything is possible here. Aman's office was a testament to his ambition, drive, and vision, and it was clear that he was not content to rest on his laurels. With every passing day, he was pushing himself and his team to reach new heights, and the space around him reflected that relentless spirit of innovation and progress.

While waiting for Murli to arrive, Aman kept pacing restlessly in his cabin.

As Murli entered the cabin, the tension brewing between the two was evident from the way they started their discussions. Without any pleasantries, they got straight to the topic and the next steps required to be taken.

Just outside Aman's cabin, the office abuzz with people returning from the cafeteria and settling into their desks. Parth's heart skipped a beat as he watched Nidhi make her way to her desk. Nidhi's beauty had been playing its charm on Parth day after day, and he had developed a huge crush on her. They had been working together for over 10 months now, but he could not muster up the courage to ask her out on a date till now. Every time he saw her, he felt his nerves getting the better of him.

As Nidhi settled into her desk, she caught Karan's eye. Parth watched as Karan flashed a smile at her, and Nidhi smiled back. Parth felt a twinge of jealousy. He had never seen Nidhi smile at him like that.

Nidhi Joshi was a carefree and laidback 24-year-old lady working in the support project at HealthTech. With a striking beauty that could turn heads, Nidhi was also a skilled opportunist, using her charm to make a way out of any situation.

She loved her job, relishing the freedom and independence it offered her. While Parth was a trouble-shooter for her in any challenges she faced at work, she was never really attracted to him, but she always kept him on ice so that she could get things done from him.

During Karan's first day at the office, many heads had turned in his direction. It wasn't just because he was a new face but also because of his remarkable physique and striking good looks. Nidhi couldn't help but feel a rush of excitement knowing that a handsome and eligible bachelor like Karan would be working in the same office. Till date, no one in the office was attractive enough as per her standards of an attractive man.

Murli came out of Aman's cabin. He seemed visibly stressed. He went straight into his cabin without even looking at the people in the office.

The day went on, and Parth tried his best to focus on his work, but every time he looked up and saw Karan laughing with Nidhi, he felt like being left out, like he didn't belong there anymore.

In the evening, as Parth was packing up to leave early, he overheard Karan and Nidhi talking. They were discussing something, and he couldn't help but listen in.

"I was thinking we could go to that new restaurant that just opened up," Karan said.

"That sounds like a great idea," Nidhi replied, her eyes sparkling.

Parth felt a knot forming in his stomach. He knew he had to act fast if he didn't want to lose Nidhi to Karan. He walked up to their desks clearing his throat.

"Hey, guys," he said, trying to sound casual, "what are you

up to?"

Karan and Nidhi turned to him, surprised.

"Oh, hey, Parth!" Karan said, "We were just talking about going to that new restaurant this evening."

"Really?" Parth said, trying to sound interested. "I, too, have been wanting to check that place out."

"Well, we can all go together then," Karan responded spontaneously.

Nidhi smiled, but Parth could tell that her smile was forced.

Parth knew that he had to make a move, and he had to do it now. He took a deep breath and looked straight at Nidhi.

"Alright then, I'll go ahead and book a table for us." Parth was quick to respond, hoping that this gesture would make him appear cool in front of Nidhi. Apparently, he even thought that this outing could be his opportunity for that social interaction he has been looking for with Nidhi for a long time now.

Nidhi looked at him, surprised. Parth held his breath, waiting for her answer.

"That sounds cool, Parth," she said, her eyes sparkling. For Nidhi, it was just an offer to enjoy drinks and meals with her talented office colleagues, who were potential helpers too, to make her life easy at work.

Parth felt a huge weight lifted off his shoulders. He looked at Karan and saw a hint of disappointment in his eyes, but Parth didn't care. He was getting an opportunity to spend time with Nidhi, and that was all that mattered. As he walked out of the office, he felt a sense of satisfaction. He had stood up to his insecurities and come out on top. He knew that he still had a lot of work to do, but he also knew that he had taken the first step towards gaining his confidence back about winning Nidhi's attention.

Later that evening, just before leaving the office Nidhi was having tea with her best friend Daksha in the cafeteria. They were sitting on bean bags in their favorite spot in the corner, which was carefully chosen so that no one would hear them.

"I had planned to go out to dinner with Karan today to get to know him better." Nidhi said as she was munching her cookie with tea.

"Wow, that's fantastic!" Daksha was ecstatic.

"But this Parth appeared out of nowhere and asked if he could join us." Nidhi was visibly upset.

"Nidhi, that guy has been hitting on you for the past 9—months, and you're just keeping him at bay. Now that he sees Karan as competition, he appears to be desperate," Daksha observed.

"Yeah, I could sense his desperation," Nidhi acknowledged.

"What's wrong with Parth? Don't you like him?" inquired Daksha.

"He's a really nice guy, but I'm not attracted to him!" Nidhi confessed.

"So then, why do you keep him interested? I know you keep sending him subtle signals," Daksha confronted Nidhi.

"My parents have been pushing me to get married for months now; I have been evading them, but soon I will have to give in. Instead of marrying someone of their choice, I would prefer Parth. He is settled and has recently purchased his own house. He can be excellent husband material," Nidhi added, smiling.

"And now that Karan has entered the picture, you're drawn to him," Daksha retorted, laughing loudly.

Everyone in the cafeteria began staring at her. Nidhi shook her head. Daksha's laughter was muffled as she realized she was being too loud.

"I couldn't get enough of Karan ever since I first saw him," Nidhi blushed. "He's such a handsome hunk."

"Just be careful. You've only just met him. Parth has been tried and tested, so consider your options carefully," Daksha suggested.

Nidhi agreed with Daksha as they sipped their tea and left the office.

In the evening, Parth found himself nervously checking his appearance in the mirror before heading out to meet Karan. They were to meet Nidhi directly at the restaurant.

As they walked into the restaurant, Nidhi was already there waiting for them. With a black one-piece dress, she looked stunning. The light breeze in the restaurant by the pool was blowing her hair into her face. She had applied just enough makeup to bring out her natural beauty.

As soon as Parth and Karan saw her, their hearts skipped a beat. They couldn't take their gaze away from her. They hadn't seen Nidhi like this before. With bright expressions on their faces, they made their way to the table to meet Nidhi.

As they perused the menu, Karan chatted excitedly about the items, while Nidhi listened attentively, occasionally interjecting with her own thoughts. Parth found himself struggling to decide what to order. Being an introvert, he felt like he was not able to keep up with the conversation, and he couldn't help but feel a twinge of jealousy as he watched Nidhi laugh at Karan's jokes.

"I've heard the *paneer tikka* here is really good." Karan said, looking over at Nidhi, "What do you think, Nidhi?"

"That sounds delicious, Karan," she said. "But I think I might try the *Paneer Malai Kabab*; is it OK with you, Parth?"

Nidhi smiled, her eyes flickering over to Parth.

Parth couldn't help but feel a sense of relief wash over him as Nidhi seemed to be including him in the conversation. As they waited for their food to arrive, the three of them chatted about everything from their favorite movies to their weekend plans.

But as the night wore on, Parth found himself increasingly distracted by Karan's constant attempts to impress Nidhi. He kept trying to one-up Parth with stories about his travels and his job, and Parth found himself feeling more and more intimidated.

But Nidhi was the ultimate winner in this situation, as she deftly managed to keep both men interested. She laughed at Karan's jokes, listened intently to Parth as well, and kept the conversation flowing. She was playing both men with ease, giving them equal attention and emotional support, all the while enjoying the attention, she was receiving from them. But make no mistake, Nidhi was no fool. She was evaluating both Parth and Karan, carefully weighing the pros and cons of each man. She knew that she had to choose wisely, as the man she ended up with could potentially be her future spouse.

Parth and Karan, meanwhile, were doing everything in their power to win Nidhi's attention. They would go out of their way to help her with work, make her laugh, and do anything they could to spend time with her.

As they left the restaurant and said their goodbyes, Parth couldn't help but feel a sense of admiration for Nidhi's poise and grace. And while he still hoped to win her heart, he knew that he had some tough competition in Karan.

It was ten o'clock when Parth walked into the opulent 2-bedroom apartment he had recently purchased. He had been staying with his parents till then, but he was an independent and driven young man who wanted to live his life on his terms. Though he didn't have much money on hand, he managed to put down the least amount necessary on the house and borrow the remainder from the bank.

He gave his best to his work and was very good at what he did. After achieving the highest marks in his engineering degree, he got a lucrative offer during his campus interview. His life was going nicely after seven years of experience. When compared to his peers, he had all he needed to consider his life complete. His accomplishments in life were the stuff of envy among his friends and classmates, especially when he landed a job at HealthTech.

His parents, especially his father, would tell that a good heart, rather than material wealth, was the true measure of a man's success. Parth tried his best to follow their advice, but he couldn't help but be drawn into the materialistic view of success.

His parents had been trying to find him a suitable life partner, but Parth was adamant on finding an accomplished urban partner, unwilling to settle for anything less than what he desired. After he met Nidhi, he was certain that she was the one he was seeking for, and he was willing to go to any length to win her.

4

## THE SELFISH DRIVE TO SUCCESS

It was nine o'clock at night, and Aman was still in his office, lost in his thoughts about next steps. A phone call from his wife, Anita, jolted him back to the present.

"Why do you keep calling me? I've already told you I will be late; don't wait for me!" he shouted as he answered the phone. Frustrated by the situation he was in, he left the office immediately and sped away in his car, leaving a trail of noise in his wake.

As Aman drove into the main road, Socialite Maya noticed him racing past her. Eager to introduce herself to the powerful businessman, she decided to follow him. She spotted Aman's car parked outside one high-profile bar.

She entered looking out for him. He was right at the bar counter, having a scotch all alone.

Maya rushed towards him and sat by his side. She placed an order for a traditional screwdriver. Aman did not recognize her and smiled at her casually. He was still sulking and had no clue that Maya was trying to get his attention by sitting next to him.

He was quite focused on having his drink, frustrated over his family and business falling apart. It wasn't that Aman did not love his family; he wanted the best for them. But he only loved himself more, which was pushing him away from his wife and child.

Maya noticed that Aman was deep in thought, his gaze fixed on the glass of scotch in front of him. Curiosity getting the better of her, she couldn't help but ask, "Hi, what's wrong? You haven't kept your glass down once; you can't enjoy scotch in this manner."

Aman turned towards Maya, surprised by her sudden interest. With a sad smile, he responded, "I am not here to enjoy my drink, Miss."

Maya leaned in, intrigued by Aman's vulnerability. "If I may ask, what's troubling you?"

Aman hesitated, but the alcohol had already loosened his tongue. "It's my family and business," he said, his voice barely above a whisper. "I love both of them, but I just can't seem to make things right, no matter how hard I try."

Maya's eyes widened in surprise, and then she let out a laugh. "Please don't get me wrong, Sir. I'm not laughing to undermine your pain. I only find it amusing that the city's most powerful personality is limiting himself to a glass of scotch to help him overcome his problems."

Aman raised an eyebrow, intrigued by Maya's bluntness. "What do you mean?" he asked.

Maya leaned in closer, her eyes twinkling with mischief. "Well, you're a man who has everything, power, influence. And yet, here you are, seeking solace in a glass of scotch. It's such an interesting juxtaposition, don't you think?"

As soon as Maya made her statement, Aman's eyes widened

in surprise, and he leaned in to hear more. "Do you know me? Who are you?" he asked, his curiosity piqued.

Maya replied nonchalantly, as if she had just made a casual observation. "Yes, I know you, Mr. Aman Rajput. You have never noticed me, but I cannot overlook the fact that one of the most successful personalities in the business world is my neighbor."

Aman was now completely taken aback. "What? Are we neighbors?" he asked in disbelief.

Maya nodded with a grin and said, "Yes, we are! And it's about time we got to know each other, don't you think?"

Aman remained silent and continued with his drink.

"So, what's bothering you? You can be open with me. I am a lawyer and know how to keep secrets!" Maya attempted to elicit information from Aman.

Aman still favored silence and his scotch.

Maya, as a lawyer, knew how to get people to talk, so she began with casual conversation. "Tell me about yourself. How a young boy from Delhi decided to swim against the tide and achieved such great success?" She was well aware that Aman enjoyed compliments.

The trick worked and Aman began opening up to Maya.

"I was always a bit of a rebel from childhood on, and despite my parents' medical background, I was more interested in computer engineering. My parents didn't try to persuade me to become a doctor, knowing it would be fruitless, and I landed at the prestigious Indian Institute of Technology in Delhi. After spending a couple of years in my first job, I realized that I didn't enjoy working for others and took the plunge to pursue a Master's in Business Administration, which would help me start my own venture."

Maya was listening carefully.

"After finishing my MBA with a perfect score, I accepted a campus job offer and moved to Pune to work for a new company as a business consultant."

"But why did you take the campus offer if you didn't want to work for others?" Maya inquired.

"I have grown up in a middle-class family. I didn't have the money or contacts to start a new business, so I resolved to work until I acquired all of the resources I needed."

"Very thoughtful!" Maya was aware of Aman's hunger for compliments, she didn't miss an opportunity to lavish him with praise.

"Due to my parent's background, I planned to start a venture in the healthcare industry. In my new job, fortunately, I got the chance to work on a healthcare-related project, which broadened my horizons and changed my perspective on the industry.

"I was always enthusiastic about my work, and in a short span of time I became the most crucial member for our customer. My colleagues found me self-centered and difficult to work with, but I didn't care about them. My goal was to create good relations with my client even at the cost of my own employer." Aman was high on alcohol and compliments, so he was spilling all his secrets.

Maya was all ears, and Aman continued his story. "I regularly worked beyond business hours, even when there wasn't much project work going on, as I was keen to know how to run IT projects in the healthcare industry. After 2 years, having got a good understanding, I decided to quit.

"During the notice period, I took special interest in the support area, despite being a business analyst for the development project. On the day of my departure, I left the office with a sense of accomplishment, knowing I had made the right decision to pursue my dreams."

"I don't understand. Why would you work overtime during the notice period?" Maya was confused.

Aman gave a wicked smile to Maya as he continued, "That was all part of my strategy, which I had meticulously crafted over the years. I was secretly working on automation tools that could cut efforts by 35—40%. When I had traveled to Germany for a workshop with a customer, I discovered that they are incredibly cost-conscious and would go to any length to decrease the cost of their project. I already had an excellent relationship with Gregg, who was the major decision-maker. Upon my resignation, I contacted Gregg and offered him the same support work at a 30% cheaper rate as part of my new firm, leveraging the automation tools I had created. I also offered him a portion of the profits. Gregg went all out to persuade his management to terminate their running agreement with my previous employer and construct a new one with HealthTech, my start-up."

"You are a cunning genius, Aman," Maya appreciated Aman's business acumen.

A smile appeared on Aman's face. He went ahead, "Starting a business and keeping it going and growing it are two entirely different things, therefore I was picky about who I employed. I wanted the finest from the market, so I offered them 35—% more than the market."

"How big of a team do you have now?" asked Maya.

"I have 25 people engaged on a support project for Gregg. I hate support projects, but it provided me with running capital. I have two teams, each with 20 people, striving to make my innovative idea of *Unified Healthcare Platform* a reality."

"What is this new platform?" Maya asked.

"Well, believe me when I say that this platform will forever transform the healthcare business, and nothing can stop HealthTech from becoming a Unicorn once it is implemented."

Maya could hear the excitement in Aman's voice as he spoke about his idea.

The phone rang as Aman was engrossed in talking with Maya. It was Anita again.

'Why did she have to call right now, God?' Aman mumbled in annoyance and answered the phone. Aman's "Yes, Anita!" sounded more like a sigh than an actual response.

Anita's tone was formal and intense as she said, "Today is our son's sixth birthday, and I had called you earlier to remind you. But you hung up on me. The birthday party has ended at 11 o'clock, and now you may come home whenever you want."

"I'm sorry, Anita; I totally forgot! Work has been keeping me so busy lately that..."

But Anita wouldn't have any of it. She exploded at Aman, accusing him of being driven by selfish goals that stopped him from spending time with his family, which she and their 6-year-old son valued more than money or success. Aman did what he could to soothe her, but it was too late. Anita cut off the call.

"Oh no, it was my son's birthday," he said. "How could I have forgotten? I must leave now," Aman murmured as he rose from his chair, disappointed.

"It's already 11 o'clock," Maya tried to pacify him. "By the time you get home, he'll be fast asleep. Please stay; we are having a great conversation here."

Aman sat back in his chair, and they embarked on a captivating conversation that lasted late into the night. Over drinks and stories, they discovered that they had much in common despite their different backgrounds. As the bar began to empty out, they decided to leave together and hail a cab.

The ride back to Aman's villa was filled with lively banter and playful teasing. As they said their goodbyes, Maya was beaming with joy, happy to have finally caught the attention of one of the most sought-after men in the city. Aman, too, felt a sense of excitement and intrigue, wondering what other surprises life might have in store for him.

# 5

# THE DARK CLOUDS GATHER

Murli, as usual, woke up at 5 o'clock in the morning and went about his routine of meditation, physical exercise, and reading. He then dropped Radha off at her school bus stop, as he did every morning at 8 o'clock.

It had already been two days since Aman broke the news to Murli. While Murli was disturbed initially, he was now coming to terms with the inevitable.

Ruchi checked on him as they were having breakfast, "How do you feel now?"

"Much better!" He spoke in a much more relaxed tone and asserted, "I know the road that lies ahead is arduous, but I know what I need to do."

"Do you want to tell me what's wrong? You have been so disturbed for the last two days," Ruchi asked in a concerned tone.

"Ruchi, I don't keep any secrets from you, but I wanted to be alone for a couple of days. What we keep thinking about gets attracted to us. That's why I didn't want to discuss it, because discussing challenges leads to more negative mental patterns.

For the last 2 days, I intended to focus exclusively on solutions and dealing with the current situation." Murli clarified why he had been quiet for the past couple of days.

"I completely understand, Murli; I know you better than anybody else." Ruchi attempted to downplay the issue.

Murli started explaining the problem to Ruchi in greater detail, "You have heard reports of an ongoing pandemic in Europe. We all assumed it was simply a storm in a teacup. Several pandemics have occurred in the past. This, too, we thought would be handled in due course, but it appears that we were mistaken."

"Why? What happened?" Ruchi inquired, worried.

Murli told her about what had transpired in the office.

"Last week, Aman got a call from our client, Gregg. He informed that things are pretty bad due to the pandemic and their corporate office has demanded a reduction in spending. As a result, the support team needed to be ramped down by 50%. He also directed Aman to work only on critical issues in order to keep the lights on and said that no change requests or nice-to-have features would be considered.

"Aman was stunned to learn of this news as the ground slipped beneath his feet. He spent the next few days planning to mitigate the effects of the ramp-down, but then he got another bombshell. His investors called to tell him that they were pausing all investments due to the pandemic and had no idea when they would resume.

"Aman was completely bewildered and frozen at this point. He summoned me to his cabin two days back and informed me of the company's impending difficulties. I tried to calm him down, but he had already decided to reduce both our support and development teams.

"I told him to avoid a knee-jerk reaction, and we could think of something else; there would certainly be some other option to handle the crisis, but he was in no mood to listen to me. With his company at stake, he was ruthless in his decision-making. He has planned for 50% layoffs."

"Oh, my god!" Ruchi was shocked.

"I begged him to take into consideration the employees' point of view'. They have families to support and loans to pay! In such a market, where would they find a job on such a short notice? But he just didn't care. He was furious and told me that he no longer had the energy to argue with me. He was more concerned about business and least bothered to look after his employees!" Murli explained, his voice still trembling thinking about that conversation.

"What a selfish person!" Ruchi said it with disdain.

"I was speechless since I know Aman does not listen once he makes up his mind. I just got out of Aman's cabin! I felt helpless."

"This is a disaster. That guy is so self-centered! Why would you ever choose to work with someone like him?" Ruchi was equally taken aback by the event.

"Yes, our opinions and values are completely contrary to each other, yet his vision regarding a unified healthcare platform is truly fantastic and might help millions of people worldwide. Also, I have decided to stick around, as I want to act as a barrier between him and the team, or else he would not hesitate to exploit them for every penny paid."

"Hats off to you for working with such a person for the past 12 months! Just keep your cool, Murli. Don't let your emotions overcome your rational thinking or you'll end up making wrong decisions," Ruchi warned.

"Yes, I know, and that's why I am trying to avoid meeting the team. I don't want to deal with them unless I have some clarity on my next steps." Murli agreed with her.

"It's good you are taking time to think rationally about this situation." Ruchi advised.

Silence filled the room for some time as if both were trying to comprehend the situation. As both of them were sipping tea, Murli asked in surprise, "Ruchi, you never once questioned about what will happen to my job."

Grasping his hand, she replied, "Murli, I love you for who you are. Having you by my side makes me want to drop everything else. Also, I'd rather not weigh you down with my expectations."

"I can't believe my good fortune to have you and Radha in my life." Murli's eyes began to well up with tears.

As he sat in his chair, Ruchi stepped out of her seat and embraced him from behind.

Calming down, he stated, "Aman said that my job is not at risk."

"And now you feel even more guilty about keeping your job while fifty percent of your team will be laid off!" guessed Ruchi.

"I keep wondering how you know everything there is to know about me, Ruchi." Murli said with admiration for his lovely wife.

"Because I am your other half," Ruchi said with a grin. "It's time to get up and go to work; you have a team to take care of."

Murli got up from his chair and gave Ruchi a bear embrace before heading to the office, but little did he know that there was another shock coming from Aman.

As soon as he reached office, Aman entered his cabin and

said, "Good morning, Murli! I know you're not happy with my decision, but…"

"I understand, Aman," Murli interjected. "So, what's the next step?"

"Look, support team; I've got it covered. I already have a list of the names. I will finalize and notify the team." Aman now had complete clarity on what needed to be done.

Murli said, "Alright," completely at a loss for what to say.

"You must interact with the development team. We have a one-month notice period. You know, nobody works during the notice period, but I don't want the team to squander this time, so let's issue termination notices to all 40 members!"

"What??" Murli was taken aback.

"Murli, pay attention to what I'm saying. We have two scrum development teams of 20 people each. Let us set a stretched goal for both teams. For the next month, you have to allocate 25% more work than their normal efficiency. The team that accomplishes the goal with high quality will be retained. Of course, we may substitute an excellent member from the losing team with an average person from the winning team."

"This is insane! I disagree with forcing them to stretch during this period of notice. When will they have time to hunt for a new job?" Murli resisted Aman's proposal.

"Once again, Murli, I don't care. I'll be paying them for one month, and I want the best for the company." Aman replied ruthlessly.

Murli avoided any more debate with Aman since he knew it would be futile. Aman was least concerned about people. His company was more important to him than anyone else.

"Let's work together over this week on a strategy to execute this plan. I will collaborate with HR and Legal to ensure that the procedure is carried out smoothly in order to avoid legal squabbles. You will be working on project assignments for both teams for the next 30 days.

"Today is Wednesday, so let's both finish our tasks by this Friday and next Monday, i.e., on the first of next month, let's share layoff news with the team. I'll ask HR to send out termination letters by Monday evening itself. So eventually the team will have time until the 29th of next month to finish the project task allotted to them. On the 30th, we will make the final decision on who to keep and who to let go."

Murli was speechless after hearing Aman's bizarre proposal.

"Do you get the plan, Murli?" Aman made sure Murli was listening.

"Hmm..."

Aman walked out of Murli's cabin before Murli could say anything.

Once Aman had left his cabin, Murli sat in his chair lost.

He then got up and gazed out his cabin window at the team members, who were working calmly but Karan and Parth drew his attention.

Murli always got the feeling that Parth was a distinct shadow of Aman. Parth was only focused on his own work and would not engage with anyone unless compelled to. He was excessively concentrated on himself rather than on anyone else. Murli noticed only one difference between Aman and Parth, and that was about emotions. Parth was more emotional, and he had some empathy for others at the back of his mind.

On the other hand, Murli had noticed that Karan was a seasoned technical lead, with the kind of calm and level-headed attitude that seemed to be in short supply. Karan had a certain wit and charm that endeared him to everyone he met. Yet it was his razor-sharp mind and vast knowledge that distinguished him, particularly when it came to navigating the high-pressure seas of the IT industry.

Murli remembered how Aman was furious that Karan had turned down his offer, he was one of the best talents in the industry. Aman had then tasked him with getting Karan on-board. He remembered how intense anticipation had built up inside him as he perused Karan's outstanding LinkedIn profile. He thought to himself that Aman was absolutely correct about Karan. After conversing with Karan, he understood that he was mistaken about his assumption that Karan had turned down Aman because of his desire for a large salary. Instead, he discovered that Aman's notoriety as a demanding manager, deterred Karan from joining HealthTech. Karan had blindly trusted Murli while he joined HealthTech, and now it looked like that gamble had backfired. Murli felt an overwhelming sense of guilt as he watched Karan from his cabin.

For the rest of the day, Murli kept working on the project tasks for the team, but he was disturbed all through and decided to leave the office early.

This was rare, and the team was taken by surprise.

# 6

# FINDING STRENGTH IN THE MIDST OF ADVERSITY

It was six o'clock in the evening. Murli was seated in his study, contemplating his next course of action. Ruchi entered with a cup of tea.

"How was your day?" she said as she handed him a cup of tea.

He explained Aman's new plan to send termination notices to all 40 team members.

"Doesn't this man possess a bit of humanity in him?" Ruchi's voice was full of contempt for Aman.

"Calm down, Ruchi; he's doing what he believes is right. And why are you creating bad Karma for yourself by thinking negatively about him?" Murli attempted to remind Ruchi of the law of Karma.

"Yes, you are right! What are you going to do next?" Ruchi asked.

"While I am concerned about the entire team, I am most concerned about Parth and Karan. Others are juniors, so they can find a job sooner or later and they don't have many financial liabilities either. Parth and Karan, on the other hand, are seniors, so getting a job this quickly will be difficult, even though they are exceptional talents.

"Parth has purchased a ready-to-move-in flat a few months ago and has gone over budget, resulting in a massive EMI load for him. Also, he mentioned a few days ago that his sister's wedding is coming up in a few weeks and that his parents are completely reliant on Parth for all expenses.

"Karan just started last week, and he had great hopes for this job based on my promises during the interview. If he loses this job, he will face immense social pressure and may even be humiliated by his ex-colleagues." Murli was quite concerned.

Ruchi attempted to comfort Murli by grasping his hand. "This is a terrible circumstance for everyone, but you must rise above it and deal with it."

"But how, Ruchi?" Murli still hadn't come up with any plans.

"Do you remember the Bhagavad Gita session we attended last month?" Ruchi inquired.

"Yes, it was nicely delivered."

"Let's have a little brainstorming session." Ruchi created the figure below on one blank page of paper.

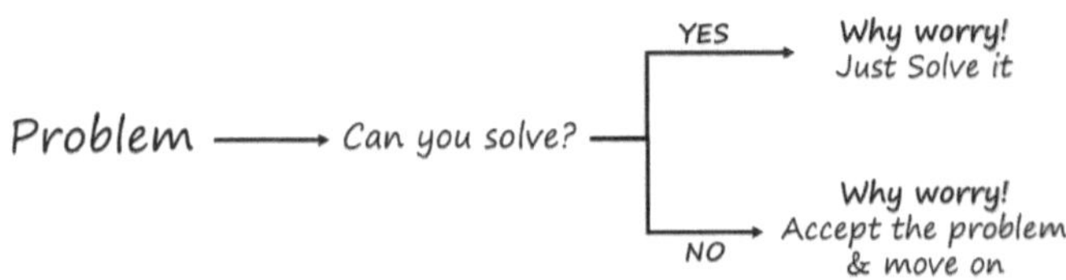


Looking at Murli, Ruchi explained, "Isn't this what he explained? If you have a problem, first ask yourself if you can solve it. Why get stressed thinking about it if you cannot? You must accept the situation and move forward to deal with it.

If you can solve it, then do whatever it takes to get the problem solved. You may not know how to fix it right now, but if you have an inner belief that you can, you will eventually find a way. Now, tell me can you solve your current problem?" She asked.

"Yes, I believe I can do something about it, but I'm not sure what," Murli pondered for a moment. "But then I find that I can't stop the pandemic, change Aman's mind, or get HealthTech financing!" Murli's expression was filled with frustration once more.

"Murli, you are always thinking about how to solve the problem entirely, and you have already figured out that you cannot do it. Consider whether you can lessen the impact of the outcomes. Do you recall the Circle of Influence and Circle of Concern from Stefan Covey's book, *7 Habits of Highly Successful People*?"

"Of course! What a fantastic book!" Murli stood up and took the book from his bookshelf. He then opened the book to the figure below.

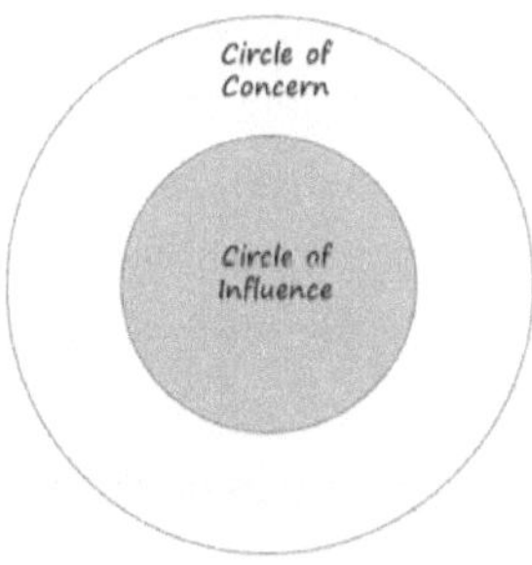


Murli continued to expound with zeal.

"These circles distinguish between proactive people, who focus on what they can accomplish and influence, and reactive people, who focus their efforts on matters beyond their control.

The first is our circle of concern. This is the bigger one as it encompasses a wide range of factors such as the state of the economy, global politics, societal attitudes, the organization you work for, what your co-workers do, how people drive their automobiles, and so on. The list may go on and on, but the important thing to remember is that you may have little control over many of these issues since they are outside your control. Devoting energy to control them will be a waste of time.

On the other hand, our circle of influence will be significantly smaller. It contains the things that we can change, like your health, skills, project work which is assigned to you etc. The idea is to focus your energy on the things you can control in order to create effective changes. If you do this, you will see that your circle of influence starts expanding slowly; others will regard you as an effective person, which will boost your influence. If you focus all of your energy on things you can't change, your circle of influence will narrow. Not only will you deplete your energy, but others may begin to perceive you as overly negative and judgmental.

In a nutshell, reactive people have smaller circles of influence, whereas proactive people have larger circles of influence."

Murli explained everything in one breath.

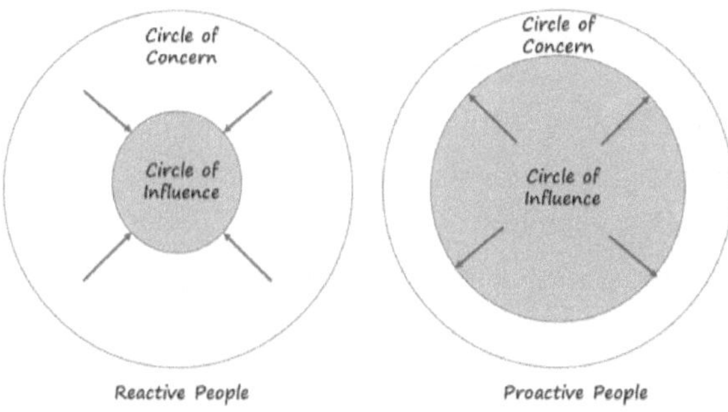


"You have a great deal of information, and I am so proud of you; nevertheless, I do not understand why you do not put it to use, Mr. Murlidhar." Ruchi teased him.

"Oh no! So, all this while I was focusing on the circle of control," Murli exclaimed. "When conditions are difficult, the clutter in our minds overpowers our intellect," he admitted.

"Yes, and it can happen even to someone as knowledgeable as Mr Murlidhar," Ruchi replied with a smile.

Murli got up from his chair and embraced Ruchi in his arms, staring at her sweetly.

"Thank you, Ruchi, for putting me on the right path. I am so lucky to have a life partner like you who helps me walk the path of spirituality," he added lovingly.

"No, Murli, I consider myself fortunate to have you as a companion. When we first met, I was a non-spiritual person like most out there. You never forced me to pursue any spiritual path over the years. You simply continued to demonstrate how to live life on that road. Unknowingly, I also started walking down that path because I saw how balanced your life was."

"Thank God I proposed to you in college; otherwise, I used to fear I wasn't good enough for you," Murli replied slyly.

"And the way you had proposed was unique. From the third year onwards, you were a completely different person." stated Ruchi smilingly. "Oh, it's seven o'clock; I need to pick up Radha from her Karate sessions," Ruchi replied, breaking free from Murli's embrace.

As she left, Murli reclined back in his chair, and that mention of college by Ruchi took him back into his past as it started flashing in front of his eyes.

Sitting in his study, Murli recalled moving to Pune to pursue his engineering degree.

Still searching for answers to many of life's problems, he attended several talks by many spiritual gurus while studying for his engineering degree in order to find answers to his issues. He received some and kept looking for more. He had always felt the Bhagavad Gita was more about theoretical philosophy and not practical to follow in today's contemporary, competitive world, but a part of him still wanted to learn more about it.

In fact, it wasn't until one of life's challenges hit Murli hard in college that he was able to open up more to understanding how spirituality was not simply wrapped up in books but could also serve as a practical solution to dealing with life's small or big problems.

Back in college, Murli was extremely dedicated to his studies but somehow was never able to get good grades, which used to frustrate him a lot. In addition, he was also the victim of severe bullying by Sahil and his gang. They made fun of his non-urban mannerisms and straight-edge lifestyle, calling him a geek and a loser. He tried his best to ignore them and focus on his studies, but their taunts and jeers were constant.

Over the course of time, being treated as an outsider, Murli couldn't help but feel a sense of disappointment and hurt.

One day, as Murli was walking to class, Sahil and his group appeared out of nowhere. They surrounded him, laughing and jeering.

"What's up, Murli? You still living like a country bumpkin?" Sahil sneered.

Murli took a deep breath, trying to remain calm. "I'm just trying to focus on my studies," he said quietly.

"Aw, poor little Murli," Sahil chimed in. "Maybe if you dressed a little cooler and hung out with us more, you wouldn't be such an outcast."

Murli felt his face heat up with anger and embarrassment. He had always felt like an outsider in the city, but he had never expected to be treated like this. However, as he felt his frustration reaching a boiling point, he took a deep breath and reminded himself of his purpose: to aid his family in altering the trajectory of their present lifestyle. He took a deep breath and closed his eyes. As he opened his eyes, he felt a sense of calm and detachment. The jeers of Sahil and his group faded away, and he felt as if he were watching the scene from a distance.

He turned and walked away, ignoring their taunts. As he walked, he felt a sense of pride and self-assurance that he had never felt before. He knew that he was on the right path, and nothing could stop him from achieving his goals.

From that day forward, Murli continued to study hard and tried to excel in his classes. The bullying from Sahil and his group continued. Murli's calmness made Sahil even more fierce in his torture. Just when Murli thought that he had almost become immune to the torture unfolded on him by Sahil and his gang, they became increasingly harsh and relentless. They would follow him around, taunting him and making fun of his accent and clothing. It seemed like there was no escape from their cruel words and actions.

One day, as Murli was walking home from class, Sahil and his gang appeared out of nowhere. They surrounded him, pushing him and laughing.

"What's wrong, Murli? Can't handle the big city?" Sahil sneered.

Murli felt a surge of frustration, but he had tried to ignore them and rise above their bullying. But before he could say anything, Sahil took it to a whole new level. He grabbed Murli's backpack and dumped its contents onto the ground, scattering his books and notes everywhere.

"Oops, looks like you dropped something," Sahil said, smirking.

The other members of the gang erupted into laughter, and Murli felt a wave of humiliation wash over him. He bent down to gather his things, but the gang kicked them away, sending them flying. Murli's heart sank. He had enough. He couldn't take it anymore. He felt like a failure, like he had let his family down. He didn't know what to do.

That evening, Murli sat on the edge of his bed, staring at the wall in front of him. The bustling sounds of Pune city filtered in from the window, but he hardly noticed them. Instead, his mind was consumed with thoughts of home - lush green fields, the cows grazing in the pastures, and his mother's loving smile. He missed it all terribly. But he had made a promise to himself and his family: he would study hard, become an IT professional, and give them a better life. He had come to Pune with a single-minded determination to achieve his goals, no matter what.

But the bullying by Sahil and his gang had left him broken.

He called his mother from a phone booth.

"Hello, Ma!" he said, his voice barely above a whisper as he struggled to hold back tears.

"Murli, my son, how are you?" His mother replied, her voice filled with warmth and love. She was strict but equally loving toward her son.

"I'm not good, Ma," Murli said, his voice cracking. "The bullying...it's just too much."

His mother's voice grew concerned, "What bullying, Murli? What's going on?"

Murli took a deep breath and explained everything -bullying, the taunts, the humiliation. He told her how he felt like a failure, like he couldn't handle the pressure of the city.

His mother listened patiently, her heart breaking for her son, but she knew that she had to be strong for him.

"Why has God been so unfair to me, Ma?" Murli continued. "We perform all of his rituals and adhere to all of his traditions. You are so devoted to him; why is he continuing to put your son through this? Does God truly exist?" He was frustrated.

"Murli, my son," his mother replied firmly yet gently. "Just have faith in God. Can you truly enjoy the day if there is no night? Also, keep in mind that you are not a failure. You are strong and capable. You can manage whatever comes your way. All you have to do is believe in yourself and God."

Murli felt a glimmer of hope in his heart. He knew that his mother was right. He couldn't give up. He had to stand tall and face his problems with dignity.

"Thank you, Ma," he said, his voice filled with gratitude. "You always know just what to say."

His mother started laughing, "That's what mothers are for, my son! I can be strict at times, but I am always there to love and support you."

On weekends, Murli never stayed back in the hostel to avoid bullying from other students. He would find out if there were any spiritual lectures happening in the city and then spend his time there understanding the spiritual knowledge.

His friends used to mock him for attending the spiritual meetings instead of "enjoying life," as they defined it by watching movies, wandering about the city, and running after girls. They used to refer to him as 'Grandpa'.

Murli, on the other hand, was unconcerned. It was more important to him to discover answers to his questions than to care about what other people thought. Little did he know that his thirst for discovering the deepest secrets of life was about to be quenched.

# 7

# THE MEETING THAT CHANGED EVERYTHING

It was a quiet Sunday morning, and Murli had plans to attend Dr Ram's Bhagavad Gita lecture.  Since he was so pumped up, he left the hostel before 8 o'clock, long before his sleeping roommates were up.

It was a small group of about 15-20 people in Dr Ram's session, and Murli stood out as the lone young man among the elderly audience. Dr Ram lectured widely on the Bhagavad Gita's profound spiritual lessons and was a famous scientist in retirement.

Murli had great hopes this time because it was delivered by a scientist, so he expected a scientific examination of the Gita to pacify his logical mind, but instead the session took a typical turn of merely explaining passages from the Gita.

This frustrated Murli, and he shouted, "Why should we believe in the Bhagavad Gita?  There is very little scientific evidence that anything preached in it works!"

Everyone turned to stare at him, and Murli realized he had been rude to both the speaker and the audience.

He apologized and said, "Ummm, I'm sorry, I didn't mean that, I......."

Dr Ram cut Murli off and asked, "What is your name, young man?"

"My name is Murli, and I am studying engineering here in the city." Murli replied, still embarrassed.

"Murli, I'm pleased to see a young man of your age taking so much interest in the Bhagavad Gita. Now tell me in detail, what are your questions?" asked Dr Ram in a calm voice.

"Sir, I just do not believe that following Lord Krishna's path is realistic in today's ever-changing life. The Bhagavad Gita seems to be out of date."

Murli's question astonished everyone.

"OK, fair enough," Dr Ram responded. "Let's take it one step at a time. What actually bothers you, son?"

"Sir, I am not able to comprehend that we are not the body, but we are souls, which are immortal and only leave the body after death, like changing the clothing. I don't believe in Karma either. There are many evil people in society who are happy and prosperous while doing heinous crimes." Murli was uninhibited in expressing his opinion.

"Interesting questions! Let's take a break; it's lunchtime, and Murli, let's talk over lunch. Everyone, let's catch up in an hour." Dr Ram said as they took a break.

They proceeded to a neighboring tiny café for lunch. Dr Ram found a quiet spot for Murli and himself and ordered for the lunch. While they were eating, a small girl, perhaps about 4-5 years old, appeared on the sidewalk with her mother begging for food.

Dr Ram pointed to her and asked Murli, "Why do you think that young girl is so impoverished that she doesn't even have anything to eat?"

Murli was perplexed, yet he remarked with sadness in his eyes, "God has been cruel to that poor little girl."

"Well, it's always easy to blame God for our pain since we know he'll never come to justify himself," Dr Ram remarked with a laugh.

Murli felt embarrassed as he remembered blaming God for all his troubles to his mother the other day.

"Why is it that someone is born into a highly affluent family, and someone is born into an incredibly poor family?" Dr Ram fired another question at Murli.

Murli had no answer to this question either.

"OK, tell me why certain 3—-year-old children can swim, sing, dance, solve hard mathematical problems, and speak various languages at such a young age without any formal education?" Dr Ram shot another question.

These questions baffled Murli, and he had no idea how to respond.

"Well, now let me answer those questions for you, one by one. I'm guessing you're worried about two things: first, who we are, body or soul; and second, what is the law of Karma, correct?"

"Yes, these questions have been baffling me since childhood" nodded Murli in affirmation.

The Bhagavad Gita, at a high level, may be broken down into three sections. Section one deals with our distinct identities as souls. The second section elaborates on the nature of the ultimate reality, or God. Finally, section three describes how our soul relates to God." Dr Ram started explaining the Bhagavad Gita. "Let's talk about the first part. So, tell me who you think we are?"

"This is me sitting here talking with you." Murli tried his best to give an answer.

"Are you saying that you are this body with all these parts, legs, head, eyes, etc.?"

"That's right," replied Murli confidently.

"What if someone chops off your hands? Would you still be alive?" asked Dr Ram.

"Of course, I will be alive." As Murli responded, he thought to himself, *'What a silly question!'*

"That means you're not your hands?" Another question came from Dr Ram.

Murli shook his head in affirmation.

"Assume someone removes your legs, ears, nose, and eyes; you will still be alive, indicating that you are not these body parts. Is that correct, Murli?" Dr Ram continued with his questions.

The more inquiries Dr Ram asked, the more perplexed Murli became.

"I'm confused," Murli said. "What are you trying to say? One will still have his brain, heart, lungs, and so on."

"Are you saying that you are only these parts and not the entire body?"

Murli was stumped.

"OK, let me make it simple for you," Dr Ram said, smiling. "So, if someone dies naturally, his entire body will be intact, with all of its parts, right?"

"Yes, right!"

"But why do we call him dead?"

"Because he can't move or do anything." Murli answered with some confidence this time.

"Correct, do you now believe that there was something in

his body that has now left? Murli, what could it be?"

Murli responded, "Energy?" after a brief moment of thought.

"Bingo!! The energy that was driving the body left, and that energy is known as 'the soul'."

"Hmm. Yes, that does seem plausible," Murli said, "but I am still unable to fathom this soul notion. I believe what I see."

"OK, fair enough." Dr Ram said, "Let me explain in scientific terms. What is Einstein's energy theory?"

"Energy can never be destroyed or created. It can only be converted from one form to another." Murli replied confidently.

"Right!! This means that the same energy can sit as a table, lie as mud, and stand as a tree. Although everything in the universe is made of the same energy, it vibrates at different frequencies and takes on different forms. Everything in the universe is made up of energy!" Dr Ram finally got to the point he intended to make.

"Oh, I see!" Murli was surprised.

"This same energy propels our bodies. This can be referred to as the soul, spirit, or simply energy. When this energy leaves our bodies, we are declared medically dead. This body has all of its parts intact, including the heart, liver, and kidneys, but it cannot function on its own without this energy. It's like a light bulb: as a physical object, it is visible, but it won't work unless we turn on the invisible electricity. Our bodies, like light bulbs, require energy or soul in order to function."

Murli was all ears.

Dr Ram continued, "In verse 27 of Chapter 2 of the Gita, Lord

Krishna says:

जातस्य हि ध्रुवो मृत्युर्ध्रुवं जन्म मृतस्य च।
तस्मादपरिहार्येऽर्थे न त्वं शोचितुमर्हसि।।

**Jatasya hi dhruvo mrityurdhuvam janm mritasya cha I**
**Tasmadapariharye'rthe na tvam sochitumaharsi II**

**Because one who is born will undoubtedly die, and one who dies will undoubtedly be born. As a result, you should not lament this unavoidable fact.**

"Therefore, while the body dies, the soul lives forever. Murli, are you getting the point?"

"Yes, sir, I think I'm getting it now," Murli replied, "but my rigid mind still has some doubts."

Dr Ram and Murli talked at length on this topic. Dr Ram was the one being questioned this time, and his responses were straightforward and unambiguous. Murli found the man's understanding of the Bhagavad Gita and life to be astounding.

Dr Ram realized it was time to get back to his lecture. "Murli, that was a great talk! Now that time is up, I must resume my lecture. I know I have yet to respond to your questions about Karma. Please contact me later this week."

"I appreciate your time very much, Sir. Can we meet next Sunday, if I'm not bothering you?" Murli requested.

"No problem; I've never had a curious student like you before; I'll be happy to explain," Dr Ram replied warmly. "But I have one exercise for you during this week."

"What exactly is it, Sir?" Murli asked with curiosity.

"For the next week, until we meet, imagine yourself as energy that is using this body to do your work. Attempt to separate yourself from this body. Will you do it?" asked Dr Ram.

"I will definitely try," Murli replied with enthusiasm.

Dr Ram took a food parcel as he was leaving the cafeteria and gave it to the little girl outside.

Murli was so captivated by his newfound guru's words that he didn't notice the time passing as he walked back to the hostel from the lecture. As was the norm, the moment he checked into the hostel, the teasing began. "Look! It's Grandpa!"

Murli disregarded them and went for his studies.

He started working hard on the exercise assigned to him by Dr Ram. But he was unable to continuously let go of his body consciousness. However, whenever he was able to do so, he experienced a new sensation: one of lightness. He tried to maintain that level of soul consciousness but found it impossible and used to get frustrated. He was a committed student and he persisted with the practice.

Murli's lifelong curiosity about the world around him finally started to get satisfied, and he was better able to concentrate on the lectures in the college. He had found the right direction, and now he simply needed to follow it with commitment.

One day, Sahil started making fun of him while he ate lunch in the college cafeteria, as he always did. Murli, like usual, chose to ignore him, but this time he was struck with an idea. 'There isn't much I can do to change things here. Why not try soul consciousness?' he wondered to himself. Then he imagined that Sahil was a soul, a manifestation of the same creative energy that produced everybody. He felt like he was observing the scene from a distance: a person named Sahil was bullying a person named Murli. He was so fascinated that he began to smile to himself.

Sahil was enraged when he saw Murli smile; he became even more violent and began ridiculing Murli more.

Murli's smile became bigger. Sahil became irritated and exited the canteen. Murli felt more empowered than ever before.

After that incident, Sahil and his group stopped harassing Murli since they realized it would be futile. Murli learned an essential life lesson that week: *Situations only have control over you if you let them! They lose their power if you simply accept them and do not feed them with energy through your emotions.*

Murli had been looking forward to meeting Dr Ram all week, so on Sunday morning he headed out of the hostel to meet him in a garden close to his residence. It was a beautiful garden with lush green lawn, exotic flowers, and pathways to walk. Murli reached the garden sharp at 8 o'clock as agreed with Dr Ram. As he waited in the garden, he saw people exercising and speaking with one another.

He made the deliberate shift to thinking of people as souls rather than physical beings. He experienced something newsensation of oneness.

Dr Ram arrived and cheerfully greeted Murli, "How are you, young man? How was your exercise?"

"I am fine, Sir. The exercise did not go well. I couldn't concentrate and frequently forgot to see myself as a soul rather than a body. I tried to refocus my attention, but I got off track again and again," Murli said, disappointed.

Dr Ram began to laugh. He said, "Don't worry, young man, this is normal; at the very least, you tried to refocus your attention, which takes practice. When you begin to see yourself as a soul, you will begin to see everyone else as a soul as well.

Just keep practicing."

"But it is not easy," Murli complained.

"Who said it was going to be easy? Please give yourself some time as you strive to break years of conditioning. Don't be hard on yourself. Even if you can't focus all of the time, strive to be soul-conscious anytime you're in a challenging situation and feel lost. That will be a good starting point for you," advised Dr Ram.

Murli was listening carefully.

"If you begin to see yourself as a soul and not a body, you will not do anything for your body that may darken your soul because you will be leaving your body on mother earth but taking all your Karma recorded on your soul, which will define your fate."

"Ok, got it," Murli responded.

"That brings me onto Karma, but before we get started, let us first understand the second part of the Bhagavad Gita, namely, God."

"Yes, please; I've been waiting for this for a week." Murli enthusiasm could be seen in his eyes.

"Who do you think our creator will be if we are energy?"

"More powerful energy," Murli responded.

"That is correct, so God is a supreme soul with a powerful source of light energy that has no shape or karmic bonds. And if you read holy books from any religion, they all preach the same thing: *God is light, and God is one.*"

"Then who is Krishna if God is light?"

"Because the supreme soul is non-physical, it requires a body to convey the message. Krishna is a physical manifestation of the Supreme Soul, as Lord Krishna states in verses 7 and 8 of Chapter 4 of the Gita:

"यदा यदा हि धर्मस्य ग्लानिर्भवति भारत। अभ्युत्थानमधर्मस्य
तदात्मानं सृजाम्यहम् II
*yadā yadā hi dharmasya glānir bhavati bhārata*
*abhyutthānam adharmasya tadātmānaṁ sṛijāmyaham*

परित्राणाय साधूनां विनाशाय च दुष्कृताम् । धर्मसंस्थापनार्थाय
सम्भवामि युगे युगे II
*paritrāṇāya sādhūnāṁ vināśhāya cha duṣhkṛitām*
*dharma-sansthāpanārthāya sambhavāmi yuge yuge*

**"Whenever there is a decay of righteousness and an exaltation of unrighteousness, then I myself come forth. Whenever virtue subsides and wickedness prevails, I manifest myself. From ages to ages, I have come to establish virtue, destroy evil, and save the good."**
Dr Ram waited for a moment and asked Murli, "Is this clear to you now?

"I suppose," murmured Murli.

"Let us now discuss the third part of the Bhagavad Gita, which is about the relationship between us as souls and God. Here, Lord Krishna says that God is in everything, and everything is in God. We are all part of the same universal energy; we just have different forms depending on the frequency at which we vibrate.

"So we're just a speck of energy in the vaster energy system of the universe. You know what SOUL means: Source of Unique Light. This universe is just one big organism. Your life is not independent of it; everyone is a source of unique light. We are made of the same energy and dissolve into the same energy." Dr Ram explained everything to Murli passionately.

Murli was captivated by this explanation.

"Now, let us return to your question about Karma. First, let us define Karma. What do you think Karma is?" asked Dr Ram.

"Karma is the actions we take in our daily lives," Murli answered confidently.

"Well, that's the half-truth. Let me tell you a story:

*"Every weekend, two friends used to go to a bar. They would drink, smoke, and have fun with girls every weekend.*

*"When they were on their way to the bar one weekend, one of their friends noticed a Bhagavad Gita lecture going on. He was deeply ashamed of his actions. He asked a friend to accompany him to this lecture, rather than the bar. His friend mocked him for trading the bar for a lecture on the Bhagavad Gita and tried to persuade him to come to the bar with him, but the first friend refused and went into the hall to attend the lecture while the other friend went about his routine in the bar.*

*During the lecture, the first friend became restless, thinking about the other friend and how much fun he must be having in the bar. Throughout the lecture, he kept imagining his friend having fun in the bar.*

Now tell me who created good karma?"

"Obviously, the one who went to the lecture! While the other friend who went to the bar, he at least tried to follow the right path." Murli responded boldly.

"That's the problem, Murli; most of us don't know what Karma is, and we're always under the impression that Karma is simply the actions we take."

"What do you mean? Isn't that true?" asked Murli with surprise.

"What if I told you that the first friend who went to the lecture created more bad Karma?"

"How? That's not possible!" objected Murli.

"Allow me to define Karma for you in its true sense. Karma is more than just our actions; that is only a tip of the iceberg. Karma is also the thoughts we create."

"How? My thoughts do not harm anyone." Murli objected again.

"That's what you think!  Tell me, what exactly are thoughts?"

"Thoughts are created by the mind."

"True, but what are thoughts?" Dr Ram asked the question again.

Murli was perplexed by this query.

"Let me explain. Thoughts are simply the energy that we create. So, when we create a thought, we create energy, and that energy vibrates from us and reaches the person or thing about which the thought was created. This is a more subtle process than actions that have an immediate impact." Dr Ram explained.

"Wow, that's fascinating but difficult to believe!" Murli responded.

"Have you ever noticed that when you meet some people, you feel uneasy even though they haven't done anything wrong to you?"

"Yes, that happens frequently with me. Is it because of the kind of thoughts they have about me?"

"Exactly!!"

"Now I understand."

Dr Ram continued explaining further, "The law of Karma states that you will reap what you sow, what goes around eventually comes around. While we are concerned with our actions, we completely disregard our thoughts, not realizing how much Karmic baggage we are accumulating through our thoughts! And believe me, this is the law of Karma, my friend, and it always works. Our souls are like tape recorders; they record all of our Karma, and we get what we deserve in this life based on our Karma from previous lives. It's as simple as that: good Karma brings good fortune, and bad Karma brings bad fortune."

Murli and Dr Ram were having an animated conversation about various facets of the law of Karma. It wasn't even ten o'clock yet, and the nice morning sun rays had been taken over by a hostile sun blazing with all his cannons.

Dr Ram decided to call the meeting to a close. "Are you now clear on the Karma, Murli?" he inquired one last time.

Murli paused for a moment before saying, "Yes Sir, while this all makes perfect sense, this could be one theory, but there could be other reasons we don't know about."

"Your point is valid, but for me, the Bhagavad Gita is the ultimate truth that I have discovered over my lifetime by experimenting with its laws," the old scientist said. Dr Ram further said, "As a scientist, I believe in experimenting, so I would like for you to experiment with the learning from the Bhagavad Gita and not take my words as final. For example, how do you solve mathematical equations to prove the formula is correct?"

Murli said, "We start with an assumption, like a=b, and then we solve the questions with this assumption. Once it is solved, we prove that our assumption was right."

"Excellent. Now, please assume the Bhagavad Gita is right and start experimenting with your life and see where Lord Krishna takes you," the scientist said with a smile.

It was nearing the end of the session when Dr Ram said to Murli, "As William Shakespeare has said: *All the world's a stage, and all the men and women are merely players; they have their exits and their entrances.* Don't take life too seriously; instead, focus on doing the work that truly brings you joy, and remember that we're all just actors in this grand drama."

"Thank you, Sir," Murli said, his voice filled with gratitude. "I feel so much better now. Thank you for showing me the path of spirituality!"

Dr Ram smiled, patting him on the back. "I always knew you had it in you, Murli," he said. "Now go out there and show the world that you are the true son of God. Your every action should be in line with what Krishna has taught in the Bhagavad Gita!"

With Dr Ram's words ringing in his ears, Murli stood up, feeling more confident and determined than ever before. After that day, Murli experienced a renewed sense of purpose and determination, but his journey of embracing spiritual truths and principles had just started.

Because Dr Ram had piqued his interest during that visit, Murli made certain that he did not miss any opportunities to hear him out. He had been struggling to understand the deeper understanding of spiritual keys the Bhagavad Gita had to provide until he obtained answers to his questions. He had numerous discussions with his scientist mentor. He felt liberated from all the questions that had plagued him since childhood. The direction of his life was now completely evident to him.

Murli discovered he didn't want to be religious; instead, he desired to be spiritual. Religion was created to help mankind pursue a path of spiritual values like peace, love, and compassion, but Murli has seen how religion is now being exploited to foster enmity among individuals who share the same source of energy. He began to see everyone as a part of the broader universal energy.

His college life transformed drastically; instead of being always stressed, he felt liberated. Murli also discovered why he hadn't been receiving good grades despite his efforts: he was constantly held back by expectations from himself and his family. He began to improve dramatically in academics as he began to let go of the burden of expectations. In fact, he became the class topper starting in his third year. He was fun to be around. He was helpful and compassionate toward others. Everybody loved him. Instead of Grandpa, he was now called the rock star of the group.

While Murli was immersed in his thoughts, Ruchi knocked on the door, "Murli, it's 11 o'clock; are you coming to sleep?"

"It's already 11 o'clock? I completely lost track of time." he was surprised by how much time had passed.

As he was going to bed, he reflected on the hardships he had endured. He had learned that unprecedented challenges can either make one stronger than ever before or shatter them into pieces that are difficult to reassemble, depending on the mindset of the individuals.

He was not sure whether this impending storm was going to make his team stronger or blow them out of their feet!

8

# UNFOLDING THE HARSH REALITY

I t had only been four days since Aman had informed Murli of the layoffs, but it felt like an eternity to him. For all those days, Murli had been fighting conflicts between his mind and brain. He was finally clear on what he needed to do next, thanks to clarity from his wife and guru.

The next morning, as usual, Murli and Ruchi were having their breakfast.

"Did you think about your circle of control, Murli?" Ruchi inquired as she sipped her tea.

"Yes, I also reflected on the lessons Ram Sir had taught me during my college days. I have realized that I can't change the situation entirely, but I'll make sure Karan and Parth are prepared for this jolt by explaining some fundamental principles from the Bhagavad Gita."

"How about the other team members?" Ruchi inquired.

"First and foremost, disclosing such information to 40 members may jeopardize the entire goal. We don't know how these many people will react to such sessions, when we break the news to them. Aman will also not let me 'waste' so many people's time. As I mentioned yesterday, if Parth and Karan lose their jobs, they will have the greatest impact, so I'm focusing on them." Murli further explained.

"I agree that you should have targeted sessions with them." Ruchi nodded in agreement.

"However, Ruchi, I am not a spiritual guru. How can I educate someone about the Bhagavad Gita when I am not qualified for it?" Murli expressed his concern.

"No one is better qualified than you, Murli. You live by those principles day in and day out. Just ensure that you don't overload them with more than what they can chew!" Ruchi advised.

"What do you mean?" Murli inquired.

"Look, these guys will be really upset once they know that their job is on the line, so they would like to use all their time focusing on the project so that they can save their job. Secondly, they will not be in the mindset to listen and absorb Bhagavad Gita teachings as they will think that it's not going to help them deal with their current challenges." Ruchi explained.

"Do you want to say that I only explain what is required to deal with the current situation?" Murli inquired.

"Exactly!"

"It will be difficult to extract simply a few droplets from such an ocean of knowledge." Murli responded with apprehension.

"Don't worry, honey, I'll help you." Ruchi assured him.

"I appreciate you always being there for me, Ruchi." Murli said as he looked lovingly at his wife.

Throughout the week, Ruchi and Murli worked in the evenings preparing the information sharing sessions with Parth and Karan.

On a lazy Sunday morning, Murli was ready with a plan for his knowledge-sharing sessions. He dialed Parth and Karan and invited them over for coffee in the evening at his place.

This surprised them, as Murli had never invited anyone to his home before. They gladly accepted the invitation and arrived at 5 o'clock in the evening. When Murli opened the door, his 7-year-old daughter Radha greeted them.

Parth and Karan noticed a stunning 2-foot-tall statue of Lord Krishna as they entered the house. Murli explained that the statue reminded them that their house was nothing short of heaven and that they should always display their finest selves to each other and any guests that come in.

"That's fascinating," Karan responded spontaneously.

Looking around in the house, they could see Murli's personality reflected in it: humble, principled, and grounded. It was a moderately furnished three-bedroom apartment. The walls were painted a warm, earthy color, and the area was brightly lit by natural light, providing a friendly and welcoming atmosphere. They could see statues and art prints ranging from Buddha to nature.

"Let us go to my study." Murli warmly invited them inside.

As they entered Murli's study, they could feel the space's wonderful vibes, and there was a lovely aroma in the room that was refreshing. Ruchi walked in and served them water.

"Murli keeps mentioning both of you and your amazing work." Ruchi complimented Parth and Karan.

They in turn expressed their gratitude to Ruchi for her warm words.

"Ruchi, could you please bring us coffee and some snacks?" Murli made the request.

"Sure, coffee is ready; just give me a few minutes!"

They settled on the cozy sofa around a center table and exchanged usual pleasantries.

"Murli, you and Aman both appeared disturbed this whole week. I've never seen you two like this before. What's the problem? The entire team is concerned," Parth suddenly inquired.

Ruchi arrived with snacks and coffee before Murli could respond. He asked Ruchi to take Radha for a walk outside in the garden because he knew the evening was going to be tumultuous and didn't want them to be exposed to the negative energy.

"Grab some coffee and snacks first, and then we can have discussions." Murli insisted. He knew they would not have their meal after hearing about the layoffs.

They had coffee with snacks while talking about things other than office.

"Your observation is right, Parth. Things are not good at office!" Murli brought the topic back.

"What's the matter?" Karan inquired, visibly concerned.

"Change is continuous, guys! There are certain things in life that we cannot control; there will be events that make us believe that this is the end of the road; nonetheless, we should view such situations as opportunities," Murli tried to be calm.

"What are you talking about, Murli?" Karan, bewildered, questioned.

Murli didn't know where to start but eventually began informing them about the company's financial troubles. He explained that the company was in jeopardy due to budget cuts and a halt in funding from investors. Aman had instructed him to keep only one team and release the other.

"Seriously!! What does that signify for us?" Karan inquired, his voice trembling.

Murli explained what Aman had told him about the competition between the two teams.

"This is not fair. You can't treat us like this. I have contributed so much to this company, so many efforts, so much of my personal time and you are just going to throw us away now? You should have protested, Murli! I didn't expect this, at least, from you!" Parth shouted at the top of his lungs.

"Yes, you guys are behaving incredibly selfishly. You cannot do this to us. Murli, I left my previous organization to join HealthTech because you painted a rosy picture for me. Now you are telling me that I may be fired within one week of joining! Please tell me this is just a joke." yelled Karan, on the edge of tears.

Murli kept quiet. He had no words or courage to console them.

"Murli, please do something about this. I've been working with you for the past ten months. You were always there to help us get out of the trouble. Please help this time too!" Parth was practically begging.

"Yes. Murli. I've heard nothing but positive things about you from the team. You are not the type of manager who abandons his team. I'm confident you'll find a way out, if you try." Karan pleaded from the bottom of his heart.

"I tried everything to avoid this catastrophe and tried several times to persuade Aman. I decided to inform you only after I knew there was no way out," Murli explained, demonstrating he was as helpless as they were.

Parth and Karan were both taken aback. They got up and departed in rage without speaking to Murli anymore.

Murli had anticipated their reaction, and there was nothing

wrong with it. He sat in silence for a few minutes. And then he prayed to Lord Krishna for them before beginning his evening Pooja.

Ruchi and Radha returned an hour later, when Murli had just concluded his pooja. He was sitting quietly at his desk when his wife said, "Was there a problem, Murli? How did it go?"

He told Ruchi everything that had transpired. She remarked, "Oh, that's very sad, but we saw this coming. This is a huge shock for them. Please don't get offended."

"Of course not, Ruchi. I can understand the pain they must have been going through."

"Did you offer them help by conducting sessions about the Bhagavad Gita?" Ruchi inquired, intrigued.

"They were both so agitated. Talking about such sessions would have enraged them even more. I will try to talk to them tomorrow in office" replied Murli.

Ruchi cautioned, "Just a piece of advice: don't anticipate them to accept your offer for the knowledge sessions, so don't feel bad that whatever work we've put together over the course of this week may finally not be used at all."

Murli nodded in confirmation.

Both Karan and Parth were in a state of shock while they left Murli's residence. When they had heard what Murli had to say about the uncertainty of their jobs, they were deep in shock. They both came from different walks of life, and their jobs were important to both of them for their own specific reasons. It meant the world to them to be stable and rooted in their current positions at work.

After Parth reached his apartment, he broke down in tears, which he had been holding since leaving Murli's house. He felt the weight of responsibility on his shoulders as the sole breadwinner for his parents.  He was worried about their financial security and wanted to make sure he could continue to support them. The burden of his home loan was constantly on his mind, and he worried about how he would manage to pay it off. He had a deep sense of duty towards his family, which made him regret bitterly his decision to leave his previous organization to join Aman's startup.

The situation was not much different with Karan either. He was grappling with his decision to leave his well-established job to join Aman's company. He wondered if he had made the right choice and whether he should have listened to the advice of his friends. The thought of facing his friends and admitting that he might have made a mistake was daunting for him. He worried about what they would think of him and whether he would lose their respect for him.

As the night drew on, Karan's heart felt more pierced with betrayal and despair.  His image among his peers was everything to him, and this sudden turn of events threatened to put a dark mark on his impeccable reputation. As he sipped his drink, a sinister twist began to gnaw at his heart, filling him with an ominous foreboding of what was yet to come.

Both young men were seething with rage and resolved to fight to the end if necessary to keep their jobs.

# II

# THE JOURNEY FROM CHAOS TO UNDERSTANDING

9

# MAKING LEMONADE FROM LIFE'S LEMONS

The dreadful day had finally arrived; the day Aman had planned to notify the team of the layoffs. Murli went through his regular morning routine, but his energy was entirely missing, and he was merely going through the motions. His distress was palpable, and Ruchi could feel it.

While Murli was having breakfast, Ruchi walked towards him and put her hand on his shoulder in an attempt to soothe him. She said, "I know today is difficult for you, but understand that it's just part of your job. Nothing you can do will stop this from happening; all you can do is be there for your team and support them through it."

Murli nodded and was ready to leave for work with a clear mind, knowing exactly what he needed to do. He bowed to Krishna as he left the house and prayed for the strength to do the right things.

Aman and Murli had scheduled simultaneous meetings with the support and development teams for 10 o'clock in the morning to break the news of the layoffs. Even though other team members were not aware of the agenda for these meetings and were startled to be invited to them, Parth and Karan were aware of what was going to transpire. Tension was visible on their faces, and one could see that they hadn't slept adequately last night. Their team members continued asking them about what was wrong, but they decided to keep quiet.

Even Nidhi attempted to get information from Karan, "What's the issue, Karan? Is everything alright?"

"You will know in some time," Karan said flatly.

While waiting for Aman and Murli, both the teams were talking about what they thought the agenda would be in their respective conference rooms.

It was roughly 9:30 a.m. when Aman made it to work. The fight he had with Anita that morning had already put a damper on his mood. Anita was frustrated by Aman's habit of returning home drunk from work every day for the past few days. She made an attempt at confronting him, but he ignored her and left for the office in frustration. As he got to the office, he convened Murli and the HR departments in his cabin to review the strategy one last time.

After a brief discussion, they decided that the HR group should be present with both Aman and Murli while they hold meetings in the respective conference rooms.

When Aman entered the room with the HR group, the entire support team was tense.

"Hello team!" Aman said as he greeted them. "I am aware you all are curious to know the agenda for this urgent meeting. Let me get straight to the point: The pandemic in Europe has driven the economy to its knees. Even our customer has been hit hard and they have planned budget cuts. They have requested a 50% reduction in the budget. I'm sorry to inform you that we must reduce the team by 50%, which means I must let go of 13 team members from the support team."

Everybody was shocked to hear the news, there was complete chaos in the room.

Aman tried to calm them down, "Guys, guys, hear me out first. I understand the situation is difficult, but as the owner of this business, I sometimes have to make difficult decisions. You are all fantastic talents, and whoever does not make the list will undoubtedly find another job within the notice period."

Everyone's heart was racing after hearing the news from Aman. Along with the rest of the team, Nidhi began sweating in the air-conditioned room.

"So, I will tell you the names of 13 members who will receive a termination notice from HR today and will have a one-month notice period," Aman began dictating the names.

Nidhi was relieved that her name was not on the list along with her best friend Daksha, but she felt sorry for other team members with whom she had worked for months.

Rasika, a member of HR, took over from Aman, "Today is Monday and the first day of the month. Folks who couldn't make it to the list have time until the 30th of this month with HealthTech."

Nobody had the guts to question Aman, so they just kept quiet, still not able to believe what was happening. The meeting was over in just 10 minutes.

Aman left the room without even attempting to console the team members; he had his own problems to deal with, both professional and personal.

On the other hand, Murli was compassionate while explaining to his development team the current market situation due to the pandemic. He informed them of the decision about the ramp-down plan and that left everybody shell-shocked. He also informed them about the one-month challenge and stated that the team with the best performance would be retained.

Murli spent an hour pacifying the enraged team members, trying to answer their queries, and motivating them to deal with the situation. A look of immense sadness spread across his face as he requested that HR notify all 40 members of the team of their impending dismissal.

He tried to inspire his team members one final time before wrapping up the meeting. "Let me tell you something: We never have control over everything in life. Your attitude towards challenges determines your fate. Just know that I will always be there for you for any help, whether at work or in your personal life, and that my doors are always open to everyone."

He requested Parth and Karan to stay back for a while.

He waited for everybody to leave the room and then said, "Guys, I know this is difficult for you and the rest of the team. I can't change the existing circumstances, but I can help you deal with this difficult situation."

"How?" Parth inquired.

"Have you read the Bhagavad Gita?" Murli threw a question in response.

They both nodded in negative.

Murli was nervous about telling them about the Bhagavad Gita because he had decided not to preach it to anyone. He was well aware that this could potentially go the same way as in the college and he may become the target of ridicule in the entire office, especially when everyone was upset with management.

He recalled what Ruchi had told him in the morning and eventually gathered the courage to speak out since he cared more about the boys than his own reputation.

"The Bhagavad Gita does not preach religion but rather tells us how to conduct our lives. If we can incorporate this wisdom into our daily lives, we will not suffer, regardless of the circumstances. Even though it was written 5000 years ago, the wisdom contained in this book is timeless and applicable even in today's modern world. The battleground of Kurukshetra is indicative of the mental warfare we fight every day. *We can only win this fight of life if we have spiritual understanding of the principles and the fortitude to live by them.*" Murli said in a single breath, which didn't seem to have any impact on the boys.

"Why are you telling us this?" Karan was enraged.

"I understand you're in a difficult situation right now. I can help show you the path outlined in the Bhagavad Gita so you can deal with this situation in a better way." Murli's response seemed to be one of borrowed confidence, which was highly out of character for a man who normally beamed with confidence during official meetings.

"Murli, are you insane? We're on the verge of losing our jobs, and you want to teach us the Bhagavad Gita? Seriously?" Parth yelled back.

Murli remained silent since he was unsure how to respond, although, in the back of his mind, he had anticipated a similar response.

"I'm sorry, Murli. I didn't intend to yell at you. You are aware of our mental state," Parth apologized after gaining control over his emotions.

"Don't worry, Parth. I absolutely understand. I'm just trying to help you in any way I can. Just one piece of advice from my side; *remember not to blame others for your problems. By blaming others, you miss out on an opportunity to assess and better yourself.*

*Please recognize that changing your mindset will put an end to all your sufferings."*

"No philosophy, please! I think it was a blunder to join this company," Karan said in frustration.

"Calm down, Karan! You can't go back and change the beginning, but the boat can start sailing from where it is right now, and you can definitely change the times to come. Please let me help you, and I promise you won't regret it." Murli pleaded.

Karan and Parth ignored his words as they stormed out of the room. As they walked towards their desks, they looked at each other with furious competitiveness; it was now survival of the fittest. While they always exchanged icy vibes, they never showed it openly. Now that this competition was official, they were determined to offer everything they had in this one month.

Murli walked out of the conference room with a blank expression. He was disheartened that Parth and Karan had refused his help. Not because he took offense at their sudden outrage, but rather because he was aware that this knowledge would have transformed their lives. He closed his eyes and prayed to Lord Krishna to give every member of his team the strength they needed to deal with this time of turmoil.

Once a hive of youthful excitement during lunch, the cafeteria was now sitting silent and lifeless.

The office, which used to be full of enthusiasm, has devolved into a place of worry and anxiety. Everyone had a worried expression on their face.

Murli rushed to Aman's cabin to express his dissatisfaction with the entire situation.

"Have a look at the team, Aman! They have toiled for you

for months; do you feel justified in being so unkind to them?" Murli was plainly upset.

Aman was about to explode, but he restrained himself and asked Murli in a cool but frustrated tone, "So, tell me, if you were in my shoes, what you would have done. Let the business sink?"

"That's not the case, Aman. The success of our business is our topmost priority, and we will do everything in our power to see to it that it thrives, but never at the cost of the people who make up our organization. I would have waited for a couple more months before making such a decision, and in that time, I would have subtly encouraged some of the team's under performers to start looking for new jobs. If the situation had not improved, I would have given those under performing team members one month's notice. This would have allowed them at least three months to seek jobs. And the very idea of two teams competing against one another is absurd!" Murli was quite vocal about his opinion this time.

"Why didn't you tell me this before?" Aman inquired gently.

"Because I knew you wouldn't agree to this," Murli explained.

Aman grinned and asked, his tone going up, "Since you know me so much better, why are you here again playing the same team-related tape recorder?"

"Because I thought you still had some humanity in you!" Murli responded to Aman with disdain.

"Watch your language, Murli! I am a businessman, not a human rights activist. I will do what is best for my company," Aman yelled at Murli, getting up and pounding his palms on the table in rage.

Murli realized that arguing with Aman was a waste of time

and energy, so he left Aman's cabin without a single word further.

While the support team was under no pressure to work overtime, the development teams started working 12—hours per day to meet the deadline before the opposing team. Murli was feeling terrible for them. He used to stay in the office till the teams were through working for the day to see if they needed any help.

It had only been two days since the team received the termination notice, but Parth, who was normally calm, was already losing control. He was heard yelling at one of his teammates as he had messed up the entire module by using incorrect reasoning in the code. When every minute counted for survival, he now had to spend hours redoing everything.

Karan and his team felt happy since the competing team would now trail them.

Parth left in frustration and walked outside into the lobby. Murli came looking for him.

"Don't worry, Parth; these things happen; you are not new to this. Clear your mind and get back to work." Murli tried to console him.

"Murli, I've been under a lot of stress for the past few days. I haven't been sleeping or eating well. I'm really depressed. All of the bad thoughts concerning the ramifications of not keeping this job keep running through my head." Parth's voice trembled as he felt helpless. With his head in his hands, he plunked down on the lobby chair.

Murli trying to support Parth, sat on the adjacent chair, patted him on the back, and tried to pacify him. He said, "There is nothing like the end of the road in life, Parth. This is just a phase; there is always a new beginning waiting. *Always remember you have to fight through the bad days to make the best days."*

"But Murli, these negative thoughts just don't stop!" Parth seemed hopeless, with tears rolling out of his eyes.

"Negative thoughts are sure to come in the life of every human being, Parth, but it depends on us human beings as to how much importance we give to these thoughts. Instead, focus only on the positive aspects of your life. That's a sign of a strong character." Murli was continuously trying to pacify him.

"Murli, you know how much I respect you as a mentor, and I look up to you when it comes to work. A man of your IQ and EQ would certainly not give me empty advice. You mentioned that the Bhagavad Gita might assist me in coping with this problem. I require help!" Parth pleaded to Murli helplessly, showing his desperation in a circumstance that certainly felt beyond his capability to deal with.

"Sure, Parth, I will be delighted to help. I promise you will not be disappointed if you have the strength to follow that path. My guru once told me: *When hopes are low and no way is visible, one should follow the footprints of the Bhagavad Gita so that God himself can show him the way.* Let's meet in the evening to talk about it."

Parth thanked Murli and rushed back to his desk to continue his work.

Murli was on his way back to the office when the security guard stopped him and begged, "Sir, whatever is going on is unfortunate. This is the first time these young kids have encountered something like this. If you can, lend a hand to these kids so that they don't succumb to the pressure and do something terrible." The guard's eyes welled up as he folded his hands in front of Murli.

Murli held his hands. "Don't worry, uncle; I will take care of them". Murli was thinking, 'I wish Aman had at least some level of empathy as the security guard,' as he made his way back to his cabin.

Karan was keeping track of everything that was happening around. As soon as he saw Murli approaching Parth, he assumed that Murli would soothe him and therefore create a soft zone for Parth. And because Murli was one of the final decision-makers, he didn't want Murli to have any soft corner for Parth, so he had followed Murli to hear their talk.

He thought to himself after listening to their talk, 'This may not be good for me. They already know each other well; I just joined the company last week. I am already on the back foot. Now they will be spending even more time together, and it's possible Murli will develop an affinity for Parth during this period.'

The normally lively cafeteria was rather quiet even during lunchtime. Everyone was quietly having their lunch. Parth opted not to eat and continued working at his desk while Karan was having his lunch by himself at the corner table, lost deep in thoughts. Nidhi observed the dejected look on Karan's face. She went up to him and said, "Karan, this is unfortunate. If you give it everything you've got, I have no doubt you'll come out on top."

"Indeed, I have to give it all!" Karan whispered.

Later in the afternoon, Karan went to Murli's cabin and said, "Before anything else, I want to apologize to you, Murli, for my rude behavior the other day. Losing this job would be a nightmare come true, and I'd be humiliated in front of my friends and family who opposed my relocation to Pune."

Murli placed his hand on Karan's shoulder and said, "That's not an issue, Karan. In fact, I apologize that I was unable to fulfill my promise. It seems I misunderstood Aman, because I never expected him to do something like this."

"I can't take much more of this tension, Murli. Kindly help me in regaining emotional control." That was an attempt on Karan's part to convince Murli that he actually needed his assistance.

"I'm going to start teaching Bhagavad Gita lessons to Parth this evening; you're welcome to participate if you wish." Murli's offer of help came from a place of sincerity.

"If that may help, I'll gladly participate."

Karan was relieved that his mission was accomplished. He did not want to waste his time on spiritual teachings; instead, he would have preferred to spend that time on efforts that would boost his chances of winning, but he was pleased with the fact that he would not be missing any action between Parth and Murli. As a result of his participation in these sessions, he would be able to ensure that Parth was not benefiting from Murli's favors.

A guru emerges when the moment is right, as the saying goes. Murli could be that guru for Parth and Karan; now it was up to them to decide if they would embrace or reject his wisdom.

# 10

# INTO THE UNCHARTED WATERS OF DIVINITY

In the evening, Parth and Karan entered Murli's cabin with different motives, but they both were curious about what exactly Murli was going to teach them.

More than Parth and Karan, Murli was looking forward to these sessions. He had seen how even a few droplets of wisdom from the Bhagavad Gita had helped him transform his life, and he wanted Parth and Karan to benefit from it as well.

"Good evening, guys! I am glad that you both accepted my offer to understand the Bhagavad Gita." Murli greeted the guys with compassion. "The Bhagavad Gita contains 700 verses in 18 chapters and includes all the essence one needs to experience this life to the fullest. But don't worry; I am not going to blast you with all that knowledge. I'm just going to share some key principles with you so that you can live a more balanced life, irrespective of the circumstances. We will just have one-hour sessions every day so that you do not lose much of your productive time. I hope that's okay."

Parth and Karan both nodded in agreement. Karan was only

there out of desperation, but Parth was holding out a thin hope that these sessions would help.

"I realize you guys are here not by choice but by circumstance, and you must be wondering how these sessions are going to help you deal with this situation, but believe me, these droplets of wisdom from the Bhagavad Gita will save your soul from drowning in the thunderstorm of challenges." Murli didn't notice much enthusiasm. Hence in an attempt to perk up the guys' glum faces, he decided to start with a story.

"Let me begin with a little story I read somewhere:

*Ajay and Vijay, two close friends, lived in a tiny village. Ajay worked in a field for daily wages while Vijay cut wood in a nearby jungle. During their discussions, Ajay complained about his low wages. Vijay persuaded him to join him in woodcutting because the money was good and the more he cut, the more he made.*

*Ajay agreed and returned home, sharpened the saw, and packed all the tools for the next day. He rushed to work the next day excited. Vijay showed him various woodworking methods before departing for his own work. Ajay returned in the evening after chopping seven trees.*

*"Great job!" Vijay was surprised, "No one has cut these many trees before."*

*Ajay went home happy, vowing to work harder to support his family. He worked hard the next day to beat his record, but he could only chop six trees. He could only cut four trees the next day.*

*"What's wrong?" asked Vijay. "Why has your efficiency dropped so drastically?"*

*"I'm not sure, I labored hard but couldn't chop more than four trees." Ajay was disappointed.*

*"Did you sharpen your saw?" asked Vijay.*

*"No, I didn't want to waste my time," Ajay said.*

*Vijay then explained to Ajay that on the first day as the saw was sharp, he was able to chop seven trees even as it was a new work he was doing. However, with every passing day the tools lost their sharpness and even though he continued to work hard, the output kept going down."*

Murli paused briefly before saying, "The moral of the story is that working hard is not enough; we must learn to work smart by renewing all aspects of our lives. You are not wasting your time here. All you're doing is sharpening the saw."

Although Parth and Karan kept quiet, Murli could now see some interest on their faces.

He then continued, "Let's see how we can use this learning in our situation. Today is Tuesday, the second day of this month, and we will start learning right away. We'll take a three-step strategy, called K-T-P."

"What is this K-T-P strategy?" asked Karan with curiosity.

"In our projects, we have Key Performance Indicators, (KPIs) as a benchmark to evaluate our performance. If we meet and exceed these KPIs, we get better ratings and compensation, leading to a successful career. Similarly, in our day-to-day lives, if we follow the KTP strategy, which I have derived based on the Bhagavad Gita, no one can stop us from living an extraordinary life." Murli replied with conviction in his voice.

"What does KTP stand for?" Parth inquired impatiently.

Murli smiled and opened the PowerPoint presentation he and Ruchi had diligently prepared over the previous week. He displayed the image below and began explaining his three-step strategy.

"The first step is to learn the key knowledge from the Bhagavad Gita. As I previously stated, I will concentrate solely on the knowledge you require to deal with difficult situations in life. We will have six knowledge-sharing sessions over the course of next six days.

In the second step, we will learn some techniques for applying this new knowledge in our daily life and changing our old thought patterns. These techniques will take three sessions.

And with that most of my work will be completed in 9 days, because the step 3 is all about you putting this knowledge to practice in your daily lives using the techniques. Remember one thing: *If you are able to put this information to use when the chips are down and situations are challenging, it will stay with you for the rest of your life.* So, don't let stress and doubt take over your emotions. Just continue on the path shown by Lord Krishna in the Bhagavad Gita." Murli tried to warn them.

There was no response from either of the two.

Murli continued after a brief pause "While you are attempting to practice this knowledge, I will be available to help and support you until your notice period expires."

Parth felt reassured with the words from Murli, and he had some idea as to what he would be getting into with the 3-step strategy.

Karan, on the other hand, exhaled a sigh of relief when he realized that he would only be required to waste 9 hours over 9 days on these stupid teachings.

Murli continued, "Do you believe it will be a waste of time for you, especially in these times of crisis?"

Parth and Karan only glanced at each other and opted to remain silent.

Murli recognized the boys were still unsure how these sessions would benefit them. But he chose to initiate them nonetheless. He said, "So, let us begin with the first step in understanding some important Bhagavad Gita knowledge pieces. However, before we start, I'd like to ask both of you to set your logical minds to rest for a while. There are several things that can't be grasped through reasoning. I know we're science students, and we've been taught to think rationally our entire life.

"Have you ever witnessed a magician perform some bizarre tricks? Some techniques are impossible to explain logically. There is science behind those tricks, but we as the audience don't understand it; whereas the magician knows it well, which is why he can do them. Similarly, there are some things that we as humans cannot comprehend owing to our limited understanding of scientific logic, yet God, who created everything, has science behind them. It's just that we don't fully comprehend that science.

"Simply put, logic kills magic! So, if you want to experience magic in your life, you must first put logic aside and have faith in the teachings of the Bhagavad Gita. While I will try to explain everything logically to the best of my ability, there are certain things that cannot be explained logically and must be experienced to be believed. It's like the aroma of beautiful flowers that can only be experienced rather than explained. Are you guys with me?" Murli wanted to see if it made sense to them.

"Yes, Murli, I am completely with you," replied Parth enthusiastically.

"Yes, me too," Karan replied hesitantly. While this made sense to Karan, he didn't want to divert from his main purpose.

"Great, let's start with the first step of understanding knowledge from the Bhagavad Gita."

Murli opened the image below on his laptop and asked, "Can you guess what this image represents?"

Parth and Karan started looking at this image and tried to make sense of it.

"Let me explain. We human beings have four different layers of existence." Murli continued.

"In verse 42 of the chapter 3, Lord Krishna describes these layers as below:

इन्द्रयियाणि पराण्याहुरनिन्द्रयियेभ्य: परं मन: |
मनससतुपराबुद्धरियोबुद्धे: परतसतुस: ||

*indriyāṇi parāṇyāhur indriyebhyaḥ param manaḥ*
*manasas tu parā buddhir yo buddheḥ paratas tu saḥ*

"Lord Krishna describes the order of superiority among the instruments provided by God. The body, he says, is made of gross matter; superior to it are the five knowledge-bearing senses, which grasp perceptions of taste, touch, sight, smell, and sound; beyond the senses is the mind; superior to the mind is the intellect, with its ability to discriminate; and even beyond the intellect is the divine soul."

Parth and Karan were listening carefully.

"To understand these in further detail, let me explain these

4 layers further.

"Our physical bodies and sense organs make up the first layer of our existence.  Unfortunately, we only associate ourselves with this level, despite the fact that it is the most basic one we possess. The physical body is merely the conduit through which the other layers of us operate.

"The second layer is our mind, which is one level above our physical existence. The mind is constantly taking in new information, which it uses to construct our various belief systems.

"The intellect, which is the third layer, is responsible for making decisions.  It gives credence to the belief systems, which subsequently, in due course, become ingrained in our psyche.  We develop certain habits and tend to respond in particular ways based on our belief systems.

"The energy that propels our body, mind, and intellect is referred to as our soul, and it is the fourth and most crucial layer."

The two listeners were engrossed in the new knowledge.

Murli continued, "According to verses 18—in chapter 2 of the Bhagavad Gita, Krishna describes the soul as below:

"The soul, or atman, is everlasting and indestructible.  It neither kills nor is killed. It never takes birth and never dies. It never ceases to exist once it is created. It is eternal. It cannot be harmed and cannot be contaminated. At the point of death, it does not die, it simply exits the body and enters a new one. Weapons will not pierce it, fire will not burn it, water will not moisten it, and wind will not dry it. It is impenetrable, non-inflammable, all-encompassing, stable, and motionless. It is imperceptible, invisible, and unchangeable."

"If the soul is that powerful, why don't we experience it?"

resisted Karan.

"Since people are preoccupied with the activities of their senses and brains, they are unable to perceive the presence of their own souls, despite the fact that it resides within them. People get an opportunity of coming into contact with it when they are successful in isolating their senses and focusing their attention inwards."

"And how to focus inwards?" asked Parth.

"That is something we will discuss when I explain different techniques next week. Right now, try to understand this divine knowledge." Murli wanted to keep the discussions on the track so he had decided to continue.

He further said, "Now let's understand the qualities of the soul. Our soul feels joyful when we experience positive emotions such as peace, happiness, bliss, love, etc., as these are natural qualities of the soul, and we should keep nourishing our soul with these kinds of positive emotions.

"On the contrary, when we allow ourselves to experience negative feelings like hatred, worry, and jealousy, our soul is not at ease, and if we create these emotions, it depletes the power of our soul.

"If you look at this image carefully, according to the Bhagavad Gita, our body is like a chariot. The five horses pulling the chariot represent our sense organs, the reins represent the mind, and the charioteer represents intelligence. Finally, the soul or *atma*, the one at the fourth layer, is the passenger or lord of this chariot.

"Unfortunately, this is the layer that gets the least attention from us, despite the fact that it is the most crucial.

"We are living our lives exactly opposite from what has been preached by the Bhagavad Gita." Murli took a pause.

"What do you mean?" asked Parth.

"Ideally, the passenger should tell the charioteer where to go, and then the charioteer, through the reins, should direct horses in the direction that the soul is looking for, isn't it?" Murli explained.

"Right," agreed Parth.

"So, our soul should decide how the sense organs behave through intellect and mind, but unfortunately currently it's exactly the opposite. Desires of our sense organs decide where we take our soul because our soul power has depleted considerably as we never paid attention to its nourishment."

"I don't understand what you are trying to explain," Karan resisted.

"OK, let me tell you one story," Murli was well prepared for this.

*"Two young princes from India's most powerful kingdom were sent to study with a renowned guru. They were both outstanding students who studied the Bhagavad Gita in addition to military training.*

*"They returned to their kingdom after finishing their studies. Because the empire was quite large, the king divided it in two parts and gave one each to his sons. Thus, both princes became kings of their own kingdoms.*

*"The elder brother saw food, booze, women and power all around him and got engrossed in enjoying them. He knew what he was doing was harmful for his soul as a Bhagavad Gita student, but he couldn't control his cravings. His sense organs' longings were beyond his ability to control. He gave up control of his mind and intellect to satisfy his desires. As a result of his neglect, rampant corruption, a sluggish military, and poor financial management jeopardized his kingdom's governance.*

*"The younger brother too enjoyed his life as king, but unlike his older brother, his happiness was founded on the principles that governed his soul rather than the five senses. He acted in accordance with the teachings of Bhagavad Gita and did what he considered was best for his spiritual well-being. As a result, his land and its people flourished under the wise leadership of their king.*

*"A powerful long-term enemy of the old king invaded both the kingdoms. As the enemy army was too large, both the brothers were defeated.*

*"The elder brother's army was so lethargic that they couldn't even save their own lives, let alone protect the kingdom. The kingdom was looted, plundered, and was completely destroyed. The ruler committed suicide because he got depressed and humiliated.*

*"Although the army of the younger brother was skilled and fought bravely, but it was outnumbered by the adversary. Despite losing, they suffered less damage. The king managed to have an agreement with the invader and retain his rule. He had enough resources to rebuild his empire. He revived his kingdom by motivating his people." Murli paused.*

Parth and Karan were both paying very close attention to the story.

"Isn't that what we also do?" Murli's question jolted them back to attention. "We know particular types of food are not good for us, yet we eat them, as we don't have control over the carvings of our tongue. We see and hear things that we should not! In a fit of rage, we say certain things and then regret saying them. Later on we try to justify them by saying I was out of control and didn't mean it.

"So, the bottom line is, our sense organs go out of control because our soul doesn't have much power left to get only the right things done from them." Murli concluded.

Parth and Karan remained silent.

Murli waited for a few moments before resuming the session.

"Lord Shri Krishna says in the verse 64 of chapter 2:

रागद्वेषवियुक्तैस्तु विषयानिन्द्रियैश्चरन् |
आत्मवश्यैर्वधियात्मा प्रसादमधिगिच्छति ||

*rāga-dveṣa-viyuktais tu viṣhayān indriyaiśh charan*
*ātma-vaśhyair-vidheyātmā prasādam adhigachchhati*

To put it simply, it means that *"Being consumed by desires and wishes of the five sense organs all of the time is the root of all human misery. One who gives up all the cravings, becomes free from them, and simply continues to perform their karma honestly is guaranteed to find peace."*

"Why do you think this fourth layer of the soul is that significant?" Karan questioned with skepticism. "It is possible to lead a happy life if we only focus on the first three layers."

"That's a good question. You are talking about an outside-in approach. If you take this approach, you can certainly lead a happy life, and if you are doing the right things outside; it will undoubtedly have a beneficial influence on inner self."

Karan smiled, satisfied with his modest triumph over Murli's expertise.

"Can you tell me what your favorite food is, Karan?"

Karan was surprised to be asked this question, but he responded, "Pizza, I absolutely love them!"

"But you already know that pizza is junk food that is bad for your health. Will you quit eating pizza right now if I tell you to?"

Karan stayed deafeningly silent.

"See, that's the issue. We have a lot of knowledge about what is good and bad, but we can't inculcate that knowledge since our soul has grown so weak, and our actions are being controlled either by our senses or at max by our mind.

"That is why I recommend an inside-out approach in which you begin working on and nurturing your soul from within. When it is strong enough, it will gradually begin to change everything outside. Do you get it, Karan?"

"Yes," Karan replied.

"So, out of the four levels of life, we will spend most of our time strengthening our spiritual layer. And when we learn about the techniques, we will concentrate on the mind and intellect. We will keep physical dimensions aside for this discussion. It's not that it's unimportant, but there's plenty of information available on the internet to assist you in getting into better physical shape."

"I am quite excited to get all of this information from you, Murli," Parth exclaimed. Karan, who had come to these sessions solely to keep an eye on Murli and Parth, was also getting intrigued by the conversations now.

"All right, team, let's take a break for today. It's already been more than an hour. We'll continue discussing further tomorrow."

Parth and Karan thanked Murli as they exited his cabin.

Both of them were completely blown away by what Murli had to say, and in a very different way. As they listened to Murli, they couldn't have been more different. One was inspired, uplifted, and excited for the future. The other was calculating ways to be ahead of the game. But both were learning, and both knew that they had a lot to gain from Murli's words.

For Parth, listening to Murli was like a revelation. He felt like he was seeing the world in a completely new way, as if a veil was being lifted from his eyes. Suddenly, he was inspired to think bigger, to dream bigger, and to see the larger picture. He knew that Murli's words would stay with him for a long time, and he couldn't wait to put them into practice.

Karan, on the other hand, had been listening to Murli with a different agenda. He was hoping to apply every bit of knowledge that Murli was sharing for his immediate gain. He was looking for shortcuts, for ways to make quick success, for ways to get ahead. He wasn't interested in the larger picture, only in what he could get out of it right now.

Murli's joy was evident in the bear embrace he gave to Ruchi as soon as he got inside after reaching home. He beamed with joy, which Ruchi could clearly perceive.

"It appears," Ruchi surmised with a grin, "that the boys have agreed to participate in your sessions."

"That's right! I am excited that I can assist these boys in some manner." Murli couldn't keep his excitement in check.

While still in Murli's arms, Ruchi gazed lovingly at his face.

"What are you staring at?" Murli exclaimed in amazement.

"I am just wondering if this is the same person who left the house in the morning." Ruchi said with a smile, "I have never seen you so happy even when you achieved something for yourself, but now look at you! You are such a pure soul, Murli."

She grabbed Murli tightly, telling him, "I love you for what you are," and wishing she could stay in his arms forever. Then, she looked at a statue of Krishna and thanked him for giving her such a wonderful life companion.

# 11

# EMBRACING THE UNKNOWN: NAVIGATING THE WINDS OF CHANGE

On Wednesday morning, the office was bustling with activities. At this point, teams had come to terms with the situation and were making every effort to keep their jobs.

Nidhi sauntered over to Karan's desk and gestured him to follow her for a cup of tea. Parth, who was seated nearby, couldn't help but feel uneasy as he watched the two of them leave together. But he decided to focus on his work and pushed any thoughts of them out of his mind.

As they walked to the cafeteria, Nidhi couldn't help but ask Karan about the mysterious meeting he had with Murli. At first, Karan tried to evade her questions, but Nidhi was persistent and wouldn't let him off the hook.

Finally, Karan relented and told Nidhi about the Bhagavad Gita sessions that Parth and he had been attending. Nidhi was not impressed. She couldn't believe that Karan was wasting his time on something so trivial when his job was on the line.

"Karan, are you insane? Your job is at stake here, and you're wasting time on silly spiritual lessons. Have you really gotten that old?" Nidhi teased him, trying to lighten the mood.

Karan wasn't amused. He knew that he had to convince Nidhi that he had a valid reason for attending the sessions. "Nidhi, hold -on! For attending these meetings, I have a separate agenda. When Murli offered these sessions, both Parth and I declined. But that weak Parth couldn't manage the pressure and went crying to Murli for help. I have joined this company only recently, so I am already at a disadvantage in comparison to Parth. I don't want Murli to become more inclined towards Parth due to these sessions, so I decided to attend merely to stay in Murli's good books," he explained.

Nidhi was impressed with Karan's strategic thinking. "Smart young man! I admire your cleverness," she said, giving him a sly smile.

As they sipped their tea, Parth watched from afar, wondering what was going on between the two. He couldn't shake the feeling that something was off, but he didn't want to jump to conclusions. For now, he decided to focus on his work and wait to see how things played out.

In the evening, Murli could see some level of excitement in Parth and Karan's expressions as they entered his cabin. It drove him to give the sessions his all.

"How are you guys?" Murli said welcoming them.

"As usual, stressed," Karan remarked, and Parth nodded in agreement.

"I see what you're saying. So, what exactly is stress?"

"Pressure to succeed," Karan said.

"As well as societal pressure to be accepted," Parth added.

"What if you don't have stress?"

"Then we'll be happy," Karan answered.

"So, is it fair to say happiness is what we're all seeking for?"

"Yes!" both Parth and Karan agreed.

"Everybody's primary goal in life is to be happy, and that goal has been the driving force behind nearly every other aspiration. The ultimate goal of all our actions, decisions, and endeavors has always been to bring us happiness. Isn't it?"

"Absolutely!" replied Karan.

"My reading of the Bhagavad Gita leads me to believe that in order to revitalize the spiritual aspect of our lives and achieve the ultimate goal of happiness, we need to focus our attention on four guiding principles." Murli said before he opened his PowerPoint presentation and projected the image below onto the projector.

"Understanding the fundamental principle of *Change* and how to manage it successfully will serve as the starting point for the knowledge-sharing sessions. In the second session, we'll talk about why it's important to adopt an *Acceptance* mindset in the face of adversity. The third session, one of the most crucial overall, will focus on *Expectations*. We'll then discuss what *Gratitude* is and why it's so crucial to put it into practice. The last session on *Happiness* will be the culmination of these four sessions. The understanding of real happiness will be our main topic of discussion." Murli explained.

Parth and Karan were looking intently at the screen.

"During the course of the next few days, I shall explain one topic per day. Are both of you cool with the plan?" asked Murli.

"That looks interesting!" replied Parth.

"Let us start with the first principle of change. First and foremost, tell me what is Change?"

"Change is when something out of the ordinary begins to happen," Parth tried to put his thoughts together.

"All right, we also perform change management in our projects; what precisely do we do as part of that process?" asked Murli.

Karan was quick to jump in to answer this, "We plan for any changes that may arise during application development or after the application has gone live. We have an established comprehensive workflow and approval process. We also prepare all stakeholders within the organization to deal with the change that may affect how they work. We notify them of impending changes and then assist them in adapting to those changes."

"Excellent Karan!! We can utilize you as a change champion in our projects," Murli joked, making Parth nervous.

"We always expect and plan for change in our project," Murli continued.

"Yeah, we have to, or else it will cause mayhem in the application operationally as well as organizationally," Parth responded, adding his two cents.

"We anticipate change and then plan to handle it in a project that may continue for a few years, right! Then, why don't we anticipate it in our lives? Why do we usually assume that things will always go smoothly, and then when something unpleasant happens, we are horrified and begin blaming others?" Murli tried to put things in perspective.

Parth and Karan were not sure how to respond.

"With this, let me introduce the principle of change:

**Joy and sorrow, like the seasons, come and go throughout one's life. Constant change is a universal truth of nature.**

"Nothing in our lives is permanent. Embrace change and use your power to deal with difficult situations in life, such as the one you are now in. The wise man adapts to change, whereas the irrational one persists in forcing others to adapt to him. Haven't we heard this principle before? But we never attempted to understand it."

"You make an excellent point, Murli. So, even if we anticipate change in our lives, how do we deal with it?" Parth inquired.

"Managing change in a project is not the same as managing change in life. In a project, we can anticipate what sorts of changes will occur and then plan for those changes, but life is so long that it's nearly impossible to foresee what kinds of changes might occur.

"Yet, it also simplifies dealing with change in life because we can cope with any change that life throws at us with a single basic strategy."

"What is it?" Parth inquired impatiently.

"Before going there, we must understand how change impacts our minds." Murli then proceeded to the next slide.

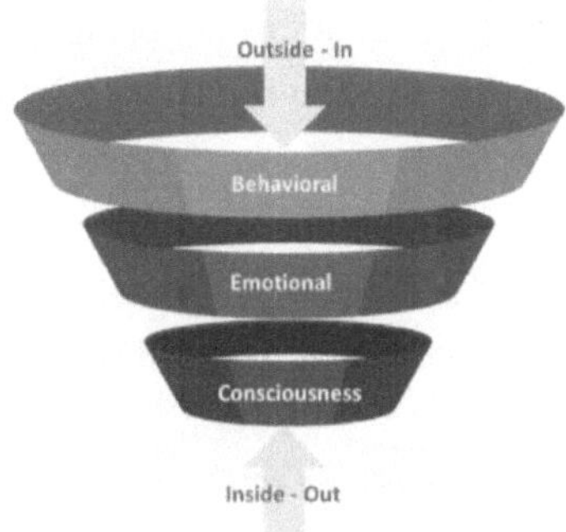


"These are the three basic types of adjustments that an individual might make in his or her life.

"The most visible type of change is at the *behavioral level*, which involves changing our actions or activities. We alter our conduct in response to societal norms, circumstances, and knowledge. It is simple to modify behavior, but it is always transient. For instance, you can get angry with your own child, but you cannot be angry with your neighbor's child and start shouting at him. As a result, we modify our behavior in response to the circumstances.

"We also adjust our behavior based on the knowledge we gain as we begin to perceive things differently. I'll give you a quick and entertaining story:

*There was once a storm in the ocean, and several ships were diverted from their regular path in a different direction. A battleship was also pushed off its path by the storm. When the storm settled down around midnight, the captain of the ship directed one of his officers to go on deck and determine the ship's course. The officer climbed up and far off on the same course as their ship he saw a blinking light. Probably it was another ship. So, the officer sent a message asking that ship to adjust its course by 20 degrees.*

*A quick flashing notification returned, advising the officer to adjust his ship's course by 20°. The message was delivered to the captain by the officer. When the captain received the message, he became enraged and delivered the message himself.*

*"I am the commander of a battleship. I order you to modify your route by 20 degrees."*

*An instant flashing message returned, "But I am a lighthouse, how can I change?"*

"When the captain realized it was a lighthouse that couldn't be changed, he changed his behavior.

"Sometimes we modify our behavior after getting a different comprehension of the situation, but it is just for that moment. Otherwise, we constantly expect others to adapt." Murli took a pause.

"That was an interesting perspective," responded Parth.

"The second degree of change is at the *emotional level*, which affects our feelings. For example, if you have an important delivery and one of your team members does not arrive at the office, you call him and accuse him of not showing up, but when he tells you that there is a death in his house, your feelings go from rage to empathy. Again, emotional transformation is completely based on the situation, so it is also temporary." Murli went ahead.

"So, if I understand correctly, both behavioral and emotional changes occur as a result of social conditioning and situational knowledge, is it?" Karan inquired.

"That's correct, Karan, and that is why both changes occur from the outside to the inside as they are caused by external circumstances; thus, they are just temporary and do not reach your consciousness. For example, when we talk to our boss, we let go of our ego, but our ego causes us to behave differently with our subordinates since the shift in ego is superficial and does not reach our consciousness, so we let our ego dictate our behavior depending on the circumstances surrounding us."

"What you are saying makes sense, Murli, but what is the ideal way to manage change then?" asked Parth.

"We should focus on an inside-out strategy, Parth. When we focus on being transformed from inside, i.e., changing our consciousness, our ego will not control our actions no matter who we are talking to or what situation we are in, rather our consciousness will.

"Parth, the simple strategy I was talking about is this: We should concentrate on bringing about change at the root level, which is to transform our consciousness . The term 'consciousness' refers to one's mental state. To alter our thinking process, we must first change our consciousness."

"I understand Murli, but how can we change our consciousness?" Parth inquired.

"This is where character development helps. Everyone thinks you should develop a personality, but no one asks you to develop a character."

"What's the difference? I think they're the same," Karan resisted.

"I assure you that they are not. What exactly is personality development? Public image, attitude, behaviors, talents, tactics, and anything else that smooths out human interaction are all part of this. And I'm not denying their significance but maturing one's personality ought to follow naturally from strengthening one's character."

"I am still confused!" objected Karan.

"Let me explain further. Adhering to the universal value system of peace, love, honesty, acceptance, etc. is at the heart of character development. Those who are strong enough to live in accordance with the universal value system always achieve inner peace and happiness, as well as external success."

"So you're saying that personality development focuses on how we interact with the world on the outside, whereas character development focuses on creating a universal value system within ourselves?" Karan tried to convey his understanding.

"You are getting there, Karan. Let me elaborate further. These days, schools place less importance on building strong moral fiber and more on cultivating unique, interesting personalities. The way we look on the outside isn't always indicative of our true nature. As a result, we always have two faces: one for the world and one for ourselves. Building your character from the inside-out will have a profound effect on your life. The Bhagavad Gita teaches you how to develop a character that will lead to success in your personal, professional, and social lives."

Karan was taken aback by this new perspective and said, "This is a very intriguing point of view, I never thought along these lines. There are tons of teachers and academies who teach personality development, but no one teaches how to develop character."

"This is due to the fact that improving one's personality yields visible benefits right away, whereas building one's character takes time, and, unfortunately, no one is willing to wait that long. You see that tree over there?" Murli indicated towards a large mango tree in the garden. "What you can see above ground is your personality, and the roots that no one can see is your character. Unless you put down some firm roots, your emotions will always be subject to ups and downs based on your external situations. Any storm may easily uproot even a huge tree if it has shallow roots. If people are not able to cope with the challenges in their lives, they end up taking their own lives because they put all their effort into becoming charismatic show-offs rather than building solid moral roots."

Parth nervously confessed, "I have to be honest with you; when I got this news of layoffs, I started getting suicidal thoughts thinking about the ramifications in my life."

"Thank God that you didn't do that idiotic thing, Parth!" Murli was stunned, and so was Karan.

After a few seconds of tense silence, Murli decided to wrap up the session. "Enough for now, gentlemen. I appreciate your patience. I have homework for you today. Go home and think about what kind of character you want to build and what traits you want to instill in your life."

As Parth and Karan left Murli's cabin, they found this information intriguing and walked back to their desks lost in thoughts. Parth decided to spend more time reflecting on the personality and character he would like to establish, as Murli had recommended, whereas Karan decided to focus on his project without wasting any further time.

As Karan was working on his desk, Nidhi approached him and inquired, "What is going on? What were you guys talking about for so long?"

"Nothing; forget about it. I have a meeting with my team; please excuse me," Karan continued with his work.

Having been brushed off by Karan, Nidhi marched towards

Parth's desk, and he couldn't help but feel a rush of excitement at the sight of her.

"Hey, Parth!" Nidhi said cheerfully, taking a seat next to him. "What's up?"

Parth smiled, trying to hide his nervousness, "Not much. Just trying to finish up some work."

Nidhi leaned in with a mischievous glint in her eyes. "So, I heard you and Karan have been attending these spiritual meetings with Murli. What's that all about?"

Parth took a deep breath. He knew that Nidhi was a city girl through and through, and he wasn't sure how she would react to the deeper truths that were being shared in these meetings. But he decided to give it a shot.

"Well, it's about gaining a deeper understanding of life and our purpose here," he explained. "Murli is like a spiritual guide and is helping us connect with our inner selves and find meaning in our lives."

Nidhi laughed, interrupting him, "Seriously, Parth!? You're spending your time on this stuff when we have a project to finish? Come on, man, get your priorities straight."

Parth felt his heart sink. He had distant hope that Nidhi would understand the value of these meetings, but it seemed like she was completely closed off to the idea. He tried to hide his disappointment as she got up to leave.

# 12

# SURRENDERING TO LIFE: THE BEAUTY OF ACCEPTANCE

On Thursday morning, Aman was having tea at his home. While he had given the news straight up to his working staff about the layoffs, creating havoc in their lives, his own personal life, relationship with his wife Anita was falling apart. Anita was preparing for a divorce from him. She had not reached or hired a lawyer yet, but then she had decided to tell Aman about it.

Anita sat across the table from Aman, her eyes red from crying. Aman, on the other hand, looked furious.

"How could you do this to me, Anita? How could you spy on me like that?" Aman's voice boomed across the room.

"I didn't spy on you, Aman! I stumbled upon those messages by accident," Anita replied, her voice shaking.

"And you couldn't give me the benefit of the doubt? You couldn't trust me?" Aman sneered.

"I trusted you, Aman! I trusted you with my life. But how can I trust you when you've been flirting with Maya?" Anita retorted, her voice rising in anger.

"Oh, please. Don't act like you're so innocent. You're just trying to plot the divorce so you can extract money from me. You're nothing but a gold digger!" Aman snapped.

Anita's eyes widened in disbelief. "What are you talking about, Aman? I've never asked you for anything apart from what is needed to run this house."

"Then why are you trying to divorce me?" Aman challenged.

"Because I can't trust you, Aman! Because you've broken my heart! Because I can't live with someone who cheats on me!" Anita replied, tears streaming down her face.

Aman leaned back in his chair, a cruel smirk on his face. "You're the reason our marriage is failing, Anita. You don't trust me. You don't appreciate me. You don't respect me."

"How can I respect you when you don't even respect our marriage and flirt with other women behind my back?" Anita shook her head in disbelief.

"It was just harmless flirting, Anita. You're blowing it out of proportion," Aman replied, his voice dripping with contempt.

"It wasn't harmless, Aman. It has already harmed me. It has broken my heart. And now you're blaming me for it," Anita cried.

Aman stood up from his chair, his face twisted in anger. "I'm done with this conversation, Anita. I have work to do. And as for our marriage, we'll see what my lawyer has to say about it."

Aman exploded out of the room, leaving Anita to deal with her broken heart and dreams while their baby kid watched them from a corner of the house, too young to understand what was happening.

Aman stormed out of his house, his mind in a tumult. He couldn't believe what had just happened. He had tried so hard to convince Anita not to go through with the divorce, but she was adamant. And now, he had lost his temper and had said things he regretted.

As he walked down the street, he found himself drawn to Maya's house. He needed someone to talk to, someone who understood him. He had been messaging her for a while now, and she had always been there for him.

Maya opened the door, and Aman stepped inside. He collapsed on the couch, his head in his hands.

"What happened, Aman?" Maya asked, her voice soft and soothing.

Aman looked up at her, tears in his eyes. "Anita found out about us. She saw our messages. She's going to divorce me."

Maya's eyes widened in surprise. "I'm so sorry, Aman! I had no idea it would come to this."

Aman shook his head, his anger rising. "She's just a dumb woman, Maya. She doesn't understand me. She doesn't appreciate me. She's too simple for a man like me."

Maya took Aman's hand, her touch comforting. "I understand you, Aman. I appreciate you. I know what you're capable of. You're ambitious, driven, and passionate. You need someone who can match your energy."

Aman looked at Maya, a glimmer of hope in his eyes. "Do you really think so?"

Maya nodded, her smile reassuring. "Of course, Aman. I know you and I believe in you."

Aman felt a surge of emotion, his heart racing. He knew what he wanted to do.

"I'm going to divorce Anita. I can't stay in a marriage where I'm not appreciated. I want to be with someone who understands me. Someone like you!"

Maya's smile widened, and she leaned in to kiss Aman. "I want to be with you too, Aman. I'll support you through this. We'll make it work."

Aman felt a sense of relief wash over him, his doubts fading away. He knew that he had made the right decision. He thought he had found someone who understood him, appreciated him, and believed in him. And he was going to do whatever it took to be with her.

While so much was happening with Aman, his employees at the office had not the faintest idea about what was going on in his personal life. They were totally occupied with the crisis at hand and were trying to handle the things in their own way. Murli, in particular, was totally invested in helping Parth and Karan.

It was lunchtime, and the cafeteria was again buzzing with youthful energy. The main difference was that teams were now talking about projects and issues during lunch instead of everything else. After lunch, Murli returned to his cabin, relieved to see that his team had accepted reality and was working together to deal with the disaster.

It was time for the session, and the boys were right on time in Murli's cabin as they were excited to learn more from him.

Murli started the session with a question to Karan, "Let's start with one interesting question. What irritates you guys most? Karan, let's start with you".

"When people behave really stupid, it irritates the hell out of me!" Karan replied.

"Any example?" Murli asked.

"While driving, I come across so many stupid people. They will keep honking even though they can see that there is a traffic jam. They cut the lanes, which makes the traffic jam even worse. On highways, some people drive so slowly it's like they are driving a bullock cart!!" replied Karan, showing irritation.

"How about you, Parth?" asked Murli.

"Yes, some people for sure irritate me too, but if things don't go as per my plan, it freaks me out. I get nervous and anxious," replied Parth.

"Why do you guys think these things irritate you?" asked Murli.

"Not sure exactly why, but they irritate me for sure," replied Parth.

"They irritate you because you don't accept them, you start resisting them as they don't fit into your acceptance criteria. Today's session on acceptance is going to be really interesting."

Murli walked towards the whiteboard and started writing.

Murli began to explain, "Acceptance is the core of spirituality. If you can practice acceptance, then your journey to happiness is half covered. It can be practiced on two levels: embracing people as they are and accepting situations as they are.

"Let us begin with the first principle of human acceptance:
**Live and let live.**

"Isn't this something we've heard before? What does this

mean exactly? Any ideas?"

"It's simple; I will live my life the way I want, and you can live your life the way you want. Let's not meddle in each other's lives," Karan said flatly.

"Yeah, I agree with Karan," Parth added.

"In that case, Karan, why does the example you mentioned regarding traffic delays annoy you? They want to honk or cut lanes, so why not let them live their lives as they wish?"

"One may live as he or she likes, but they must take care not to annoy others," Karan argued.

"So, honking or lane cutting may aggravate you but may not be irritating for somebody else; so, who decides what is acceptable or not?" asked Murli.

Karan was not sure how to respond.

"Let me now explain this principle in its right spirit."

Karan and Parth started listing carefully.

"We've all developed acceptance criteria for people in our lives according to the role they play in our lives. Your boundary of acceptance will differ for your spouse, children, and co-workers, and when these people cross their boundaries, we become upset. Does that make sense?" asked Murli.

Karan and Parth nodded in agreement.

"*Remember one golden rule: People are not born to fit your acceptance criteria. Everyone has their own upbringing, habits, and belief systems. We can't change them, can we?*" asked Murli.

"Sure, we can't change them, but how do we live with them without getting irritated, Murli?" Karan wondered.

"If you have to walk through a jungle full of thrones, how will you traverse the jungle, Karan?" Murli inquired.

"I'll wear appropriate shoes, so those thrones don't hurt me," Karan answered.

"Isn't it simple? You wouldn't carpet the entire jungle." Murli inquired.

"Only a fool would do that, Murli," Karan responded.

"But isn't that exactly what we're doing? If our life is a jungle and the people in it are thorns, instead of protecting ourselves, we want them to adapt according to our acceptance criteria, much like trying to cover the thrones with carpet. How's that for stupidity?" Murli quipped with a smile.

"What do you mean?" Karan said, perplexed.

"Live and let live means accepting people as they are and not wasting our energy trying to change them to fit our acceptance criteria because it will never happen. Instead, we should concentrate on improving our tolerance so that their behavior does not disrupt our peace of mind."

"But is it possible to develop that power to tolerate everyone around us?" Karan inquired.

"Hundred percent possible! Let's take your example once more. Assume you're driving your car at a speed of 70 km/h; this is the ideal speed for you, and you're having a good time. Now there's a car in front of you going 40 km/h. You become agitated since there is no space to overtake, and you begin honking and criticizing that driver.

"Consider another scenario. You are driving at 70 km/h when someone in an old car overtakes you at 100 km/h. It hurts your ego as you start the race to overtake that car.

"In both scenarios, you were enjoying your journey with your family until someone outside, whom you were unfamiliar with, grabbed your peace of mind. Instead, you may always choose to let them continue their journey while you enjoy yours by being tolerant of their behavior. But this is only possible when your soul is powerful enough to ignore such people without creating negative thoughts."

"So, I should just let people do whatever they want to do?" resisted Karan.

"You need to understand the difference between acceptance and being indifferent. What you are talking about is letting people do whatever they want and being indifferent to them. That's not what acceptance means. We still need to do our duty as parents, spouses, managers, etc. If somebody is doing something wrong, we still need to tell them and show them the right path, but while doing that, we should not create feelings of irritation or stress."

"How is that possible? If somebody doesn't listen to me after I tell them repeatedly, it will obviously upset me," answered Karan.

"You make a conscious decision that I will tell somebody three times with a positive intention so that I will create good vibrations. If that individual still doesn't listen, then I will just accept him or her as it is and learn to deal with them in future."

"Wouldn't that classify as weakness?" asked Karan.

"If that individual doesn't listen to you three times, then no matter how many times you try to explain to him, it will be a waste of energy. Our objective is to protect our energy and stop depleting our soul energy. This will be your strength, not your weakness.

"We have been raised with the principle of 'tit for tat'. It is like copy-paste; somebody does something, and we just replicate the same behavior and respond in the same way. Unfortunately, these days we refer to it as strength, but is it really a strength? Think about it. Will you still think highly of a developer if he or she copies code from the public domain and incorporates it into their own?"

"Not at all!" responded Parth.

"Then why do we praise someone as strong if they always follow the crowd and never have their own unique personality? True strength is to live life with moral principles, which will nurture your soul, and only a few people can do this. It's up to you where you choose to keep control of your life, within yourself or outside with hundreds of people."

"I understand Murli, but it's easier said than done," replied Karan.

"Totally with you, Karan! We can't change our behavior of so many years overnight. It will need practice, which we will discuss in the technique sessions."

Karan and Parth nodded in agreement.

Murli continued, "Now let's discuss the second principle of accepting situations as they are.

**"Whatever occurred happened for a reason. Whatever is happening is for the best. Whatever happens will only be for the better. Practice acceptance and move forward.**

"If you read the Bhagavad Gita, you will realize that the essence of many verses is accepting the situation as it is. Every situation can bring us something good if we have an eye to look for it."

"What good will come from the existing situation? One of us is going to lose our job," Parth joked sarcastically.

"Wouldn't you be qualified as God if you knew what was going to happen in the future?" Murli inquired.

Parth remained mute. Karan, too, was silent.

"Whatever has transpired has to be for a reason. You're going through a hard patch. There must be a reason for that, just that you guys are not able to comprehend it right now,"

Murli attempted to inspire them.

"Let me tell you an amazing story about Buddha.

*As a prince, Siddhartha had everything he could want. Seers who were present at the time of his birth predicted he would become a great emperor or an enlightened teacher. They foretold that the prince would give up his royal existence and seek enlightenment if he saw the four passing sights - old age, disease, death, and asceticism. The king wanted his son to succeed him on the throne. Hence, he king shielded Prince Siddhartha from these four painful realities.*

*When Sidhartha was 29 years old, one day, accompanied by his charioteer, he sneaked out of the safe confines of the palace grounds. He saw a dead body, an old man, a sick person, and a traveling ascetic. That was the first time he experienced suffering and realized it was part of everybody's life.*

*He searched religious books and asked royal gurus for answers to human misery but found none. Siddhartha decided to abandon the comforts of the palace. He lived ascetically in the woods with some of his time's most famous gurus and ascetics. He tried several meditation techniques from many teachers. But their teachings did not answer his questions about human suffering or how to end it.*

*Siddhartha spent seven years away from home seeking answers to human suffering. He used to resist rage, lust, and stress when meditating. One day, he decided to accept his feelings while meditating under a peepal tree, and then a miracle started unfolding. He stopped being controlled by his thoughts when he accepted them all. After realizing that, as humans - pain is inevitable but the choice of suffering is completely ours, he became enlightened.*

If Siddhartha can become Buddha just by accepting life as it is, can't we attain peace of mind with a little bit of practice?"

Parth and Karan were listening carefully.

"Okay, let's discuss the second angle of acceptance: that whatever happens, happens for the good.

"Imagine both of you getting everything you wanted as teenagers; how would your lives have turned out if you had them all?"

Murli paused for a long while.

Karan considered all the girls he liked. Blushing, he smiled to himself. He wondered what would have happened if all the girls had said yes to his proposal. He imagined their demanding outbursts like a nightmare.

Murli began to smile as he saw Karan's reaction.

At the other end, Parth was reflecting on how he worked hard to pursue his MS from the United States, obtained admission, and even raised a loan worth lakhs of rupees, but his student visa was denied. He recalled his heartbreak and six months of depression. He blamed everything on God and even stopped praying. Now, while thinking about it, he realized that it was probably best that he didn't receive a visa because several of his friends who went for higher education couldn't find work after getting their MS because the recession had occurred at the same time and their parents had to pay off huge student loans. After MS, some came back to India and worked, but it took a long time to repay the loans.

He had never gone deep into his life events, but now he realizes that it was the best thing that happened, even if he was miserable at the time. A glimmer of relief swept through his face.

"What are your thoughts, guys? Don't worry, I'm not going to ask about all of this," Murli smiled. "Just tell me, how would your life have been different if you could have had all of those things?"

"My life would have been a horrible hell," Karan said, remembering all the girls.

"My life would not have been any better either," Parth said.

"Is this principle clear to you now?" Murli inquired.

"Yes, it is, but how do we see the bright side when we're presented with a difficult situation and just accept it to move on?" Parth wondered.

"Look, you can't change the past or write the future. You don't have to be concerned about the future or linger on the past. You only have power over the present moment, so embrace it with an open heart and work hard.

"Happiness is only attainable when we are able to accept everyone and everything as they are, which involves putting an end to resisting others, moaning, and playing the victim card, as well as criticizing and manipulating others."

"That's right, Murli. This was amazing information." Parth appreciated Murli's teachings.

"OK guys, let's break for today and meet tomorrow, but I have an exercise for you."

"What is it?" asked Parth.

"I understand how tough it is to practice acceptance with people, especially those with whom we spend a lot of time since you see those bothersome behavior all the time.

"So, let's start small: try practicing acceptance with someone who irritates you but with whom you spend very little time." explained Murli.

"Sure, I will definitely try." Parth stated with zeal.

Parth and Karan left Murli's cabin and went to their cubicles for their work.

Later that evening, Aman and Murli were in the conference room with Parth and Karan to get updates from them on their teams' progress.

Parth and Karan gave their presentations, updating everyone on the current situation. In terms of development, Parth's team had a slight edge over Karan's. Having worked with the team for a few months, Parth had an unfair edge in knowing each member's strengths and weaknesses. He was able to use this information to effectively delegate jobs, enabling the team to quickly speed up.

Karan, on the other hand, had a much more limited understanding of the skill sets and experience levels of his teammates, and therefore his team's performance, while still good, fell short of that of Parth's.

Parth was pleased with the progress as they left the meeting, while Karan was concerned because his team was trailing Parth's.

As usual, Nidhi was keeping an eye on both Parth and Karan. Parth appeared to be quite relieved, whereas Karan appeared to be stressed. She approached him and inquired, "What's the matter? How did the meeting go?"

"My team is somewhat behind Parth's team in terms of progress," Karan said apprehensively.

"Don't worry, Karan, you'll catch up. It's just been four days." Nidhi made an effort to cheer him up.

"Your job is already secure, Nidhi; you have no idea how much pressure I am under." Karan stated solemnly.

"But I am sincerely concerned about you, Karan." Nidhi made an attempt to make her argument.

"I know Nidhi, and I apologize if my tone came across as rude," Karan said.

"It's fine, Karan, but just listen to me. These sessions, I believe, are Murli and Parth's attempts to waste your time. They are already quite familiar with each other. They want you to fail. One hour is plenty of time to catch up with Parth." Nidhi attempted to persuade Karan to abandon these sessions.

Karan thought for a bit and then said, "Knowing Murli for the past few days, I don't think he would plot something like this. Also, it would seem suspicious if I suddenly stopped going to those sessions."

"I considered giving you my opinion, but the final decision is yours." Nidhi replied casually and returned to her desk.

Parth was envious after watching Nidhi and Karan converse for so long. His delight at his minor victory over Karan was taken over by the pain of jealousy. He then sat back and began to take long breaths. He then reasoned to himself, 'Murli has taught us about acceptance today, so why not try to accept this situation as it is and keep focusing on the job at hand?' This one thought provided Parth with a lot of relief, and he could now focus on his work again.

As Nidhi went back to her desk, she was weighing her options. She signaled her best friend Daksha for coffee. As both of them grabbed coffees, they got engaged in their gossip.

"So, how's work going with Parth and Karan?" Daksha checked with Nidhi.

"They both seem more motivated and focused towards work," Nidhi said thoughtfully.

Daksha nodded. "By the way, what are your plans for the future, Nidhi?"

Nidhi blushed a little at the question. "Well, I'm a practical person," she said. "I want to settle down with someone who respects my freedom and can provide me with security for the rest of my life. And honestly, I see potential life partners in both Karan and Parth. So, for now, whoever manages to keep their job, I'll choose to stay with that person."

Her colleague looked surprised. "Wow, that's a bold statement. You aren't really putting all your eggs in one basket!"

Nidhi smiled confidently. "I don't take chances in life. When it comes to matters of the heart, I know what I want, and I go for it."

"Wow, you have such amazing clarity, Nidhi! By the way, who do you think can keep the job?" asked Daksha curiously.

"While I'd love to see Karan come out on top, I have a feeling Parth's team will prevail due to superior teamwork." Nidhi gave her opinion, and then she thought, 'I can't make Parth nervous, and I also have to keep him interested in me.'

She pulled out her phone and messaged him, "Heyyyy Parth, how about meeting for breakfast tomorrow morning in the restaurant downstairs before office starts?"

Parth's response was instant, "Sounds excellent, let's meet at 9 o'clock."

Nidhi looked at Parth with a grin on her face as she and Daksha headed back to their workstations from the cafeteria. As Parth saw Nidhi beaming at him, he felt an overwhelming sense of joy. Breakfast with Nidhi the following morning was already on his mind.

# 13

## THE TRAP OF EXPECTATIONS: HOW TO ESCAPE ITS CLUTCHES

Typically, Fridays were filled with anticipation for the weekend at HealthTech, but this Friday was different. It had been one week since the teams had been informed about the layoffs and the competition. Everybody knew they had to keep working on this weekend and the next few weekends too to save their jobs. Therefore, this was simply another working day for everybody but not for Parth. He was looking forward to his breakfast with Nidhi.

He groomed himself for a few minutes longer than usual in the morning. He reached the restaurant a bit early and was waiting for Nidhi.

Nidhi arrived promptly at 9 o'clock. "Good morning, Parth; I hope I'm not late. Your time is extremely precious."

"No, Nidhi, you are right on time. I arrived a little early." Parth was mesmerized by Nidhi's beauty. The sun's early morning rays shining on her face accentuated her beauty further.

When the waiter asked what they would like to have for

breakfast, they both settled on masala dosa. They got into casual conversation and spent about 30 minutes talking and having their dosa. It was Nidhi doing most of the talking, and Parth was simply soaking up every moment spent with her.

As they entered the office, Nidhi noticed Karan working at his desk. She didn't want Karan to see her with Parth, so she excused herself by saying she was going to the restroom.

Parth was having the time of his life. His team was ahead of Karan's, and as icing on the cake, Nidhi had shown an unexpected interest in him. He exhaled a breath of relief and got to work.

The day passed with both Parth and Karan working hard with their teams. In the evening, they both gathered in Murli's cabin. Murli began the talk by asking if anyone had any questions on the previous day's topic of Acceptance.

Parth started the conversation. "We read these sorts of quotes, watch motivational videos on social media but tend to dismiss them, claiming this is not practical and not for individuals like us who have to cope with so many obstacles in our day-to-day existence. I believe that your arguments are rational and realistic, given that you live by these beliefs and have achieved success. But how can we instill these principles in our own lives?" Parth inquired.

"Hold your horses, we'll talk about the techniques on how to use these principles in your daily life next week. Currently, I want you guys to focus on knowledge and get absolute clarity about these principles.

"Let us begin with today's principle. So, without further ado, tell me which is the most famous verse in the Bhagavad Gita."

Parth answered:

"कर्मण्येवाधिकारस्ते मा फलेषु कदाचन।

मा कर्मफलहेतुर्भूर्माते सङ्गोऽस्त्वकर्मणि॥"

Karmanye vadhikaraste Ma Phaleshu Kadachana,
Ma Karmaphalaheturbhurma Te Sangostvakarmani

"It's no surprise, isn't it? We've been hearing this since we were children," Murli added. "What exactly does this imply, Parth?"

"This indicates we should keep working without expecting any results," Parth responded.

"And what are your thoughts on this?" Murli asked both of them.

"This is complete rubbish and totally impracticable. We're all aiming to achieve something in life. How can we just keep working and not expect anything in return? We are not saints; we are normal humans, and when we work hard, we naturally want something in return." Karan said, mocking the verse.

"Exactly," Parth agreed.

Murli smiled as the responses were as expected. "Well, it's something we have never understood, or rather, no one has adequately explained this verse to us. But I don't blame you; I had the same reaction when I heard this for the first time until my Guru explained the core essence of this verse. Believe me when I say that this is the most insightful lesson in the Bhagavad Gita. Today, all we care about is money, a huge home, a car, and a secure future. We are so focused on achieving our ambitions that we do everything with the single goal of achieving more and more money."

"So, what's the problem?" Karan tried to resist.

"There is no issue with wanting to have more money; even I work to earn more and more money so that my family and

I can live a comfortable life. But there are two issues: one, we constantly expect things, and second, we worry too much about results, placing stress on ourselves."

"Would you mind explaining Murli?" Parth requested.

"Okay, let's see. You now have a deadline to complete your task by the 30th of this month, which has already put you under tremendous pressure. Isn't it?" asked Murli.

"We are bound to feel pressure if you anticipate delivering 25% more work during this notice period. Isn't it, Sir?" Karan asked sarcastically.

"Fair enough!! But please understand that setting targets and deadlines is part of life. If there are no deadlines, one may take many more days to finish the same work. Once we have a deadline, we start working more efficiently. In your case, the issue will arise when you guys begin to entertain worrisome thoughts such as 'if other teams finish before me, they will have a higher likelihood of retaining the jobs, and my career will suffer.'"

"But isn't that normal? These thoughts are bound to come in any competition," asked Karan.

"Well, that's the problem; whatever everybody does, we tag that as normal. Now try to think differently. These thoughts will haunt you while you perform and work. Negativity causes stress and discomfort. You and your competitor have a deadline and imagine both of you meeting it. One of you does it under pressure, while the other gives it his all regardless of the repercussions. You'll both succeed, but differently; one will have grown stronger in character while the other would have suffered psychological and physiological repercussions."

"Yet, Murli, we can't escape stress in this situation. Please be reasonable with us!" pleaded Parth.

"OK, let's understand this in a more scientific way. The simple formula for stress in science is

**Stress = Force/ Cross-sectional area**

Basically, stress is the external pressure applied on the selected cross-sectional area of an object, more the cross-sectional area, less will be the impact of the pressure. So, we can equate cross-sectional area to resilience of the object to withstand the pressure.

So essentially, in simple terms, the formula of the stress is

**"Stress = Pressure / Resilience**

"Pressure from deadlines, exams, relationships, situations, traffic jams, etc. is all included in the numerator. The ability to withstand pressure is known as resilience. We have conveniently removed the denominator from the formula today and accepted the formula as

**"Stress = Pressure**

"We don't look at the denominator because we aren't ready to be responsible for our own inner strength. Because of this, most of us think that stress is the same as pressure but if we could develop more and more resilience then no matter how much pressure the external world puts on us, we will never feel stress which will eventually help us to deal with external situations more effectively.

"Things that are out of our control will always happen and it will keep making us anxious till we have learned how to protect ourselves by developing resilience.

"Nowadays, if we do anything, we expect something in return, and if we don't get that output, we get dissatisfied and unhappy. And the irony is that most of the time, whether in our professional or personal lives, we have little influence over the outcome, so the numerator is beyond our control; but to develop resilience is for sure under our control. My experience has taught me that external pressure has 10% of the power, but the remaining 90% is based on my ability to cope.

"Do you agree or disagree?" Murli asked.

"This is a fantastic insight, Murli; no one has ever before interpreted this verse to us in this way." The explanation really astonished Parth and Karan.

"Let's dig deeper into this. Now, instead of anticipating things, isn't it preferable that you complete your work with 100% devotion every single day and leave the rest to God and destiny? In either case, you have no control over the outcome. So, while the one of you who does not retain a job will be for sure disappointed, it will be simpler for him to recover and seek alternative sources of income.

"You know, the suicide rate and depression rates among working professionals have never been higher than today simply because they can't meet their own or someone else's expectations."

Parth and Karan had worried expressions on their faces.

"Even in our personal lives, we have high expectations of our spouses and children. The marriage has evolved into a business, with constant give and take, like 'If you do this, I will love you; if you don't, I won't'.

"Kids have become the test subjects for our expectations. We attempt to compel them to accomplish things that we were unable to achieve in life. Of course, we do our best to offer them everything we hadn't got as children, but we also have expectations that they will always listen to us, and if they don't, we become furious with them. When children reach a certain age, they become rebellious, eventually distancing themselves emotionally and physically from their parents."

"I agree, Murli, but isn't it natural to have expectations?" Parth questioned.

"It's true that everyone has them, but that doesn't make it natural.  Let's say everybody in a certain government office is involved in corruption.  Does it become natural because everybody's doing it? Obviously not!! We have been conditioned by our parents, culture, and surroundings to believe it is natural. Natural things usually occur with ease; do expectations make you feel at peace?"

Both remained silent.

"Let's move on to the second demon: worry and pressure to perform.

"This is a result of expectations and comes free with it. For example, we all put in additional effort during yearly appraisals and assessments in the hopes that our manager will give us a higher rating. When you focus on the reward, you are surrounded by fears of failure, and when the outcome is negative, you get depressed.  So, it is usually advised to concentrate on your efforts rather than the outcome.

"Do not make the rewards for your actions your motivation because the rewards are dependent on external situations, hence your motivation levels will always fluctuate, resulting in poor performance. Rather, focus on continuing to accomplish your job with the same focus and dedication every single day."

"Easier said than done, Murli!" Karan remarked sarcastically.

"Well, it's not as hard as we think it is. Let me tell you a small story.

*"One day, a yogi embarked on a journey to the Himalayas with his disciple. It was getting dark, and they were in the middle of a jungle. Fear had taken over the disciple. He asked his master to*

*return because he couldn't see anything ahead of him.*

*"I agree we can't see the entire way ahead of us to our destination, but do you see your next step?" said Master.*

*"Yes, I do," the disciple said.*

*"Isn't it enough for us to keep moving forward?" asked the master as they continued walking ahead."*

Murli stopped for a moment to drink some water and then continued, "Similarly, we may not know when we will reach our goal. Instead of becoming impatient or abandoning your goal, take one step at a time."

Then he looked at his watch and said, "Let's call it a day, gentlemen. I understand that this principle contradicts our long-held beliefs, yet it can also be extremely liberating. Please think about it, and if you have any questions, we may discuss it further tomorrow."

Parth and Karan exchanged glances as they exited the conference room.

Parth inquired, "Tea?"

"Let's go; we need it badly," Karan said.

Everyone else was surprised as they both walked out of the office and into the cafeteria together. They never had tea together, and the new crisis had made them increasingly competitive with each other. Everyone suspected that something other than work was going on in those sessions.

Parth inquired over tea, "Whatever Murli is saying makes sense, but is it really realistic to live such a life?"

"Exactly, exceedingly unlikely! Only yogis who leave the worldly world and travel to the Himalayas may do so. They are not subject to employment or family responsibilities."

"I wonder if anyone in the professional world leads such a life." Parth wondered.

They didn't say anything more to each other and just sat there thinking while they finished their tea.

While a transformation was taking root in the hearts of Karan and Parth, Aman's life was going through a turmoil. He was hardly seen in the office. Murli had noticed it and he thought that Aman was working hard to find new investors to pump life back into the start-up. Contrary to these expectations, Aman was exploring the possibility of his relationship with Maya taking off.

He found himself telling Maya all of his deepest thoughts and secrets, and she reciprocated with telling him her own. They were both amazed at how much they had in common, from their love of jazz music to their passion for adventure sports.

As their connection deepened, Aman began to feel alive again. He had been so bogged down with work and family issues that he had forgotten what it felt like to be truly happy. Maya was like a breath of fresh air, reminding him of all the good things life had to offer.

Their outings became more frequent, and they started exploring new places and trying new things together. Aman felt a sense of liberation that he had never felt before, and he knew that Maya was the reason for it.

As the week went by, Aman became less and less concerned about his divorce from Anita. His lawyer was handling everything, and he was confident that he would come out on top. He was more focused on building a future with Maya.

One day, as they sat by the river, watching the sunset, Aman took Maya's hand in his and said, "Maya, I don't know what the future holds, but I know one thing for sure: I want to spend it with you."

Maya's eyes welled up with tears, and she leaned in to kiss him.  In that moment, Aman knew that he had found his soulmate, and he would do anything to make their love story work.

# 14

## WHEN PHILOSOPHY MEETS REALITY: THE AWAKENING OF KARAN AND PARTH

On the Saturday morning Murli and Ruchi were having breakfast.

"Is Radha still sleeping?" Murli inquired.

"Yes, today is the second Saturday, so it's a holiday for her. By the way, how are the sessions with Parth and Karan going?" Ruchi said. "I didn't ask you for the entire week since I didn't want to interrupt you in the middle of your sessions."

"I'm glad you asked. In fact, I wanted to talk to you about it. It appears that the knowledge is making sense to them, but knowing how we are raised with logical thinking, I have a feeling that some part of them still refuses to believe that it actually works in real life. It was comparable to how I felt while I was attending Ram Sir's sessions." Murli briefed her.

"So, what's your plan?" questioned Ruchi.

"I walk on the path of the Bhagavad Gita, but I never advertised my life to anyone. You know it better. But it appears that now is the time." Murli said, hesitantly.

Ruchi appeared perplexed.

Murli began articulating his opinions, with Ruchi interjecting her own. They developed a plan after an hour of deliberation. It was now time to put it into action.

Murli called Parth and Karan to invite them to dinner on Sunday evening.

They didn't want to bother Murli any longer, but Murli insisted, and they consented.

Saturday and Sunday were quite busy at HealthTech's office. Nidhi and the support staff were not working, and it was only the development teams of Parth and Karan who were working their tails off to keep their jobs.

On Sunday evening, Parth and Karan arrived at Murli's place about 8 o'clock. Little Radha opened the door and walked inside after seeing them, exclaiming, "Daddyyy, your friends!"

Murli welcomed them and invited them to take seat on the sofa. Ruchi greeted them and offered them a drink of water. They were both fatigued after working over the weekend, but the aroma of incentive sticks and pleasant vibrations had pumped energy into them as soon as they had entered Murli's house. While Murli and Ruchi were arranging food on the dining table, the boys began playing with Radha.

"Dinner is ready; let's get started," Ruchi remarked pleasantly.

Five of them took seats, with Radha sitting next to Murli.

Murli, Ruchi, and even Radha closed their eyes and prayed to God as everyone settled. Parth and Karan were watching them, unsure of what to do and simply waiting for them to begin.

"I'm sorry for keeping you waiting, let's get started," Murli remarked.

Everyone had a good time while eating and talking. Murli purposefully avoided discussing office or Bhagavad Gita matters.

After the dinner, Parth and Karan sat on the sofa playing with Radha, while Murli and Ruchi cleaned the dining table.

"I completely forgot to bring dessert. Allow me to get some from a nearby shop. Will you accompany me, Radha?" Murli said.

Radha began wearing her little shoes without saying anything to indicate her desire to accompany Murli. Both said their goodbyes to Ruchi, who was sitting with Parth and Karan, and walked out.

"Your family is so welcoming, it feels like home," Karan, who missed his family back home, complimented Ruchi.

"How many years have you been married, Didi?" Parth asked, using the term of respect for Ruchi.

"It's been almost 7 years," Ruchi replied with a smile.

"Wow, that's quite a long time," Parth remarked. "How did you two meet?"

"We were batch mates during our engineering," Ruchi shared.

"Interesting. Did you fall in love in college?" Parth asked with a grin.

Ruchi chuckled. "It was definitely fascinating, but it took some time for us to get to know each other."

"How was Murli in college?" Parth inquired.

"He was quite introverted for the first couple of years. I barely noticed him," Ruchi admitted, chuckling again.

Karan was surprised. "Really? I thought he would have been quite outgoing."

"No, he was always buried in thoughts, always agitated. He spent most of his time in the library studying. Despite his commitment to studies, no one really noticed him," Ruchi explained.

"How did you two get to know each other then?" asked Karan.

"It was during the third semester in second year when our lecturer assigned me to a group for a project. My friend and I were both upset to learn that Murli would be part of our team," Ruchi said.

"Why were you upset?" Parth asked curiously.

"His personality was so ambiguous. He was attractive, but his body language would stress out even a motivational speaker," Ruchi joked, making Karan and Parth burst into laughter.

"Even during project conversations, he was hesitant to present his thoughts. Actually after a few weeks of discussions, I felt Murli was a good guy with some amazing ideas but lacked confidence.," Ruchi continued.

"One day, we were having coffee in the college canteen when one of my friends asked Murli, 'Why are you constantly stressed? And why are you so preoccupied with your thoughts?' And Murli remained silent as usual, saying nothing.

"Our project went quite well and was well received by other teams and lecturers. It took first place. It was Murli's idea that we executed, but because we three were doing the most of the talking and presenting, the majority of the credit went to us. Everybody thought as if Murli was merely baggage for the team," Ruchi finished with a hint of disappointment.

"That's not fair," Karan said sympathetically.

"Yes, even I felt terrible at that time, and I was curious to know from Murli why he would not speak up for himself." Ruchi replied and further said, "As we celebrated our award with close friends, the atmosphere was shattered by the cruel taunts of a guy called Sahil directed at Murli. He mocked him and laughed at him for being a 'lucky geek.' I couldn't bear to watch it and shouted at them to stop their garbage. But my other team members said nothing, letting the mockery continue.

"Silence fell as Murli stormed out of the party. I followed him and asked why he couldn't speak up for himself. His response was heart-breaking. Coming from lower middle-class, his parents had invested everything in his education, and he was under pressure to perform well and secure a job otherwise he would fail them. Tears streamed down his face as he walked away.

"After that, we barely spoke, and Murli remained withdrawn until the third year. Then, something changed. His body language was transformed, and he radiated confidence. He made friends, aced his exams, and even discussed his opinions.

"We were all studying for the third-year final exam. I was studying in the campus garden when I noticed Murli playing football on the field. The football rolled towards me and eventually halted near me. Murli came to pick it up.

"We have a final test coming up, but you don't seem concerned. Good luck!!!" I remarked cynically.

"Hey Ruchi, good evening! I'm lucky for sure, and as for the exam, if you study consistently, you don't need to study day and night during the last few days before the exam." Murli retorted with a smile. Looking at his confidence, I was taken aback.

"Ruchi, I have something to tell you," He remarked as he

returned the ball to the playing field. "You were the only one who stood up for me last year when everyone mocked me."

"No offense, Murli, but you were that kind of geek who would be a soft target for anybody, so I don't blame them. You should have learned how to defend yourself!" I responded unequivocally.

"Yes, I completely agree with you," Murli said, yet able to preserve a smile on his face after my criticism.

"But in the last 8—months, I've noticed a significant change in you, and it makes me wonder if you're still the same boring person. How did this much change happened?" To be blunt, I asked a direct question.

"Murli burst out laughing, but when she saw my serious expressions, he stopped and said, "I met Dr Ram last year, who taught me to follow the path outlined in the Bhagavad Gita. I've felt so liberated since I started walking down that path; nothing bothers me anymore."

"Wow!" I was taken aback.

"You don't think I'm a dull geek anymore, do you?" Murli inquired, intrigued.

"Oh, you've changed so much. You are incredible; I just...." I held myself back after realizing I was giving in to my feelings. But, Murli had grasped the meaning behind it, so he decided not to waste any more time and continued, looking deeply into my eyes, and he said, "I've been observing you for the past three years. You are such a strong, independent girl. I've always admired you. Ruchi, I truly like you."

His admission surprised me. Murli continued without hesitation.

"I'm not sure if this is love or not because I'm still trying to figure out what real love is, but I like and care about you."

"My heart was racing with each passing word from Murli.

"But, Murli..." I was at a loss for words.

"Ruchi, I was only trying to express myself, and I think I deserve that one chance, just as you have every right to detest or even despise me. I'm telling you because I don't want to live the rest of my life regretting not telling you how I felt. I will respect and accept whatever decision you make. Please accept my apologies for troubling you during your exam period."

"Despite my surprise, I was touched by his honesty and sincerity. I respected his courage and accepted his confession, regardless of my own feelings. Murli had transformed, not just academically but also as a person.

"I genuinely feel our relationship deserves one chance to flourish, Ruchi, and I promise to give this relationship my all." Murli continued, his voice firm and his eyes filled with love.

"As I sat there in stunned silence, Murli wasted no time in waiting for my response. He briskly walked back to his field but turned around to deliver a remarkable proposition, "The chapter you're studying is better explained in the book by Dr Rao, pages 45 to 61. You can find it in our library's Section C." His smile was infectious, but my mind was racing with thoughts." Ruchi's flow was broken by interruption from Karan.

He couldn't resist asking, "Did you say yes?"

"I didn't answer right away, but over the yearly holidays we were in touch with each other with occasional phone conversations. During these conversations, I realized what a genuine person he is. He never pressed me to accept his proposal, but I always sensed vibes of love and care from him during our talks.

"Murli's academic excellence had made him a favorite

among his peers. On the first day of college after vacations, I watched him from a distance, looking like he was waiting for someone. As I called out his name, he turned around with a smile and asked me for a cup of tea.

"He brought up our relationship proposal when we were sipping tea: "Sorry if I appear desperate, pressuring you to accept my proposal, but I really don't want to waste a single minute of my life without you, Ruchi."

"I interrupted him, "Don't apologize, Murli! You are an amazing person; I also like you a lot, and despite the fact that we come from different backgrounds, I have decided to take chances with our relationship."

"Murli's expression lit up with love. He appeared calm on the outside, but his eyes filled were with joy betrayed his seeming calmness.

"Murli never let me down, and we had a fantastic time in college. We complemented and completed each other in every sense.

"When he received job offers, I suggested he continued his education, but his priority was to support his family. His calm demeanor and focus on his goals impressed me further.

"However, his parents did not approve of our relationship due to our different castes and cultures. Despite the stress, Murli remained calm and confident. He kept assuring me that things would fall into place. After four years, his parents finally agreed, and we got married. Looking back, those years were stressful, but our love for each other and our families made it worth." Ruchi finished the story of her love with Murli.

"Wow, what an incredible and inspiring story!" Karan exclaimed. "How old is Radha?"

"She will complete nine next month," Ruchi said.

Parth and Karan began to stare at each other, thinking, 'How can Radha be nine years old if Murli and Ruchi are married only for seven years?'

Looking at their reaction, Ruchi realized that she had been taken off guard.

She went on to share the heart-warming story of how they adopted Radha from an orphanage when she was only four. Despite her initial hesitation, Ruchi was convinced by her husband's unwavering conviction that they could make a difference in the world by taking care of at least one child.

"It takes a lot of courage and faith to adopt a child, especially when you have the desire to have your own," Ruchi smiled. "But Murli's incredible qualities of confidence and persever-ance won me over in the end."

She made a personal request to keep Radha's adoption a secret. Parth assured her that they were like her brothers and wouldn't share her story with anyone.

Murli and Radha entered while they were talking. They had brought the favourite dessert of Radha.

As they all enjoyed their dessert, Ruchi shared some words of wisdom, reminding Parth and Karan that everything happens for a reason and that tough times eventually pass.

While bidding farewell Parth and Karan thanked Murli and Ruchi for a wonderful evening.

After they left, Murli hugged Ruchi warmly before closing the door and Radha rushed over to hug them both, and the evening ended on a heart-warming note.

Coming out from the house of Murli and Ruchi, Parth and Karan hopped into the same cab. As they were driving home, Parth suddenly exclaimed, "Oh, my God!"

Both Karan and the cab driver turned to look at him in

surprise.

"What happened?" Karan asked.

Parth explained, "Earlier this week, we were debating the viability of the Bhagavad Gita teachings in today's world. We concluded that it was impossible to live by those principles. But after seeing Murli's life, I'm starting to think we were wrong."

Karan raised an eyebrow and asked, "What do you mean?"

"Well, think about it. Murli lives his life based on these teachings, and he's successful in every aspect of his life –professional, social, and personal. Doesn't that imply that these principles are still applicable in today's world?" Parth questioned.

Karan thought for a moment and nodded in agreement, "You're right, Parth. I hadn't realized it before, but Murli's life is a testament to the effectiveness of those teachings."

Parth was visibly moved and said, "I think I need to make some changes in my life and start incorporating those teach-ings. I want to see their impact on all the aspects of my work and relationships."

Karan, on the other hand, had a different motive, "I think I'll do the same, but my goal is to win the competition against you and retain my job in Aman's company."

Parth chuckled, "Well, at least we're both taking something positive away from this experience."

The fierce animosity between them had now turned into healthy competition.

The cab driver smiled and said, "It's always nice to see people inspired by the wisdom of the Bhagavad Gita."

Parth and Karan exchanged knowing glances, feeling moti-vated and energized to apply these teachings in their lives.

# 15

# THE ATTITUDE OF GRATITUDE: SEEING THE BRIGHT SIDE

It was a new week, and teams now had only three weeks to finish their projects. After the early setbacks caused by a lack of teamwork, Karan had taken matters in his own hands. He was an exceptional developer. Earlier, he had relied on his team for development, but now he was developing the most challenging features himself. He used teams for minor feature development, configurations, unit testing, and so on.

A status review was scheduled for the afternoon. Parth and Karan both gave presentations. Aman was astonished to learn that Karan's team had made tremendous progress during the previous week and that his progress was nearly identical that of Parth's team.

Parth was alarmed by this. Murli was able to read Parth's expression.

"Great work, Karan; this is fantastic progress." Aman expressed his appreciation, then moved to the quality assurance team and inquired, "How is the code quality of both teams?"

Aman was informed that the quality of Karan's team's code

was good with only minor flaws, whereas Parth's team's work was extremely sloppy, and the team had not adhered to the standard coding practices and the code was deployed without thorough testing.

This made Aman furious, but before he could say anything, Murli intervened, saying, "Parth, let's not compromise on quality to gain speed. Please halt all future development until you have resolved all of the issues raised by the quality team."

"All right, Murli," Parth said, attempting to mask his own displeasure.

Nidhi walked to Karan's desk after the meeting, when the teams were working on their tasks. "I got the news. You have now surpassed Parth's team. Congrats!! Don't let the momentum fade away, Karan."

"Sure, Nidhi, it's a win, but I'm still concerned because it may be temporary. For now, I am doing most of the complex coding, so we could surge ahead last week, but this is not a sustainable approach," Karan responded. "The upcoming features will be more complex, and I will need support from the team; I cannot handle everything by myself. Parth's team has better developers; I believe they compromised quality for speed this time, but Parth is astute. He will undoubtedly make a strong comeback." Karan expressed his concern.

"I guess, you're overthinking," Nidhi reassured Karan.

"I hope so," Karan said.

Parth was already agitated, and seeing Nidhi with Karan made him even more so. He was frustrated with the comments by the quality team on his team's work and feeling a bit of let-down. He then closed his eyes and began to reflect on the session on *Expectations.* He attempted to release any expectations from his team and from Nidhi as well through a sequence of thoughts. He decided to focus on the tasks at hand. He was now in a much better mood.

He called a meeting with his team to discuss the next steps.

In the evening, Karan and Parth reached Murli's cabin on time for the session, and Murli welcomed them with his usual warm smile as he inquired, "How are you two doing?"

"We're still under a lot of pressure to finish everything that's been assigned to us. Both the teams are giving it their all, but you know the issue with my team's code quality!" Parth replied, stressed.

"Parth, just keep going. Always remember, every cloud has a silver lining. This is a phase and will pass."

Parth felt reassured by Murli's soothing words.

"Shall we now begin the next session on Gratitude of our knowledge-sharing series?" asked Murli.

"Yes, sure. Let's get started!" replied Karan.

"How would you define Gratitude?"

"It's about thanking other individuals for the help they give us," Parth explained.

"Well, and how many times do we really mean it whenever we express it?"

"Less than 50% of the time in my situation! I say it just as a mannerism," Karan answered bluntly.

"Appreciate your candid response, Karan. *Thank you* are two of the most powerful words in the human language when used with the right intention. And Parth, what you said about gratitude is only the tip of the iceberg; there is much more to it."

"Really, what more can there be to gratitude?" Parth inquired and was surprised.

Murli got out of his chair and walked over to the whiteboard.

He began explaining while writing the text below.

"Please allow me to explain the law of gratitude.

"It operates on two levels: the emotional and the spiritual.

"Let us begin with the first law of Gratitude at an emotional level:

**"Through expressing gratitude, we improve our mental and emotional state, which allows us to focus on improving our lives."**

Murli then wiped the whiteboard clean and drew a tiny black spot on it.

"What do you see?" he inquired.

"There's a black dot!" Parth and Karan both responded at the same time.

"That's the issue, guys! We always focus on such small black dots in our lives and overlook 99% of the great things that God has provided us. A minuscule black dot on a vast whiteboard, would have been the correct response and right way to look at life."

"Does it make a difference?" Karan was perplexed.

"Okay, let me explain why it matters."

Murli launched the presentation and began explaining the figure below to explain this law.

"I assume, you must have read this quote somewhere: *I cried because I had no shoes until I met a man who had no legs.* Such a powerful line, but have we ever considered what it is attempting to say?

"Look at this image: a man without legs is condemning God for giving him such a miserable life, but he forgets to express gratitude for having one. If he can just look back, he will realize that millions of people perish every day. He stares blankly at a man who has at least one leg and can walk with some support.

"Now the man with one leg is criticizing God for giving him only one leg. While ignoring the man with no legs, he keeps looking at a man walking on both legs without any support. He has complaints about how dreadful his life is.

"The man with both legs is weeping because he doesn't have shoes and has to walk barefoot. Displaying no gratitude to God for keeping his both legs intact, he gapes with contempt at a man wearing a good, costly suit and shoes.

"Now, the man in the good shoes is unhappy as well. He is considering purchasing a new car and is blaming God for not providing him with enough money to buy a car, whereas he is utterly ignorant of what he already has." Murli explained.

"But is there anything wrong with dreaming of a better life?" asked Karan.

"There's nothing wrong, Karan! In fact, we should always try to strive to do better in every aspect of our lives. But the problem is that everyone in this picture ends up suffering because they don't appreciate what they have and keep complaining about what they don't have." Murli explained further.

"Huh," Karan pondered.

"Isn't this our life's story? We often assume the grass is greener on the other side, but you never know what someone else has gone through or is going through right now to get to where they are. As you try to live in a grateful state, you will understand that your circumstances are not as terrible as those of others." Murli continued..

Parth and Karan remained silent.

"The difficulty with the human mind is that we crave for something so much that we sacrifice our peace of mind to get it, but once we get it, we begin to take it for granted until we lose it again!"

"What do you mean?" Parth inquired.

"Say, you want to buy a house. You work hard to purchase one, and once you have one, you begin to take it for granted. Unfortunately, if you have to sell your house due to some financial problem, you will miss owning a house and will have to work hard to purchase another one. Did you ever appreciate it or thanked God for the beautiful house when you had it?

"You are correct! After living in my new home for a few months, I began to take it for granted." Parth added.

"Not only do we take things for granted, but we also take

people for granted. We only start to miss them when they are no longer in our lives. Have we ever shown any gratitude to mother nature for generating such magnificent life on Earth? Have we shown our gratitude to the Sun for shining every day without fail? Consider what would happen if the Sun chose to take a few days off; would all life on Earth not perish?

"You are aware that people are dying on the streets due to the ongoing pandemic since they do not have access to oxygen cylinders. Have we ever expressed gratitude to the air we breathe, which has never failed to supply us with enough oxygen? Why do we wait for something horrible to happen before we start appreciating the worth of the little things in life?"

"Yes Murli! As I stand on the brink of losing my house if I am unable to keep my job, I can now appreciate how important it was for me. We stop appreciating things and people once they enter our lives," muttered Parth. "But Murli, even if we had expressed gratitude, how would have that helped? Would someone not has lost their house, or would the pandemic not have hit us?"

Murli replied patiently, "That's a great question, Parth. Here is where the first law of gratitude comes into play. *Gratitude helps foster the growth of a positive mindset and frees us from toxic emotions.* In 2008, scientists conducted a study to evaluate the brain activity of individuals who were thinking about and experiencing gratitude. What they discovered astounded them. Gratitude triggers synchronized activation in several brain regions, including the hypothalamus and the reward pathways in the brain. That means gratitude can increase levels of the neurotransmitter serotonin and activate the brain stem, causing it to create dopamine."

"Sorry to interrupt Murli, but what does this exactly mean?" asked Karan to get clarity.

"As you may know, Dopamine is the pleasure chemical in our brain. When it is released in the nervous system, we feel happy and motivated. The more positive and thankful thoughts we have, the healthier and happier we feel. Owing to the brain's flexibility or plasticity, when our brain is flooded with happy thoughts, this emotion will function as a catalyst to improve every area of our life, including our relationships, health, work-performance, accomplishing our aspirations and objectives, and more."

This knowledge completely captivated Parth and Karan.

"Does that suggest that the more gratitude we practice, the more adept our brain gets at dealing with any challenges in life?" Parth wondered.

"Absolutely! I've seen so many individuals complain about their job, pay, work pressure, office politics, and so on. Whenever you experience such feelings, compare yourself to someone who does not have a job or a business to operate. Consider the lives of garbage collectors, umbrella sellers, rickshaw pullers, and street hawkers. These people struggle to earn even a subsistence wage for their families. At the very least, you have a great education to find a new job. I know it's difficult to show gratitude, especially given the current circumstances you're in, but please keep blessing all things that serve you.

"We, in general, turn a blind eye and do not express gratitude for the good things that continue to come to us; we take them for granted and keep asking for more in life. We are not content with what we have, and it is here that we must practice gratitude."

Murli took a pause and then asked, "Do you understand the

first law now?"

"Yeah, Murli! It's clear now," Karan said.

"Now, let's talk about how gratitude operates at the second level, which is the spiritual level.

"The second law of gratitude is identical to Newton's Third Law of Motion, which states that *for every action in nature there is an equal and opposite reaction.*

**"The release of your mind's energy in the form of thoughts of gratitude will always reach the universe or God, and then the universe reacts by showering its energy of abundance on you."**

Murli paused while Parth and Karan appeared perplexed.

"Let me give you a simple example. Suppose you're assisting someone, but he or she never expresses gratitude. How long will you continue to assist him?"

"Maybe another 2-3 times at most," Parth said.

"I shall quit helping immediately," Karan retorted.

"Thank God, Karan, the universe isn't as strict as you!" Murli laughed. "God or the universe has blessed you with several things in life. How many times did you express our gratitude to the universe?"

Parth and Karan remained mute.

"After all, what is gratitude? It is just a thought of thankfulness that can spread positive energy throughout the universe. When the universe realizes that we value what it has given us, it responds by showering us with more blessings." Murli continued his explanation.

"Does this law thus indicate that the more we express gratitude for the simple things in our lives, the more the universe continues to provide us, exactly as we will do for someone in our daily lives?" Parth inquired, seeking confirmation of his comprehension.

"Exactly!! Gratitude is a great multiplier, but to make this law function, you must believe that the universe is the source of our existence and that it provides us with everything we want. And a deep and genuine sense of gratitude will undoubtedly connect you to it.

"It is very disheartening to witness how many individuals, after receiving the gift of remarkable life from the universe, cut the wires that connect them with it by failing to acknowledge and express gratitude, finally leading to a miserable life. Any soul that is constantly appreciative is in closer contact with the universe."

"Is that true?" Karan inquired, surprised.

"Absolutely!! If we continue to appreciate God's supreme power when good things happen to us, more wonderful things will happen to us. The fundamental law of gratitude says: *We should not only express gratitude when things go our way, but we should also express gratitude when things go wrong, keeping faith in God who has bigger plans for us.* This attitude develops more patience within us, which is necessary in life to fight against bad situations and eventually makes us stronger. Also, feeling grateful in adversity, helps us look at the brighter side of the situation, and believe me, it will change your outlook towards life, people, and situations."

"But there are times in life when we lose control of our thoughts, such as the one we are currently experiencing. Forget about being grateful; we can't even stop the negative thoughts from flooding our minds," Parth countered.

"You should be aware that the moment you allow your mind to dwell in displeasure on negative thoughts, you lose connection with the universe. When you focus your attention on negativity, poverty, dirty politics, and so on, your mind takes on these traits and will communicate these forms, or mental representations, to the universe. As a result, more and more such things will come your way. Letting your thoughts linger on inferior thoughts is the same as becoming inferior and surrounded by inferior things.

"Please remember, as the grateful mind is constantly aligned with the best, it tends to become the best. It is critical to create the habit of being grateful for everything positive that comes your way and to appreciate it on a regular basis.

"And, to answer your question, Parth, we are always more focused on the imperfections in our lives, like the black dot, rather than appreciating what we have. This is how our parents, schools, and surroundings have conditioned us since childhood. It eventually becomes tough for us to practice gratitude since it requires us to handle and view situations from a whole new perspective. Every day may not be good for you, but there is something good in every day if you are willing to find it."

Murli noticed some uncertainty on Parth and Karan's faces.

"All right Let's perform a quick exercise. Close your eyes and think of five things for which you are grateful. It might be anything - meal you had today, certain people in your life, help you received, etc. Simply express gratitude to God for them."

Parth and Karan closed their eyes as they started pondering such things. Murli could see their reactions, which ranged from distress to gentle smiles.

"How do you feel?" Murli questioned them when they opened their eyes. "First and foremost, could you discover those five things?"

"That was overwhelming. It is the first moment when I realized there are so many things for which I should be grateful for!" said Karan.

"Same with me. I feel so light and stress-free. I forgot about all the issues in my life during this gratitude practice activity," remarked Parth.

Murli was pleased that the boys saw a shift in their emotions during the exercise.

"My day begins and ends with gratitude. If you choose to live your life in this beautiful way, I am confident that every moment of it will be filled with gratitude. Gratitude is an emotional feeling that explains how much you appreciate what you have and allows you to live in the here and now state. Over the years, I have learned how incredible it can be to practice gratitude and maintain peace of mind amid challenging circumstances." He added.

It now made sense to Parth and Karan.

"To conclude this session, let me summarize the benefits of gratitude practice."

Murli returned to the whiteboard and began describing the benefits as he listed them.

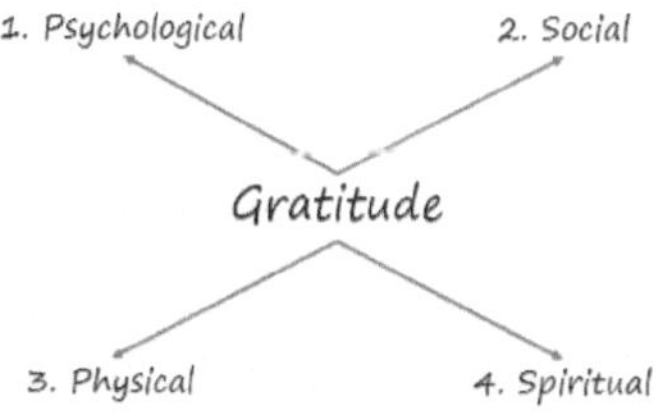


"Practicing gratitude provides benefits at four levels.

"Firstly, it works big time at the *psychological* level, as explained earlier. We become so attached to materialistic things that we forget we can't carry them with us. We came into this world empty-handed and will return empty-handed. We should pay extra attention to our dependencies on materialistic things since greed for acquiring more and more things starts controlling our actions. Gratitude helps us get rid of emotional baggage during difficult times and helps us find happiness in the simple things in life.

"Secondly, it has *social* effects as well. If you continue to help people without expecting anything in return, they will feel your energy of gratitude and will draw closer to you. You will be able to form more solid interpersonal relationships that will last for a long time.

"Thirdly, you will notice surprising improvements in your *physical* fitness. During the last few decades, positive psychology and mental health specialists have discovered an overwhelming link between gratitude and good health. When your brain continues to produce healthy chemicals, it aids in the development of a stronger immune system, the reduction of physical pains, and so on.

"Finally, the most significant advantage is on the *spiritual* level. Once you create a connection with the universe, your soul grows more powerful and aligns with the laws of the universe. Because of your steady emotional state, it will be much easier for you to inculcate the other four concepts we discussed earlier once you begin practicing gratitude."

"This is incredible knowledge, Murli! Let me express my gratitude to you by saying a heartfelt thank you!" Everyone burst out laughing when Karan said these words.

"Thank you, Murli. In the current tense situation, your

sessions are a breath of fresh air. While I was initially hesitant to participate in these sessions, I am glad that I did. I am definitely looking forward to the ways of instilling this knowledge in our day-to-day lives," Parth added.

Murli was glad that this knowledge was well received by the boys. "Yeah, the wait will finally be over soon but let me finish this session with some simple questions. Tell me, if you have to learn Java programming, what will you practice?"

Parth and Karan were surprised by such a silly question from a wise man like Murli.

"Of course, we have to practice Java programming, Murli!" replied Karan.

"OK, and what if you have to become a great batsman in cricket? What will you practice?" Murli asked again.

"Practice batting for hours!!" said Parth in response to something related to his favorite sport.

"Thank you for replying to my silly questions; now, please answer the last question. If we need to be happy, what should we practice?"

"Happiness??" Parth replied hesitantly.

"Exactly!! Why do we humans not understand such a basic equation in life? *You can never be happy if you practice worry or anxiety! If you want to be happy in life, focus on the things that make you happy.* Cultivating gratitude allows you to uncover those things that can eventually lead to a happy existence, regardless of the circumstances outside."

Murli then got up from his cabin to get a cup of coffee, leaving Parth and Karan in awe of his profound words of wisdom. The session was over and the two returned to their desks.

Parth went to Nidhi's desk later that evening.

"Hello Parth, how are your so-called 'spiritual sessions' going?" Nidhi mocked Parth.

"Please, Nidhi!" Parth expressed his disapproval emphatically.

"I'm sorry, I was just kidding!" She attempted to appease Parth.

"It's OK. I came here to make a request. You are aware of the problems with the code quality that we are experiencing. Could you please assist with the code review? That will be of great help," Parth requested.

"NO!" was the immediate response from Nidhi. After realizing she sounded disrespectful, she tried to make up an excuse, "Parth, you know how strict Aman Sir is. If I fail to meet even one SLA, he will not hesitate to put me on the firing line."

"I understand Nidhi," Parth said as he walked away from her desk.

Nidhi realized that while Karan was currently ahead, as Karan speculated, Parth had the capacity to surge ahead at any time.

She couldn't risk pushing him away.

# 16

# THE HAPPINESS PARADOX: FINDING JOY IN A WORLD OF CHAOS

It was Tuesday morning, and everybody was busy with their work in the office.

Nidhi wanted to make amends with Parth for her rude behavior the evening before. At about ten o'clock, she texted Parth, asking, "Tea?"

Parth was in the middle of something important, but he couldn't say no to Nidhi. "Okay, let's go," he replied after a brief pause.

Parth headed to the cafeteria first, followed by Nidhi. She stopped him as he was ready to sit on a table in the center, saying, "Let's sit in my favorite place on the bean bags in that corner."

Parth felt excited to know that Nidhi was now willing to share something close to her with him. She was looking stunning in blue jeans and a white top; and he, as usual, was in awe of her.

"Parth, I know you have quality issues with your code, but keep focusing on your work, and I am confident you can cross this hurdle as well. I will undoubtedly assist you once I am free from my work." Nidhi acted as if she truly wanted to help him.

Parth had been disappointed with Nidhi's response the evening before, but her calming words comforted his heart. They had a nice discussion for roughly 10—minutes before returning to their work.

In the evening, Murli greeted the boys as they entered his cabin and went right to the point, "Hey guys, let's get started on the session on happiness. By the way, what do you guys' think is happiness?"

He had planned the last and most important session for the evening. Boys were also looking forward to this session because it was about happiness, which everyone craves for.

"Whenever I get what I want, I feel happy," replied Parth. He remembered how 15 minutes of chit-chat with Nidhi over tea had made him happy, bringing a smile to his face.

"So are you saying that things and people around you bring you happiness?"

"Essentially, yes!" replied Parth.

"The definition of true happiness must be understood. It's fascinating to observe how people often search for happiness in position, wealth, health, and other materialistic achieve-ments. They have a belief that all these things will make them happy. We enter into relationships these days so that we can extract such happiness from the other person."

"That's correct. Is there any problem with this?" asked Karan.

"Yes, big problem! Let me explain the principle of happi-ness:

**"Dependence is the root cause of the world's unhappiness. This is ironic because happiness is not dependent on any-thing or anyone and it can be found only within us."**

Parth and Karan were perplexed and began staring at each other.

Murli saw their bewilderment and inquired, smiling, "What's up guys?"

"This passed over our heads," Parth answered.

Murli's smile quickly changed to laughter.

He walked towards the whiteboard and started explaining while drawing the image below.

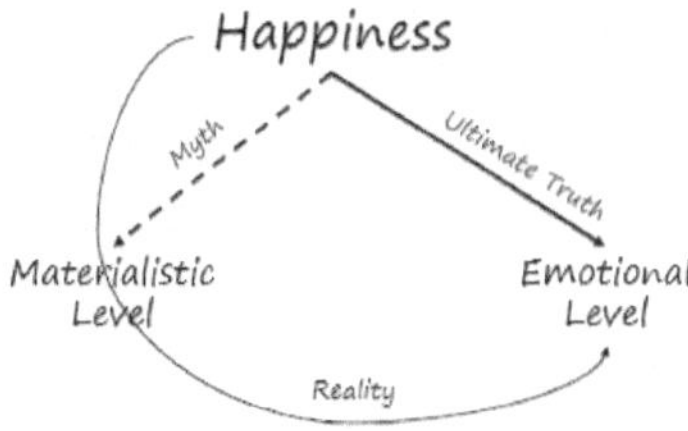


"We always believe that materialistic things can bring us happiness, which is the unfortunate myth we all are living. But, the ultimate truth is that happiness always occurs on an emotional level. Realizing that physical comfort is not the same as emotional comfort, is the first step towards achieving happiness. Happiness is just a thought we create to generate a feeling of joy."

"What does this exactly mean, Murli?" asked Parth.

"Look at this figure carefully. We believe that if we buy things that improve our physical comfort, we will be happy. We're treating happiness like a product that can be bought. It doesn't mean we should stop buying things; rather, it only means we shouldn't associate happiness with material possessions. Let's buy things for their usefulness and comfort rather than for achieving happiness through them."

"What do you mean? If I bought a car, wouldn't I be happy?" Karan protested.

"Yes, you will be happy, but is the car bringing you happiness? Think about it. It is the emotion of happiness you are creating by buying a car. Look at the arrow of *Reality* in this figure. You are trying to achieve happiness at an emotional level through materialistic achievements."

"But it is still the fact that I get happy because I bought a car," Karan tried to prove his point.

"Imagine, you bought your dream car and went on a long drive, enjoying the comfort and music. You are really happy. Suddenly, you get a call from your friend saying that the stock market crashed, and all your investments were wiped out. Will you still be happy?"

"Of course not, I will be devastated!" replied Karan.

"But why be devastated, you are driving your dream car? If a car was the one that gave you happiness, you should still be happy, right?"

"Of course, we are dependent on happiness at every stage of our lives on external situations and people. How can I be happy if I lose my investments or job? So, happiness is dependent on external factors," Karan said.

"All right, fair enough! Can you think of any additional dependencies for happiness?" asked Murli.

"Money, respect, health, family... this list could go on forever," Karan said.

"And are any of these things under your control?"

"Some are under more control, some less, and some not in control at all," Karan said.

"In that case, how can you ever be happy if you have given remote control over your happiness to hundreds of things and people around you which are not under your control?"

Karan was silent.

"Now let me reiterate the principle in simple language: *only you are capable of creating your own happiness. Your happiness lies within you.*" Murli was interrupted by Karan.

"But let's be practical. We need external stimuli to be happy. We can't be sitting here doing nothing and still feel happy!" Karan said.

"There are yogis who are always in a state of ecstasy doing nothing. They have achieved the ultimate truth and don't need any external stimulus to be in ecstasy. They are at bliss just being connected to God."

"So, you want us to be yogis now?" asked Karan irritatingly.

Murli burst into laughter, "No, no, not at all. If everybody becomes Yogi, who will drive this materialistic world? I want to explain to you how to always be happy doing what you are doing to achieve success in a materialistic world without being dependent on external factors."

"Wow, is it really possible?" asked Karan, surprisingly.

"Karan, tell me what your dreams are for living a good life," Murli asked.

"Huge home, big car, great family, lots of money, so I assume the same as everyone else," Karan responded.

"Right. In how many years do you intend to purchase your dream home and car?

"House in 2—years, then car in a couple of years."

Murli opened his presentation and projected the figure below.

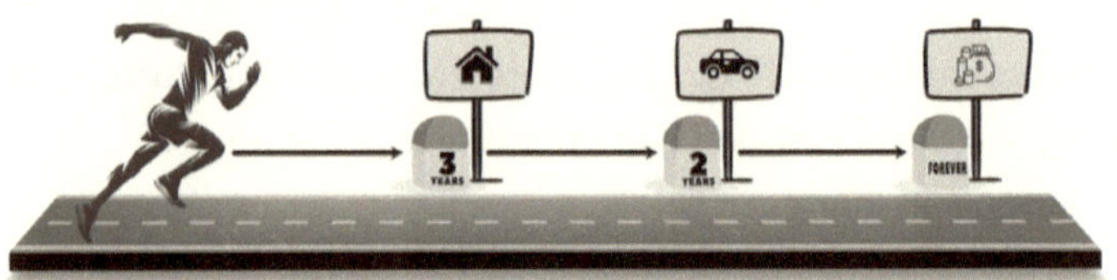

"Look at this figure closely. This is the journey of our life, always running behind something." After a pause he said addressing Karan, "Let's start with the home Karan. How will your life be for the next three years until you buy a house?"

"I will not settle until I attain my goal of purchasing a home; I will study hard and learn new skills to advance in my job so that I may continue to earn more and more money."

"I like how focused your efforts are to reach your goal. Now, suppose certain hurdles arise between you and your objective, such as the current one in which you are about to lose your job for no fault of yours. What then?"

"Of course, I'll be stressed, anxious, and even depressed." Karan said in a confessing tone.

"Right, so to conclude what I've learned, for the next three years, the quality of your life will keep fluctuating between happiness and misery since you'll be experiencing all of those unpleasant feelings if things don't go as planned, and you'll reach happiness only when you buy your dream house. Isn't it?"

Karan remained mute.

"So, this three-year path till you attain your objective will not be filled with enjoyment but rather with unpleasant feelings."

"But why think negatively? We are in an exceptional circumstance right now. There are many people who can still buy a property according to their plans with no problems!" Karan responded.

"That's true, but won't they keep postponing happiness for three years? Even if they buy a house after three years, they will be overjoyed for the first couple of months because they will receive social accolades from family and friends. Once the novelty wears off, they will take that house for granted and begin working toward a new goal: a large car!"

"Yes, like what I did," confessed Parth.

"Right! So they will postpone their happiness for three years in exchange for three months of delight.

"They will again postpone their enjoyment for two years until they reach their next goal of purchasing a new car, which again they will enjoy for 2-3 months before resuming their pursuit of the new object."

Karan and Parth were both perplexed.

"What are you trying to say?" Parth inquired.

"It's quite simple. While we ought to be focusing our efforts to attain the goal that Karan said, we should learn to appreciate the journey as well, and avoid deferring happiness till we achieve the goal."

Karan and Parth were perplexed once more.

Sensing their perplexity, Murli changed his glance towards the window and pointing to a nearby hill said, "Let's imagine you start trekking that hill with the intention of reaching the summit. You get up excitedly in the morning, completely focused on your goal. During trekking, you develop cramps or rain starts pouring in the middle of the journey, forcing you to return. What will your feelings be like? Wouldn't you be annoyed? You may feel as if you squandered your entire day.

And if there is another issue next time too, you may not even try to climb again."

Parth and Karan both nodded in agreement.

"On the other hand, if you had begun with the attitude that I would do everything to achieve my objective of ascending the hill, but I would also enjoy the journey on my way, you wouldn't have felt like you squandered your day even if you have to return from midway, because you would already have enjoyed whatever climb you completed. And you would have returned home happy.  If you have ingrained the mentality of enjoying every moment, you will keep trying to ascend no matter how many times you fail because you will not feel like you are wasting your time. And it is a natural law that if you keep striving with honest efforts, you will ultimately attain your goal.

*"Please remember: Happiness is a state that should be developed while working towards a goal, not an emotion to be experienced after the goal has been accomplished."*

Parth and Karan were staring at each other.

*Murli said emphatically, "Your happiness is under your control, and no other force can take it away unless you give them that authority."*

"Is it possible to be happy 24 hours a day, seven days a week?" asked Parth.

"Only if we take care of ourselves and accept personal responsibility. Happiness becomes sporadic when we make it dependent on other factors." added Murli and concluded the session saying, "OK, folks, that's enough for today; it was a hefty dose. Do you have any questions?"

"Thank you, Murli, for all of your wisdom throughout the last six sessions! First time, I have realized in my life that the belief systems we have created over the years are so shallow and how they make us helpless! My father always used to tell me: a good heart, rather than material wealth, was the true measure of a man's success. Never before did I grasp its meaning, but now I do." Parth responded as if he had awoken from a profound sleep of ignorance.

"Absolutely! I have no doubt that if we follow these principles, we will be able to enjoy an extraordinary life. I know you already live by these principles; I'm not sure if someone like me can actually follow them," Karan expressed his pessimism.

"Karan, we all have the same energy flowing through us. If I can do it, you can do it, and as such anyone can. It is simply a matter of employing proper techniques and remaining consistent in your efforts towards transformation. We will discuss these techniques from tomorrow. " Murli attempted to inspire Karan and Parth.

"I'm really excited to learn those techniques, Murli," Parth said enthusiastically.

With glimmers of optimism in their eyes, Parth and Karan emerged from Murli's cabin and went to their desks, only to be met by puzzled stares from their teams.

"Do you discuss the Bhagavad Gita with Murli?" Anand inquired of Parth, who was a tester on Parth's team.

"Hmm... yeah," Parth said reluctantly.

"Are you guys insane? Our asses are on fire, and you're wasting your time with this crap."

"Anand, watch your language! I realize we're under pressure, but I'm making up for lost time, so let's go back to work," Parth stated emphatically.

The scenario was similar inside Karan's team. He was enraged that Nidhi had spilled the beans about their sessions with Murli in the office. He walked down to Nidhi's desk to confront her.

Before Karan could say anything, Nidhi apologized, saying, "Sorry Karan, it just fell out of my lips, but you guys should stop wasting your time and focus on your project. Your job is on the line here."

Karan got calmed down by Nidhi's advice and went back to his desk. He started thinking, 'The only reason I decided to join Murli was because I didn't want Murli to be biased towards Parth, but knowing Murli today, I don't think he would do any such sort of act. Also, is it really possible for me to put these principles into practice? I am really not sure. Perhaps I should use that time working on the project; it will put me ahead of Parth's team.'

The story of the sessions that Parth and Karan were having with Murli in the evenings had become really viral in the office. Aman's blood was boiling as he learned about these sessions. He summoned Murli to his cabin and wasted no time in expressing his anger. "What on earth do you think you're doing? Why are you wasting Parth's and Karan's time? I want every minute of their time to be devoted to the project. STOP squandering it!"

Murli remained calm and collected, waiting for Aman to finish his rant. "Aman, you're a selfish individual," he said finally. "You've already done enough harm to the morale of the team, and I won't let you exploit them for your greed. I'll continue to do what's right."

Aman was taken aback by Murli's response. "Watch your language, Murli," he spat. "You're my employee! I pay your salary!"

Murli stood his ground. "That's true. And in exchange, I

provide my services to your company!"

Aman's ego was bruised, and he threatened to fire Murli. But Murli was one step ahead. "You'll get my resignation in your inbox in next few minutes," he said calmly before leaving Aman's cabin with a smile on his face.

Aman was stunned. He hadn't expected things to take such a serious turn. Launching their dream product without Murli would be nearly impossible. As he sat in his chair, contemplating his next move, he received Murli's resignation email.

'I can't let that jerk go. I need him at present,' he thought, 'For sure he'll be the first to go once the product is launched. But for now, I have to swallow my pride and ask him to stay.'

He rushed to Murli's cabin and apologized profusely. "I'm sorry, Murli. I lost my cool. I didn't mean to offend you. Please withdraw your resignation. Please!"

Murli remained silent, staring at Aman with a blank expression on his face.

Aman's heart sank. Had he lost Murli for good? As Aman walked out of Murli's cabin, he couldn't shake off the feeling of dread that had settled in his chest. He knew he had messed up big time. But what was done was done, he told himself, as he walked towards his car.

The first thing he did was call Maya. He needed someone to talk to, someone who would understand his ambition and drive. As soon as she picked up, he launched into a tirade about Murli and his resignation.

Maya listened patiently, her mind already ticking, plotting and planning.

"You can't let him go," she said finally, her voice low and persuasive. "Not when we're so close to launching the product.

And don't forget, you're the owner of the company. You need to secure your interest in this, Aman."

Aman knew Maya was right. He had to keep Murli around, at least until the project was complete. He thanked Maya and promised to meet her later that evening.

As he drove home, he couldn't help but think about his estranged wife, Anita. He had been dragging his feet over the divorce proceedings, not wanting to deal with the messiness and paperwork. But now, with Maya's words ringing in his ears, he knew he had to expedite the process. He wanted to be free of any entanglements that might hinder his progress.

Meanwhile, Murli had gone back home to Ruchi and shared the events of the day with her. Ruchi listened patiently, her calm demeanor soothing Murli's frayed nerves. "Remember what we learned from the Bhagavad Gita," she said softly. "You must control your rage and stay focused on helping Karan and Parth. Don't let Aman's selfishness distract you from your path."

She opened up her copy of the Bhagavad Gita and read out a few verses, emphasizing the importance of staying true to one's purpose and duty, regardless of the obstacles in the way. Murli felt his heart fill with gratitude for having Ruchi by his side.

As he went to bed that night, he felt a sense of peace settle over him. He knew he had made the right decision in standing up to Aman, and he was determined to continue guiding Karan and Parth towards spiritual awakening, with or without Aman's support.

Later that night, Karan and Nidhi walked into the club, the music thumping and the lights flashing. Karan was a bit hesitant at first, but Nidhi was in her elements, smiling and chatting as they made their way to the bar.

"Thanks for inviting me out tonight," Karan said, trying to be heard over the music.

"No problem," Nidhi replied, taking a sip of her drink. "You looked like you needed a break from work."

Karan chuckled. "Yeah, I guess I have been a bit stressed lately."

Nidhi nodded in understanding. "It's been a tough project, but you're doing great. I'm proud of you."

Karan smiled at her words, feeling a sense of warmth and gratitude towards her. "Actually, I wanted to thank you for something," he said.

Nidhi looked at him quizzically. "What is it?"

"You've been really helping me stay focused on the project," he said. "I had been thinking about skipping out on those Bhagavad Gita sessions with Murli. Today you actually reminded me about why I was even attending them in the first place. It's time to stop going into those sessions and utilize that time towards the project. It will eventually give me an easy advantage over Parth."

Nidhi's eyes widened. "Really? I didn't know I had that kind of influence on you."

Karan laughed. "You do, and I appreciate it."

They clinked their glasses together, enjoying the music and each other's company. As the night went on, Karan couldn't help but think how lucky he was to have Nidhi in his life —both as a colleague and as a friend.

III

# PLAYING THE GAME FOR EXTRAORDINARY LIFE

# 17

# THE ENIGMA OF THE MIND MAGICIAN

Ten days had passed since the entire development team received the termination letter, and the clock was ticking as they had only 20 days left to complete their tasks. The team's anxiety grew with each passing day, and the pressure was palpable.

Aman had scheduled a review meeting with Parth and Karan to evaluate their progress. In the conference room, Karan and Parth, along with the Quality Team, were waiting tensely for Aman and Murli to arrive. When Aman and Murli finally walked in, Aman immediately launched a discussion about progress reports. Both the teams had been neck-and-neck until recently, but Karan's team had made more progress in the last couple of days while Parth's team had been struggling with quality issues.

After the meeting, Aman asked Parth and Karan to stay back. "What are you guys doing? Concentrate on your work; your job is at stake!" Aman screamed, frustrated with their focus on Murli's sessions.

Silence filled the room as Parth and Karan preferred to remain silent. Despite Aman's assurances that whoever stays with HealthTech would have a bright future once the pandemic gets over, they knew he was simply trying to keep them from attending Murli's sessions and focusing on his product.

Aman's patience eventually ran out, and he stormed out of the room, leaving behind an angry cry.

"Man, such a jerk! I don't know how I got impressed with such a selfish man and agreed to join HealthTech!" Parth exclaimed with disgust.

"I completely agree, Parth," Karan said, however, he had already promised Nidhi that he would no longer attend Murli's sessions and would instead devote his time to work.

In the evening, Karan was getting anxious as it was time for the session with Murli. Despite the fact that his intellect agreed with Nidhi, his heart urged him to go ahead with the session. When he saw Parth enter Murli's cabin, he became even more agitated. He cast an eye on Nidhi. She gestured for him to skip the meeting. Even though he was feeling really uncomfortable, he decided to keep working. He was torn between following his brain and his heart. He sat for five minutes before getting up and walking into Murli's cabin, not daring to glance back at Nidhi.

"Murli, I'm so sorry for being late," Karan said, his heart still racing.

"It's great to see you again, Karan." Parth said, "I thought Aman's insightful words truly had an impact on you," and all three of them burst into laughter.

"OK, boys, let's get this party started. There will be many fascinating discussions over the next three days. As I knew you were patiently waiting for these techniques, I saved the best for last. I hope you're all set!" Murli sounded excited.

"Absolutely!" Parth and Karan nodded in affirmation.

Murli started the session with a verse from the Bhagavad Gita "Krishna states in Chapter 17 verse 3:

सत्त्वानुरूपा सर्वस्य श्रद्धा भवति भारत ।
श्रद्धामयोऽयं पुरुषो यो यच्छ्रद्ध: स एव स: ॥

*sattvānurūpā sarvasya śhraddhā bhavati bhārata*
*śhraddhā-mayo 'yaṁ puruṣho yo yach-chhraddhaḥ sa eva saḥ*

"In a nutshell, this suggests that *humans are shaped by their beliefs; they are what they believe. Your thoughts shape who you are. You are a happy person if you feel like you are. If you allow sad thoughts to dominate your mind, you will become a sad person. Man's mind is everything; what he thinks, he becomes.*"

In an effort to decipher Murli's message, Parth and Karan were deep in thought.

Murli continued, "An individual's mental strength determines how they perceive and handle circumstances. A weak mind perceives even simple challenges as problems, while a rigid mind struggles to adapt to new circumstances that arise. However, a strong mind perceives circumstances as opportunities, and with a positive attitude, it can overcome any obstacle."

"What exactly is mind, Murli?" asked Parth with curiosity.

"There is no simple answer to it, Parth. The mind is an abstract concept that is used to describe thoughts, feelings, subjective states, and self-awareness that are assumed to originate in the brain. For ages, people have debated the nature of the mind. Apart from Buddha, no one has totally comprehended the mind."

"So, Gautama, the Buddha, knew everything about the mind?" Karan inquired, surprised.

"I cannot verify the accuracy of this statement, but reportedly, Buddha divided the mind into seven sections. In modern psychology, there is recognition that the mind is not solely comprised of the conscious and subconscious but also includes the unconscious mind. This aligns with Buddha's teachings from over 2,500 years ago. It remains to be seen if contemporary science will eventually acknowledge all seven parts of the mind in the near future."

"That is fascinating!" added Parth.

"Indeed! In our discussion, we will just focus on these three components of mind." Murli continued

"Is there any specific reason we are focusing so much on the mind?" asked Parth.

"You remember the chariot diagram I had shown you on the first day of our sessions and how we will use inside-out approach? So to enhance the strength of the soul, we will utilize the mind as a tool. It's important to remember that the mind can be a great servant but a terrible master. Therefore, all the techniques that I will teach are centered around making your mind work for you. Without directing your mind in the appropriate manner, you may experience mental diarrhea, where you lose control over your thoughts and consequently, your destiny." Murli emphasized on power of mind.

"Is the mind so powerful?" asked Karan.

"Oh, yes!! Trust me when I say that the mind is nothing short of a magician. Let me tell you one story:

*Once, a frugal merchant was on a business trip. Having walked a long way, feeling tired and agitated, he stopped at a green pasture where he saw a lovely cow and wished she could give him some*

*milk. To his surprise, a glass full of milk appeared in front of him, followed by delicious meal platters. But as he enjoyed his meal, his mind started to form crazy conclusions. He looked at the cow and wondered whether it was some kind of trap. Will ghosts now come and kill him? At that precise moment, the cow transformed into a ghost and killed the merchant."*

Parth and Karan thought the story was funny.

"That wasn't any ordinary cow. It was *Kamdhenu*, a magically bountiful cow which gives anyone whatever they want. Our mind is like *Kamdhenu*; it will give you whatever you desire, good or bad. The mind can help a person rise to power, but it can also drown him in despair because it treats you as a friend or a foe depending on how you use it." Murli provided words of caution to the boys.

"Wow, is it really true?" Karan wondered.

"Absolutely! Andrew Carnegie was a wealthy American in 1900, but many suspected he obtained his wealth through illicit means. Summoned by the US government, he revealed his secret to success: the ability to focus on a single thought for five minutes without distraction. Everyone was stunned. They thought he was misleading them. When challenged by Carnegie , no one could do it.  Carnegie explained that he relied on his subconscious mind to guide him when seeking inspiration for new ideas or businesses."

This story captivated Parth and Murli.

"During the next three days, we will use the mind as a tool to enhance your soul power through some key strategies."

Murli sipped some water before continuing, "It is stated that our conscious mind comprises just approximately 2—%, our subconscious mind constitutes roughly 10—%, and the remainder is all unconscious mind.  We typically use our conscious mind so effectively that we only use around 2—% of our mind's capability, yet we have accomplished so much in life. Imagine what wonders we could produce in our own lives and for all of humanity if we could access the subconscious and unconscious minds!"

"It is incredible!" remarked Parth.

"Indeed, it is! Let us now examine these three minds and their functions. The conscious mind is the most active mind, and when we say "my mind" in a discussion, we usually mean this part." Murli displayed the image below from his presentation.

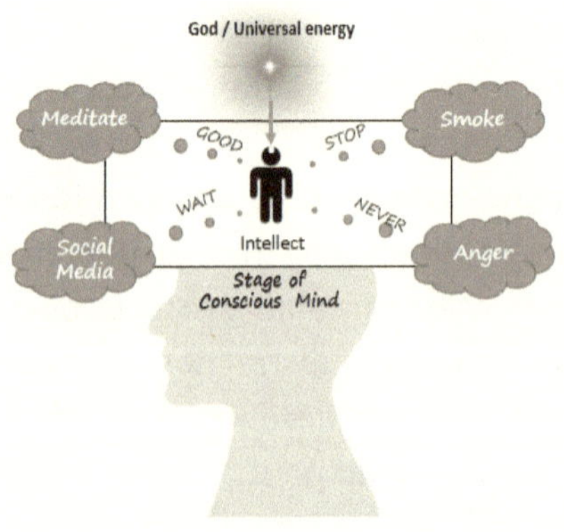


"Have a look at this image and attempt to study it thoroughly.

Our conscious mind is like a drama stage. This is where all of the action takes place. This drama is directed by our intellect, which is fueled by God or universal energy. Whatever thoughts enter our conscious mind are first examined by our intellect."

"On what basis would intellect make a decision?" Parth inquired.

"The intellect's decisions are influenced by past conditioning from its surroundings. For instance, growing up in an environment that values anger as a powerful trait may lead to using anger to complete tasks quickly. Connecting intellect to God through knowledge, prayer, and meditation leads to decisions in line with cosmic laws.

"The conscious mind is the rational and reasoning part of our mind that collects information through our five senses. It gains knowledge through observation, experience, and education. It acts as the initial filter for any information entering our mind, as our intellect decides what to accept and what to reject."

Murli continues to speak, "Moving on to the subconscious mind, there have been numerous studies in the past to gain a deeper understanding of it. While we could delve into this topic for an extended period, time constraints prohibit us from doing so. However, it's essential to note that the subconscious mind is the most crucial part of our mind, but it's challenging to access. This is where all the magic occurs."

"That is interesting." Karan was really intrigued.

"The subconscious mind cannot reason like the conscious mind; it simply accepts whatever the conscious mind tells it. Hence, the conscious mind is the first line of defense in protecting the subconscious mind from bad thoughts.

"The subconscious mind does not perceive information through the five senses but rather through intuition, commonly known as the sixth sense. Have you ever heard of telepathy? It is a technique in which the subconscious mind is used to communicate with other human minds. Doesn't this happen to us as well? When we have a strong urge to talk to anyone, that person calls us. It's all play of the subconscious mind.

"However, the subconscious mind is a two-edged sword: think good, and good will come. Think negatively, and evil will follow. Because our habitual thinking has carved deep grooves in our subconscious mind, we must be exceedingly cautious about what we think."

Murli paused for a few moments and then asked, "Do you see any patterns in your lives?"

After thinking for a while, Parth replied, "Girls always use and cheat me!" He felt embarrassed by this.

"This is because the first time someone cheated on you, your conscious mind communicated to your subconscious mind that girls cheat on and exploit you. Your subconscious mind, like an obedient servant, now makes it a reality anytime you are in a relationship."

"Do you have any patterns, Karan?" Parth inquired, seeking to elicit some information from him to which Karan chose not to speak.

"When you get home, think about the patterns in your life." Murli continued, "Do a root-cause analysis in the same way we do in the project. It will be simple to re-program your subconscious mind once you have identified the situations and thoughts that caused those patterns." Murli advised.

"How to get rid of these patterns or beliefs, Murli?" asked Parth.

"Changing our way of life can be difficult as we have formed habits and beliefs that influence our emotions as they are on autopilot. If water flows for years on a rock, it will carve a groove in the rock, and the water will constantly flow through that groove only. The same thing happened to us. We have created a certain mindset as a result of our past behaviors based on our beliefs and habits. As a result, we accept all unpleasant feelings such as rage, tension, and so on as natural.

"If we want water to flow in different directions on the rock, we must create a new mindset to change our thinking and accept new beliefs."

"But how?" Parth inquired impatiently.

"Tell me one thing. You have dirty water in your glass. How will you fill it with clean water, when you are not allowed to throw away dirty water?"

Karan and Parth continued to ponder.

Karan responded, "Continuously pour clean water into the glass until the dirty water is replaced by pure water."

"Outstanding, Karan!! The same holds true for our minds. We can't get everything out of our minds at once, so we have to constantly fill it with positive information that, with practice, will eventually develop beneficial habits for us.

"The mind is like a dustbin, which is a necessity in any house but that needs to be regularly emptied to avoid unpleasant smells. We put a lot of information into it daily, so we must be mindful of what we put in our mind and must remove negative thoughts regularly." Murli took a brief pause.

He then continued, "Andrew Carnegie hired journalist and writer Napoleon Hill to study and interview successful people to understand the secrets to their success. Hill had access to 500 influential figures, including Edison, Ford, and Rockefeller, and spent over 20 years analyzing their habits and success strategies. He discovered that these individuals relied more on their subconscious mind than their intellect to achieve their success."

The boys were astonished to hear that.

"Enough with the subconscious! I could talk about it all day.

You may recall that we discussed *Kamdhenu* in a previous story; this subconscious mind is that *Kamdhenu.* It will give you everything you ask for; we just have to ask in the proper way, which I will explain when we get to the techniques inspired by many researches done over the past few decades."

Murli started to explain about the last aspect of the mind, "The unconscious mind is like a mansion with many rooms, each containing sensations, memories, beliefs, and biological instincts that exist outside our conscious awareness. It enables us to do things on autopilot, such as breathing and digesting, and influences our actions in specific situations. We are more aware of our conscious mind, but the unconscious mind is responsible for primitive actions like sexual desires and aggressive tendencies that may result in inappropriate behavior known as unconscious conduct."

After a brief pause, Murli acknowledged, "I understand that this information can be overwhelming. The mind is a complex topic that is challenging to comprehend fully. When it takes years of study to learn about the 32 teeth in dentistry, understanding the mind is a monumental task that may take an indefinite amount of time."

Parth and Karan were listening intently, a little in awe and a little in disbelief.

Murli decided to move to the next topic, "Parth, what was your New Year resolution?"

"I don't make resolutions because I know I can't keep them for more than a few weeks," Parth replied with wit.

"Fair enough!" Murli said with a smile. "How about you, Karan?"

"I wanted to be more physically fit. I am not overweight, but I wanted to have a muscular body," Karan replied.

"Good, and are you still working on your resolution?"

"As Parth said, I could also follow for just 3 weeks," Karan said with embarrassment.

"Do you guys know the reason why most of us can't keep up with initial motivation with which we get started" Murli asked.

"Partly because we don't see results, which makes us lose motivation," replied Karan.

"Also, in the mid-way we realize this is not as important as we thought initially," added Parth.

"Those are interesting insights, but at a behavioral level. If we really need to understand the reason, we must first understand how the mind works when you make a goal," Murli explained as the boys were listening carefully.

He went on to say, "Ruchi and I have created something that I'd like to share with you. We've accumulated knowledge from various sources over the years and have put it into practice. After more than a decade of trial and error, we've developed a chart that may help you understand how the mind works. This is again purely our theory, there may be other theories around."

Murli displayed the following slide from his presentation.

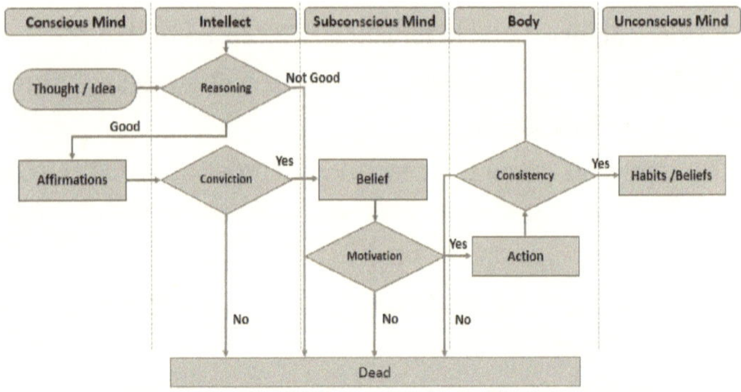


"We lose motivation when we fail to maintain high levels of motivation to achieve consistency. The process begins when an idea to become physically fit arises in our conscious mind after being influenced by different stimuli. The intellect determines whether the thought is good or bad and creates plans and affirmations to act on it. If the conviction to carry out the plan is detected, it's passed to the subconscious mind, which checks for strong motivation. If it finds higher motivation, it results in consistent exercise, which becomes a habit and is registered in the unconscious mind's chambers. However, inconsistency leads to the same resolution the following year. We frequently lose motivation by relying on external factors and expecting outcomes, making excuses like not dropping weight or not looking different, which violates the *Expectation* principle."

"Yes, continue performing your work or karma without expecting anything in return," Parth said.

"The basic flaw when we make a goal is that we relate it to some outcome with very high expectations." Murli added,

"But Murli, isn't that the right thing to do? How can we achieve our goal if we don't associate it with results?" resisted Karan.

"But that's the fundamental problem, Karan. That is the reason so many of us leave the goals midway once we don't get the expected results. Please remember: *When you are making a goal, take as much time you want to decide on your goal but once you start, do not return from mid-way, doesn't matter how hard things get.*"

"But how to keep up the high level of motivation to achieve consistency?" asked Parth.

"We need to be very careful how we define goals. Rather than associating it with outcomes, associate it with building your character. Nothing can stop you from accomplishing greater heights if you link your goals with building character rather than outcomes."

"What do you mean by linking your goals with building character?" Parth inquired.

"Instead of setting a specific outcome-based goal such as 'I will lose 10 kg', it's better to describe your goal in terms of consistent behavior, such as 'I am a person who works out for 30 minutes every day.' This helps to focus on the process of working towards your goal rather than the outcome and reduces the pressure of expecting results immediately. By consistently working out for 30 minutes every day without expectations, you will eventually become fit. The key is to focus on the behavior and consistently stick to it."

Parth and Karan were paying close attention.

"Make goals like, 'I am somebody who meditates every day,' 'I am a working professional who spends 5 hours every week learning something new in my technology,' etc." Murli took a pause, and then said, "I hope you now have a fundamental knowledge of how the mind works, guys."

"I definitely know more about the mind than I did an hour

ago! Thank you so much, Murli," Parth exclaimed.

"Right, this information was like a breath of fresh air," Karan added.

"My purpose here is not to turn you into a mind specialist but rather to show you how we may use our minds to our benefit. I am glad that you found this information useful. Let's take a break for the day and reconvene tomorrow at the same time. But before we conclude for the day, let me tell you THE most important fact about the mind.

**"Sow a thought, reap an action; sow an action, reap a habit; sow a habit, reap a character; sow a character, reap a destiny.**

"Think about what this means. I will leave this to your interpretation based on the knowledge I have imparted so far."

Karan and Parth were overwhelmed. They both believed they had learned something wonderful and were eager for the next day to study more about the mind.

As they exited Murli's cabin, Karan glanced toward Nidhi. She looked enraged. She simply ignored Karan and continued working at her desk.

"Can we quickly catch up in the cafeteria, please?" Karan texted her.

Nidhi stormed off to the cafeteria, her frustration clearly visible on her face. Karan followed her, his heart racing as he braced himself for her outburst. Nidhi didn't waste a moment and confronted him, her voice dripping with anger and disappointment. Karan's stomach dropped as he realized that he had broken his promise to her. He scrambled to come up with an excuse, his mind racing as he tried to think of something convincing to say.

"I'm sorry, Nidhi," Karan said, his voice shaking slightly. "I didn't mean to attend the session, but Murli asked me to join, and I didn't want to offend him."

Nidhi's eyes narrowed, and for a moment, Karan thought she was going to explode. But then, to his surprise, she seemed to calm down. "How many more days of this ridiculous session do we have to endure?" she asked, her tone still sharp but less angry than before.

"Just two more days," Karan replied, relieved that Nidhi wasn't yelling at him anymore. "I promise I will focus on work once it's over."

Nidhi sighed and said, her voice tired, "Okay, fine!".

"Just get me a cold coffee, will you? I need something to cool me down," she eventually said with a smile.

# 18

# DECODING PIECES OF THE PUZZLE

Nidhi arrived at the office early on Thursday morning since she had several high-priority tickets to resolve. She was accompanied by one of her team's junior developers.

Parth had overheard Nidhi telling her colleagues that she would be arriving early the next day, so he decided to arrive early as well. Even though he was exhausted from working late into the evening the previous day, he didn't want to miss out on the chance to be with Nidhi.

After settling in for a few moments, he approached Nidhi's desk and pretended to be surprised, "How come you arrived so early today?"

"Yeah! I had some urgent tasks to attend to. Nearly finished!" Nidhi responded while still working on her laptop.

"You seem so tired; let's head downstairs for breakfast." Parth offered cautiously.

"Yeah, I am truly hungry. Please give me 15 minutes and allow me to complete the task at hand." said Nidhi.

"Sure!" Parth was ecstatic. He continued thinking to

himself as he sat at his desk, 'I waste so much energy thinking about Nidhi and Karan. Today I'm going to tell her how much I like her. As Murli has taught us, while I will convey my honest feeling, I will not expect her to like me. But can I control my emotions? I'll be broken if she says no.'

"Let's go!" Nidhi's voice jolted Parth back to the present.

Parth was still perplexed while they ate their breakfast. He ultimately started the conversation hesitantly, "I have something to tell you, Nidhi!"

"What's up!" Nidhi responded while munching on her *medu vada*.

"Promise me you're not going to be angry!" Parth requested hesitantly.

"Why would I be angry?" Nidhi responded in a nonchalant manner.

"Nidhi, hmm... we've been working together for nine months now. I can't take my eyes off you; you are so charming and gorgeous. Nidhi, I genuinely like you." Parth finally threw caution to the wind while confiding to Nidhi.

Nidhi was shell-shocked, and with the *medu vada* still in her mouth, she nearly choked and coughed. Parth poured some water for her. This was something she anticipated from Karan, but not from Parth.

"Are you all right?" Parth inquired, feeling guilty.

"I apologize, Parth; I simply did not see that coming." Nidhi tried to get hold of her cough. Gaining her composure, she said, "Parth, you are a wonderful guy. I also like you as a friend, but I never thought about you from that perspective. Can you please give me some time to think about it?" Nidhi was trying to buy some time because she didn't want to make a decision until she knew who would win the competition and keep the job.

"Yes, sure, Nidhi! I will be waiting for your reply," Parth replied with hope in his eyes.

They didn't say anything to each other all through breakfast. Parth tried to look on the bright side of this development, 'She didn't say *no*, so it implies she is not in any relationship with Karan, and who knows, she will say yes to me'. As they walked back to the office, he felt so much better.

It was late in the evening, and both Parth and Karan were looking forward to the next session.

Murli began the session the moment Parth and Karan entered his cabin. "This will be an intriguing day, boys."

"Yeah, today we will finally learn the techniques to instill all of the knowledge you have taught us in our lives," Parth couldn't contain his excitement.

"That's correct! But it's a puzzle game, not just a technique." Murli attempted to build a mystery.

"Game? What game?" Karan inquired, surprised.

"It's a great game, but you must follow the rules. When played by the rules, nothing can stop you from living an extraordinary life, not even God!" Murli said confidently.

"Wow, Murli, could you kindly explain? I can hardly wait to get started!" Parth uttered it with the zeal of a child.

"All right, let's get started!" Murli began discussing the figure below as he began his presentation.

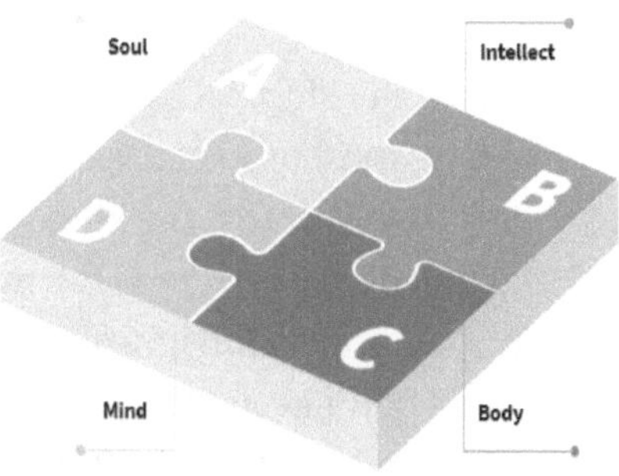


"The puzzle game has four fundamental pieces: *soul, intellect, body, and mind.* Let's see how they fit into this game. But before that tell me, do you both play chess?" Murli asked.

Parth and Karan both nodded in agreement.

"Assuming the chessboard as a stage for life's drama, let's start with the first piece - the soul. It's like the king of chess, which can't protect itself and needs its army." Murli started the explanation.

"Indeed, the King is the weakest piece in chess. Pawns have more power than him!" Karan interrupted.

"You may say that Karan, but can the game go on without the King?" Murli inquired, "After the king is eliminated from the chessboard, the game is over. Similarly, if the soul gets removed from the drama, your life will end! So, as we would take care of the king in chess, we must take care of our soul."

Parth was paying close attention.

"Now tell me which piece in the chess game is the most powerful."

"Queen!" Karan and Parth both responded at the same time.

"Our mind is as powerful as the Queen, as it defends the soul from negative thoughts like worry, anxiety, and rage. Tell me, what will happen if our queen secretly works for the opposing army?"

"That's game over for the king," Karan answered.

"Right! That's why we must protect the soul by making the mind work for it, just as we protect the king with the queen in chess" Murli explained. "In our lives, the mind teams up with negative beliefs and slowly kills the powers of our soul on a daily basis, and we don't even realize it until something hits us so hard that our soul can't handle it. Like in your case, would you have come to the Bhagavad Gita sessions if this catastrophe had not hit you?"

"Never!" said Parth.

"Right! In this game, we train our minds to serve our king and protect our soul from any storm. Our body and intellect are like pawns, capable of aiding or hindering our progress. With proper handling, they can assist our queen and benefit our soul. Without the help of the mind, they won't be useful. But if misused, they'll obstruct the mind's power. Do you understand?" Murli checked if Parth and Karan comprehended.

"Yeah, Murli, it was an interesting analogy," Karan responded.

"Credit goes to Ruchi for this entertaining idea. I could never match it," Murli chuckled, and Parth and Karan joined in.

"Like chess, this game has rules. If you manipulate or unknowingly break them, you'll lose without understanding why." Murli continued.

Parth and Karan listened with serious expressions.

"Much like chess, this puzzle game takes patience," Murli emphasized.

"But Murli, life has become so fast, it's like an F1 race, always in top gear. How can we take time out to train our mind?"

Karan asked, interrupting Murli, an avid F1 racing enthusiast.

"That's correct, but Karan, in F1 races, pit stops are used to check the state of the car and perform rapid maintenance, isn't it?" Murli inquired.

"Absolutely, they must; otherwise, they may not be able to finish the race, let alone win," Karan remarked.

A smile appeared on Murli's face, which perplexed Karan.

"I apologize, Karan," Murli said with a smile.  "I was chuckling at how astute humans can be. We excel at taking care of external matters, but we struggle to take care of ourselves."

"What do you mean?" Karan inquired, still perplexed.

"You were right about caring for the car, but what about the four vital elements I mentioned earlier? Do we pause to reflect on our lives before taking the next step? No, we keep using them without stopping and eventually complain when we are faced with challenges," Murli pointed out.

Karan and Parth were listening as they gained clarity.

"What is the basic rule in chess even before we start play-ing?" Murli inquired.

"We have to place the pieces exactly in the space allocated to them," Karan responded.

"Absolutely! Just like we correctly position the chess pieces before a new game, we need to align our scattered mind, brain, and body before playing this puzzle game of life," Murli explained.

"And what is the proper position for them?" Parth inquired.

"You just have to slow them down before you start the game, and that is the main rule of this game," Murli added.

"How can we slow them down?" Parth wondered.

"Allow me to go into the nuances of each piece to explain specific rules for that piece, where you will also learn how to slow things down." Murli continued, while Karan and Parth were paying close attention. "Let's start with the most important piece, the soul."

"The only rule for the soul is to recognize that it's the energy using your body and mind and to safeguard it at all costs. Do not compromise its integrity by indulging in unethical activities to gratify the five senses," Murli warned.

"But Murli, how do we do that? We can't see the soul! We don't even know where it is in our body! What measures can we take?" Karan asked.

"The soul is like energy, which is not visible but can be experienced. It's similar to electricity. You don't see it, but you experience it. The location of the soul doesn't matter because it's energy. However, I feel it's a small point of light in the center of my forehead," Murli explained.

"All right," Parth said, nodding.

"Moving on to the second element, the body; it's crucial to be physically ready for this game, like any other sport. However, instead of warming up, you must relax your body. When working on the puzzle, sit in a comfortable position, be it on a bed, in a chair, or on the ground. Ensure to maintain a straight spine as it represents the axis of our body, running parallel to universal power and allowing life force energy to flow freely throughout the body," Murli explained.

"I'm not used to sitting upright; if I sit upright without any support, my back hurts," Parth expressed concern.

"That's the issue for most of us; no one ever taught us the value of sitting up straight. As a workaround, you can utilize back support and, if that is too tough, sit in any position that is comfortable for you."

"Would that impact the result of this game?" Parth wondered.

"While the ultimate goal is to sit with an erect spine, for now, your comfort is crucial to playing this game. Don't worry; you still have a chance to win," Murli reassured Parth.

"Going on to the third piece, intellect," Murli continued. "Intellect is like a scissor; it dissects everything to make logical sense of it, and if not handled properly, it may be the biggest villain in the game and entirely wreck everything."

"How?" Parth inquired.

"Can you weave anything with scissors?" Murli inquired.

"Of course not!" said Parth quickly.

"Disregard logic when playing this game and focus on the experiences you will gain. We're trying to create a beautiful playground for you where your life can flourish in every way, and if you use scissors instead of needles, the playground will be shattered into hundreds of pieces.

"Let us now proceed to the final piece, our queen, the mind. Because it is the most crucial aspect of the game, and we spent a significant amount of time analyzing it yesterday. Now let's talk about how to slow this piece down so we can solve the puzzle." Murli approached the whiteboard and scribbled the text below.

"Let's begin by discussing ways to relax the mind. This is the most difficult aspect. As previously stated, our mind is like a car racing in an F1 race, and we have never trained it to take a pit stop, thus it is extremely difficult to relax the mind." Murli paused briefly before continuing. "If you look at this diagram, you can slow down your mind in two ways: first, intake as little information as possible, and second, learn to relax your mind."

"What exactly do you mean by consuming less information?" Parth inquired.

"Information overload is prevalent nowadays. It leads to unstable thoughts. Consuming negative information harms our soul. I avoid 24-hour news channels and limit my time on social media to once or twice daily. It is better to spend 30 minutes each morning reading good books or watching instructional videos that evoke positive emotions."

Parth and Karan were paying close attention.

"Can you imagine how many thoughts we have in a day?"

"1000, 5000?" Karan made a wild guess.

"According to Stanford University research, a human has approximately 50 to 60 thousand thoughts every day!"

"Oh, my goodness, why do we produce so many thoughts?" Parth responded surprisingly.

"You will find the answer if you evaluate what kind of thoughts you have," Murli said.

"What do you mean?" Parth inquired.

Murli opened his PowerPoint and started explaining,

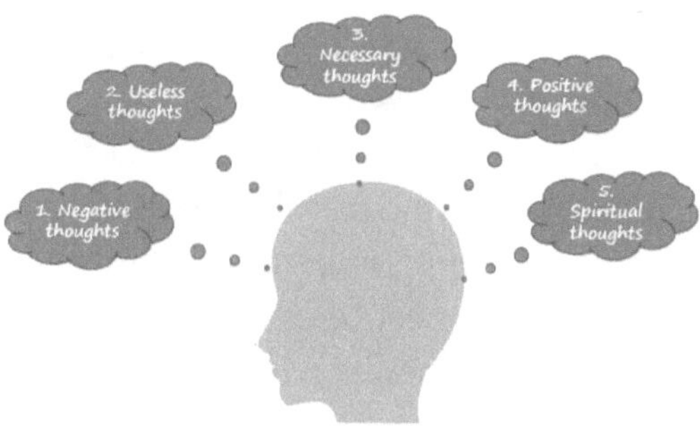


"On a broad level, we create five types of thoughts:

"*Negative thoughts* are the most dangerous type of thoughts to have because they not only hurt others but also the one who has them. They dissipate our soul's power considerably. Imagine it like a mobile app that launches automatically and consumes a lot of battery power. What do we do with these apps?"

"We forcefully stop them," answered Karan.

"Yeah, but first we investigate why our phone's battery is draining so quickly, then we investigate the cause, and once we locate this app, we forcefully terminate it. We must do the same with these negative thoughts. When we notice we are thinking negatively about anything, we must forcefully stop it."

Murli then started explaining about *useless thoughts*, "To put it simply, useless thoughts are the ones that revolve around things we cannot change or control and are often cyclical and repetitive. Studies show that up to 90% of our thoughts fall into this category, draining our mental energy without solving any problems. It's important to recognize the insidious nature of useless thoughts and their impact on our well-being."

"Oh God!" Parth was taken aback by this information.

"After useless thoughts, we have *necessary thoughts* that help us organize our daily lives, such as scheduling appointments and following daily routines.

"Then, we have *positive thoughts* that focus on finding solutions to problems, which can have a beneficial impact.

"And finally, the most important category is *spiritual thoughts*, which include concepts such as peace, love, and empathy. Cultivating these kinds of thoughts can have a profound impact on our well-being and relationships with others."

"Wow, this is a revelation; we had no idea we have so many distinct forms of thoughts," Karan exclaimed, taken aback.

"Even I was startled when I initially learned about it. Let's look at how the mind operates. As we ingest more knowledge, our minds begin to generate more and more thoughts." Murli went ahead.

"That is why we should consume the least amount of information possible." Parth added his view.

"Correct! Now consider the second aspect of mind slowing: brain relaxation. First, we need to understand how the brain operates in terms of energy flow. Do you know what the various brainwave frequencies produced by our brain are?"

"I have no idea!" Karan responded.

Murli displayed the image below from his PowerPoint presentation.

| Delta | Theta | Alpha | Beta | Gamma |
| --- | --- | --- | --- | --- |
| 0.2 – 3 Hz | 3 – 8 Hz | 8 – 12 Hz | 12 – 27 Hz | 27 Hz + |
| Asleep | Deeply Relax | Relaxed | Alert, Focused | High Performance |

"The brain communicates with our body and mind via electronic impulses called brain waves, which can be classified as fast, medium, or slow and correspond to different thought patterns. When functioning properly, the brain exhibits predictable patterns of distinct brain waves, each using specific chemicals to switch between mental states. These waves are classified as Delta, Theta, Beta, Gamma, and Alpha. These waves are experienced by people throughout the day and can change depending on the task at hand.

"Delta waves occur during meditation and dreamless sleep, while Theta waves are associated with dreamy, detached thoughts and occur during automatic tasks and deep meditation. At the other end are Gamma waves that are produced during high-level information processing, while Beta waves signify intense, focused brain activity during problem-solving or engagement with surroundings.

"Let's talk about the Alpha waves now. Alpha waves are slower and larger in amplitude, signifying a relaxed, tranquil state during contemplative or attentive activities. These are the ones we need to win our game and we need to operate at this frequency."

"Is there any reason why we need to reach the alpha wave frequency?" Karan inquired.

"Yes! Research has shown that with the first layer of our subconscious mind being dominated by Alpha waves, they play a unique role in bridging the conscious and subconscious minds. This state has been associated with peak performance, and elite athletes have been found to create Alpha waves prior to highly concentrated performances, such as shooting, a free throw or making a crucial golf shot."

It had been more than an hour, and Murli could tell Parth and Karan were exhausted, so he decided to call it a day.

"Let's wrap it up, boys. I realized the information was deep, so go have some tea before you return to work."

At the cafeteria, Nidhi was drinking tea with her friend Daksha. As she was out with Parth in the morning, she revealed the turn of events to Daksha.

"Finally, he found the confidence to open up," Daksha said, laughing.

"Yeah, but this was not what I expected from him. He's a great guy, but I have to be sensible; I can't let my emotions get the best of me," Nidhi stated.

"Nidhi, one friendly advice! Why don't you ask your heart what it desires? Allow your heart to make the decision instead of your brain." Daksha attempted to restore Nidhi's sanity.

"Daksha, I don't want to end up like my parents. They fell in love and married without considering the practical difficulties. And now they quarrel every day over little matters. That irritates me just to be around them. I don't want my relationship to end up like theirs. Let's face it: marriage is all about giving and taking, so it's better to be realistic than an emotional fool." Nidhi resisted.

Daksha remained silent while they finished their tea and returned to their desks.

After the session, Parth and Karan spent very little time in the cafeteria taking tea together.

Parth had a fantastic day. Not only was he learning so much from Murli, but he had finally been able to open up to Nidhi about his feelings after months of silence. His ability to encourage his team was the icing on the cake, and they were suddenly catching up. Quality of their work was getting better, and everyone was aware of their responsibilities.

Karan, on the other hand, has been worried since the previous status meeting after discovering that Parth's team has rectified all quality issues. He was now worried that they would zoom past his team. He decided to consult with some of the more capable developers and divide the key duties among them. He could reach the deadline only if he used his team to perfection. Karan was smart; he was now aware of his team members' skills and weaknesses. He only needed to develop strategies for task distribution.

## 19

# PREPARE TO PUT THE PUZZLE TOGETHER

As Friday morning arrived, the team felt a mixture of relief and exhaustion. They had worked diligently to meet their deadlines, and the past two weeks had felt like an endless marathon. But underlying their weariness was a sense of accomplishment and satisfaction in a job well done.

As Parth and Karan entered Murli's cabin for the final session of his discourse, they felt a surge of excitement and anticipation. They were eager to master the skills they had learned and put their new knowledge to use. They felt a sense of pride in how much they had accomplished in just a few days.

"Hello guys, are you ready to play the game?" Murli inquired, trying to energize Parth and Karan's faces.

"Yeah, Murli, we'll finally learn the secret!" Parth smiled in response.

"Wow, let's ring the bell!" Murli said, his voice full of passion.

"Yes, absolutely!" Parth and Karan both responded with equal enthusiasm.

"The game is called '*Solving the Puzzle Meditation*'. In this game, you must employ the four key pieces of the game we learned yesterday to solve the puzzle of extraordinary life through mediation."

"Can you tell me more about meditation, Murli?" Parth inquired.

"Let me ask you, have you ever done any meditation practice?" asked Murli.

Parth and Karan exchanged glances and replied together, "No."

"Do you understand what mediation is?" Murli posed another question.

"Does it have anything to do with breathing?" Karan inquired.

"Actually, concentrating on your breath is just one approach to meditation. To define it concisely, *meditation involves flooding your mind with spiritual and positive thoughts to create feelings of peace, happiness, and abundance.* It's a deliberate practice of guiding these thoughts to your subconscious mind." Murli explained.

"Do you mean to say that meditation is simply focusing on positive thoughts and then concentrating on them for an extended period of time?" Parth questioned.

"Yeah, that's right! We will use meditation as a tool to put the four pieces together in such a way that it will propel our life towards the ultimate goal of happiness. Let me explain this in more detail." Murli eventually revealed the method he intended to use to educate Parth and Karan. He flipped open his PowerPoint presentation and displayed the image below.

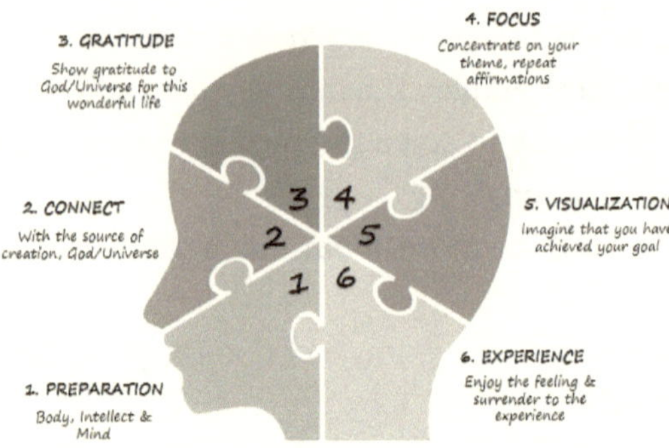


"As you can see in this slide, these are the 6 steps to this game. These steps are like a ladder to extraordinary life. Let's start with the first step of preparing for this amazing game."

### 1. Preparation

Parth and Karan were paying close attention.

Murli went to the whiteboard and sketched the flow diagram shown below.

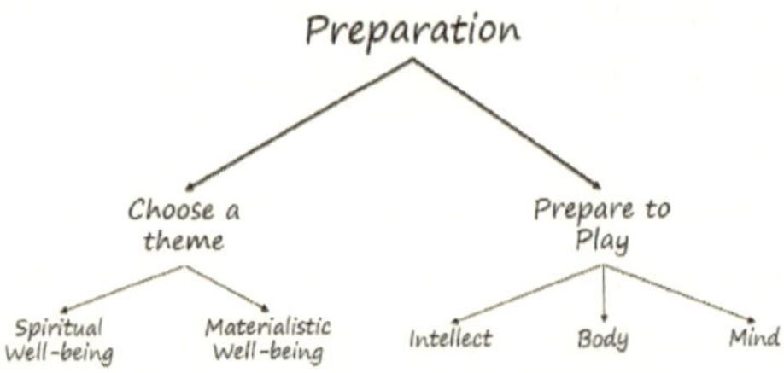


"Like any other sport, it is critical to prepare thoroughly for this game too. Preparing for this game occurs on two levels. Let's talk about them one at a time," Murli was explaining as he scribbled on the whiteboard.

### 1.1 Choose a theme

"Choose two themes for your game: one for your spiritual

well-being and the other for your material well-being. Make sure they're meaningful to you. Focus on your spiritual well-being first, as you're new to the puzzle meditation technique. Later, you can add a materialistic perspective. I'll discuss both the themes for your knowledge."

"That makes sense, Murli. But what do you mean by carefully selecting themes?" Karan inquired.

"For example, your New Year's resolution was to get a muscular body, but this was not what you truly desired. Maybe you saw some models with fantastic muscles, or some girl mentioned to you how much she likes six packs; you felt inspired to get in terrific shape for a moment, didn't you?" Murli inquired, a simper on his face, to which, Karan reddened and remained silent.

Murli explained, "If someone relies on shouting on other people to get things done and chooses the theme of being at peace just because they heard peace is good, it won't work because their subconscious still believes shouting is effective."

"I see. How can I choose a theme then?" Parth inquired.

Murli began creating the flow diagram below while still standing near the whiteboard.

Murli continued with his explanation, "This flow is how the puzzle should be solved. This is the most important hint for playing the game. You are guaranteed to win if you stick to this flow!"

"Could you kindly explain this in detail, Murli?" Parth

requested.

"As a first step, to succeed in your chosen theme, you need to feel a deep connection and possess a strong *desire*. Without a strong desire, your chances of success will be slim."

"Could you perhaps clarify on desire, it wishful thinking or goal setting?" Parth asked again.

"Desire encompasses more than just wishful thinking, and goal setting is just one facet of it. A desire with a clear purpose act as a roadmap to happiness, with goals serving as defined stages towards that end. For example, if Karan's New Year's resolution is to be in his best physical shape, his goals could include weight loss, weight gain, or muscle development." Murli explained.

"Got it!" said Parth.

"If desire was the first step, then *belief* is the second. Let's imagine you have a strong desire within you, but if you don't believe in your abilities, you'll never accomplish it. We all have a strong desire to be happy, but do we feel we can attain it?"

"Before, we believed that external conditions and other people had complete control over our happiness. However, after attending your sessions and learning the techniques you're explaining, I now believe that we can take control of our own happiness." Parth explained.

"It's great to hear, Parth. Although many of us have strong desire for joy, we think it may not be possible to be in a constant state of bliss. It's important to distinguish between wishing for something and being ready to receive it. *The universe won't grant our desires until we truly believe we're capable of receiving them.*" Murli tried to emphasize the importance of belief.

"And as you have informed earlier, for beliefs to be successful, we need to keep our minds open to new ideas, new possibilities," Karan replied.

"You're absolutely right, Karan! Now coming to the third element in selecting a theme, it is extremely important to have *faith* in God, the universe, and our own abilities. As the great Thomas Edison once said, *'The whole course of things goes to teach us faith. We need only obey. There is guidance for every one of us, and by our lowly listening, we shall hear the right words.'* When we combine faith with our thoughts, our subconscious mind quickly picks up on the vibration and transmits it to the universe." Murli returned to his seat.

"These three aspects that create a theme seem similar to fueling up the car to begin the F1 race." Karan grinned in response.

"Absolutely!" Murli responded and then decided to move on to the next task of creating affirmations. He said, "Once you've decided on a theme, you must create affirmations for that theme."

"What exactly are affirmations, and how do you create them?" Parth inquired.

"*Affirmations are positive statements that can program your subconscious mind by making suggestions to yourself.* When we combine affirmations with our thoughts, faith, feelings, and emotions, we attract similar thoughts that program our subconscious mind to manifest those realities." Murli revealed the secret of affirmations.

"Pretty interesting!" remarked Karan.

"Karan, how will you compose an affirmation for a new job?" Murli asked.

"I will not lose my current job, and even if I do, I will obtain a better one with a better role and compensation," Karan responded after some thought.

"Parth, how about you? How will you make one?"

"I think Karan's creation is really good," Parth said.

Murli returned to the whiteboard and drew the flow diagram below.

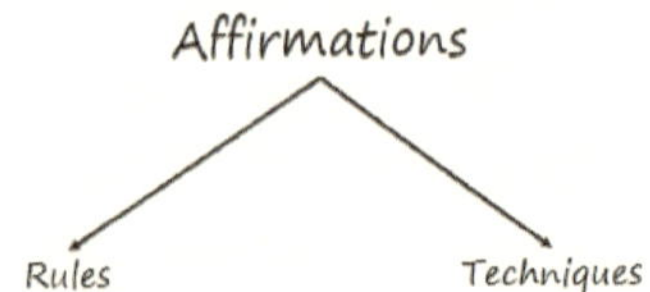


"We must exercise the utmost caution while constructing affirmations. Some rules and techniques must be followed at all times." He said and went on explaining, "Let's start with the rules:

1. Always have a short and simple affirmation.
2. It must be completely explicit and without ambiguity.
3. Be as precise as possible about your desires and timelines.
4. Affirmations should always be written in the present tense; the subconscious mind does not understand the past or future tenses.
5. Always write affirmations that are positive. Negative thoughts are not understood by the subconscious mind."

"I'd like to ask you a question about the present tense. Why must we write in the present tense? How can I write as though something happened when it didn't?" Inquired Parth

"I also have a question about why one just has to write positive affirmations," Karan remarked.

"Excellent questions, boys. As I already stated, the subconscious mind is incapable of reasoning. As a result, it follows the instructions exactly as they are. If you tell your subconscious, '*I will be happy once I get a new job*' or '*I will be fit after the next 6 months,*' you will not produce a feeling of happiness or fitness, therefore it will simply disregard this affirmation."

"Okay, so it's critical that those affirmations elicit appropriate feelings and emotions right now, so we must write affirmations in the present tense rather than the future tense, because future tense affirmations will not elicit those emotions right now, and thus will not reach the subconscious mind," Parth tried to make his understanding clear.

"That's right! What do you call someone who just keeps doing things without considering if they are beneficial or harmful for him?" Murli inquired.

"He must be such a fool," Parth answered.

"Parth, the subconscious mind is that fool. Now we must capitalize on this folly by generating a thought and its associated feeling in the present moment. It makes no difference how stressed you are; you must affirm, '*I am joyful and blessed right now.*' And your subconscious mind will work for you to make you happy."

"It will be very difficult to develop a sense of happiness when we are in the midst of tough situations!" objected Parth.

"True, but it's not impossible. When we are stressed, our thoughts can become negative and self-critical which can further escalate our stress level. Affirmations act as an antidote to these negative thoughts and promote a positive mindset." Murli tried to explain, but he could still see some concern on Parth's face. "I'll give you some tips later, Parth; don't worry. In response to the other issue raised by Karan about writing only positive affirmations, the subconscious just cannot understand negative words.

"Affirmation should be phrased in a way that focuses on what you want to achieve or experience, rather than what you don't want."

"Oh! But how is it possible?" Karan wondered, as both, he and Parth were taken aback.

"I know that sounds ridiculous, but that's how it works. You need to understand that the subconscious mind does not understand language as we do, but it can interpret the emotions behind our thoughts and actions." Murli decided to explain this with an example, so he asked the boys, "Has it ever happened to you when you are at the peak of your emotions, and you want something to happen but exactly the opposite happens?" Murli paused for a moment and then requested, "Think about it!"

After some thought, Karan said, "Yeah, it has occurred several times!"

"And what kind of thoughts did you have at the time?" Murli inquired.

"For instance, the last time I was late for the railway station. I was so worried and kept telling myself, *'I will not miss the train,'* but I did," Karan answered disappointingly.

"There you are!  In this case, your subconscious mind just interpreted your fear behind your thought and actually manifested it by making you miss the train," Murli attempted to explain.

"Huh!" Karan was taken aback.

"Parth, pardon me for using an example from your life. You told us earlier that, girls kept cheating on you, so anytime you get into a relationship, you must be thinking, I hope this one doesn't cheat on me."

"It will be the first notion that springs to mind." Parth agreed.

"You are actually programming your subconscious mind with anxiety and fear of being cheated, thus unknowingly attracting the same situations again and again."

"Can the subconscious mind achieve that?" Parth wondered.

"As I've said before, the subconscious mind is like *Kandhenu*. It can make anything happen as long as we program it with the right thoughts and feelings. We program our subconscious mind every day, but unintentionally, we often program it with negative patterns. That's why I asked about the patterns in your life earlier."

Murli tried to explain further because Parth and Karan were still perplexed. "It's the same in our projects. Programming allows you to create applications that help humanity, while some hackers use the same skills to construct something detrimental. It is in the nature of the mind to continue programming itself. We now have a choice: we may let it program unconsciously based on information we receive from the outside world, or we can make conscious attempts to program it in a way that best serves our needs."

Parth and Karan nodded in agreement.

Murli went on to say, "Let us now go over the techniques again:

1. Always begin your affirmation with gratitude, as if you've already accomplished your goal. We already know that gratitude is a powerful multiplier. That will help you achieve your goal much faster.
2. Be realistic with your desire. You cannot write that you have become CEO of an MNC in an affirmation for a new

job. Your conscious mind will reject this and prevent it from reaching your subconscious mind.

3. While uttering the affirmation, add feelings to create appropriate emotions.

4. Affirmations should be written and uttered first thing in the morning and right before retiring to bed.

5. Opportunities are created by affirmations, but you must still work. Things will not fall from the sky; you must recognize the opportunities produced by your subconscious mind and use them as steppingstones to reach your goals."

Murli was interrupted by Parth, "Murli, I have one issue! Is it necessary to elicit emotions? It will be incredibly difficult to instill feelings and emotions with regards to something that is not even genuine."

"Unfortunately, there is no way out, Parth. Because they are intended to put you in a high-energy state, these affirmations can never be effective without feelings and emotions. And as per a simple rule of physics, the higher the energy, the more quickly it reaches its destination; in our case, to the universal energy." Murli responded.

Parth was disappointed.

"But there is a workaround. If your conscious mind is resistant to the affirmation, you may fool it as well," Murli responded.

"How?" Parth inquired.

"Create your affirmations in the form of questions. For example, you can affirm something like, '*Why am I always so happy? Thank you, God, for bringing such joy into my life!*' or '*How did I acquire such a great job? It's a dream come true!*

*Lots of gratitude'.* If it is a question, your consciousness will be less resistant to the affirmation, making it easier for you to produce connected feelings."

"I can do that! Thank you very much, Murli," Parth exclaimed with glee.

"Can you kindly offer some examples of affirmations based on these rules and techniques?" Karan inquired.

"Yes, it will be fantastic!" agreed Parth.

"Alright, close your eyes for a moment, and listen to the affirmations I'm saying. Afterwards, you will let me know how you're feeling." Murli instructed them.

Parth and Karan closed their eyes, waiting for Murli's affirmations.

"*Thank you, God, for continually bringing me endless joy. I am so fortunate to be in a constant state of bliss. Thank you so much!*" Murli halted for a while to allow the boys to create their feelings.

He then recited another affirmation, "*Thank you, God, for providing me with my desired career, which allows me to thrive both professionally and financially. Lots of gratitude!*"

Murli asked, "How does this sound to you guys?" after a few more moments of silence.

"They are incredible; I felt so much better after listening to them," Parth added.

"Yeah, I forgot about all my problems for a few moments," Karan admitted.

"That is exactly my point! If you feel better after reciting the affirmation, it's the right one for your subconscious mind. These are only a few ideas of how to create affirmations that sound good to you, but you must follow the principles!" Murli warned them.

Karan and Murli were paying close attention.

"Look, gentlemen, there is no scientific device that can test how the subconscious mind operates; it all comes down to trying and experimenting. If you continue to think logically, you will, as I previously stated, eliminate the possibility of magic in your life." Murli provided words of caution.

"Murli, I have a question. You taught us not to expect anything from our actions, but now you're urging us to cultivate a strong desire to do anything. Isn't this process in conflict with the expectation principle?" Karan said.

"This is a great insight. As humans, we all have desires, and it's natural to want things. However, we must not let our lives and thoughts be overshadowed by our desires. When we use affirmations to manifest our desires, we mustn't become attached to them. Getting entangled in the web of desires can lead to melancholy, stress, and sorrow. Instead, we should give our desires to the universe, like releasing a balloon, and trust that the universe will do what's best for us."

Karan and Parth tried to comprehend Murli's advice.

**1.2 Prepare to play**

He went on to explain, "Let us now proceed to the second phase of preparation, which is to prepare your body, intellect, and mind for the game. In chapter 6 at verses 10 to 15, Lord Krishna discusses the importance of physical preparedness including steady posture and breath control. This is where the actual 'solving the puzzle meditation' techniques begin. We have already discussed the pieces of the game -ascertain that your intellect is not interfering with your affirmation, that your body is in a comfortable position, and that your brain is operating at alpha frequency."

"But Murli, you never explained to us how to achieve alpha

level frequency," Parth pointed out.

"Yes, now is the time. There are numerous ways to reach Alpha frequency. I use three levers to get there:

1. I relax my entire body from head to toe.
2. I begin counting backwards from 50 to 1 to relax my mind.
3. I begin to concentrate on my breathing and attempt to slow down as much as possible.

You will notice that when your breathing rate slows, so will the number of thoughts."

"That's fascinating! Could you please elaborate?" Parth was inquisitive.

"Sure! Relax your body by starting from your head. Focus on your scalp and you will notice a tingling sensation. Let go of any tension while affirming, '*My scalp is currently in a profound state of relaxation.*' Repeat for your face, neck, shoulders, arms, chest, stomach, thighs, legs, and feet."

"Wouldn't that take a long time?" Karan expressed his dissatisfaction.

"With practice, you can relax your entire body in 5–7 minutes, but I have a shortcut as well," Murli explained.

"What is it?" Karan inquired.

"After using the above method to relax your body, affirm '*My body is completely relaxed now*' and link this feeling to something tangible, something like using Gyan Mudra, touching your thumb to your index finger. Try it for 21 days. Your mind will associate this gesture with relaxation and eventually your body will relax automatically when you use Gyan Mudra, allowing you to experience a relaxed sensation."

"Wow, does that actually work?" Karan inquired, surprised.

"Try it out for yourself!" Murli said with a smile, before moving on to another technique for reaching the alpha phase. "Now let's focus on relaxing the mind. To use this method, imagine yourself in a peaceful location, such as a beach or a forest or anywhere you've been and imagine you're sitting there perfectly comfortably, enjoying the moment, and begin counting backwards from 50. Visualize the numbers in front of you to stay focused. By the time you reach 0, you should have reached the alpha phase. To make the process faster, after having practiced for 21 days, associate the location with relaxation, so that the next time you envision yourself there, you'll quickly reach the alpha phase. Remember to keep your breathing slow, as it helps with physical and mental relaxation."

"That's incredible," Parth exclaimed.

"Similar to any sport, it takes effort to master the basics the first time around. However, after that, it's a matter of fine-tuning your technique. While you'll need to put in some effort initially, with experience, you'll be able to relax within seconds." Murli explained further.

"That's cool," responded Karan.

"I'm hoping the first step is understood." Murli checked with the boys, who nodded in agreement.

Parth and Karan felt a renewed sense of motivation as they heard the divine words of wisdom from Murli. They were inspired by the idea that they had the power to control their minds and achieve a state of deep relaxation.

Murli allowed them time to brood over the inputs so that the learning may sink in.

## 20

# READY, SET, SOLVE: PUTTING THE PUZZLE TOGETHER

After a brief silence, Murli went on to scribble on the whiteboard.

**2. Connect**

He then continued with his explanation. "Now, let's move to the second step. Nikola Tesla, the great scientist, once said, *'Our brain is only a receiver, in the universe there is a core from which we obtain knowledge, strength, and inspirations....'* Our goal is to connect to that powerhouse, which you can call God or just a source of energy.

"You can use prayer if you believe in any god, else can just imagine a powerful source of light that is thousands of times more powerful than the sun. Imagine that God or that source of light is showering you with golden light, and that light is filling your aura, your body. You have now transcended your body; you are beyond the body, and your whole body has now become a pool of light.

"Feel the positive energy flowing through you; enjoy this feeling. You are now connected to the source of creation itself, and you, yourself have become the source of creation. You have become as powerful as the creator. Enjoy your power, feel your power, and feel blessed to be in touch with the creator." Murli's eyes got closed automatically, and his face was filled with joy as he was explaining this.

Parth and Karan were trying to follow the instructions.

Murli opened his eyes after a few seconds and asked, "Is this clear?"

"Yes, Murli, the process is clear, but how will it help?" asked Karan.

"We have already learned, as per Einstein's theory, that all matter is created by energy. We humans have limited energy, so we can create limited realities from our thoughts, but when we connect to the powerhouse of the universe, we get unlimited energy, which helps to manifest more and more realities." Murli explained.

"For how much time do we need to be in this phase?" asked Parth.

"There is no time limit as such. Once you get a feeling that you are connected to God, you can move on to the next phase. I personally stay in this state for 3-4 minutes" replied Murli.

### 3. Gratitude

"Moving onto the next step of gratitude, we have already talked at length about why to practice gratitude. While you are connected to God, thank him for everything he has given you from the bottom of your heart. Feel your heart with gratitude; spend 2-3 minutes with this feeling. Once you are done with these three steps, you are all set to consecrate your mind and fill it with blessings from the universe." Murli explained.

"So, you mean to say, we are ready to program our subconscious mind?" asked Karan.

"Yeah, you now have all the hardware and the software you need to start programming," Murli replied as the three of them burst out laughing.

## 4. Focus

He continued explaining the process, "The next step is very important, where you need to focus for 10-15 minutes on the theme you have selected. This is the trickiest part of the game."

Karan interrupted him, "As you said, this is the most difficult task; how to concentrate for 10-15 minutes? Mind will take us all over the world during that time!"

"That's right, Karan. We are told to concentrate but are not given any instructions on how to do it. However, concentration can be mastered with a simple practice. It involves focusing your attention on a specific thought. Imagine your mind as a dark space, with awareness being a soft light. To concentrate on a particular subject, such as thoughts of peace, simply focus your attention on that soft light and develop those thoughts. It's natural for your mind to wander back to old patterns, but don't give up. When you realize your mind has drifted, return to the thoughts of peace and continue practicing."

"That is interesting but will be challenging," Parth also raised his concern.

"Mastering concentration is like learning chess - it takes patience and practice. Don't expect to become an expert in a single day; it could take months or even years. The key is to continue practicing, even if your mind wanders from your focus. When you notice your mind has strayed, bring it back to your theme's thoughts. With practice, you will improve your concentration abilities. Even just two minutes of focused concentration on your theme, during a 10–15 minute session is a big accomplishment that will lead to fantastic outcomes."

"Oh, really?" Karan asked with surprise.

"Yes! The restless mind can be tamed by persistent efforts. Those who do not control the mind, it acts like an enemy for them. The mind is an obedient slave but a destructive master, so train it to take instructions from you and don't let it be your master."

Parth and Karan were listening with all their attention.

Murli came up with the fifth step.

## 5. Visualization

Putting it down on the whiteboard he explained, "To help you keep your focus and also create feelings, you can use the next step - Visualization. It acts like a propeller, which will help expedite results for you. There are many ways of visualizing; I prefer the mental movie technique."

"What is this technique all about?" asked Parth curiously.

"Think of it like creating a movie in your mind about your theme. Parth, you mentioned how to create feelings for something that hasn't happened yet. When we watch movies, we know it's all drama, yet we laugh and cry with the characters. Creating your own movie about your theme can help you stay focused and generate those emotions. You are the writer, director, and actor of this movie, so you can create any kind of movie you want that aligns with your goal."

"That will be interesting," excited Karan replied.

"Indeed! To increase the effectiveness of your meditation, immerse yourself in pleasurable experiences and let go of any resistance. This will erase any doubts and increase the potency of your practice. Have faith in your abilities and in

God. *Your faith can move even a mountain, but the doubt in your mind can create another mountain of troubles.* With conviction and experience, any reservations or hesitations will disappear, leading to a continuous and engulfing meditation experience."

"That is fascinating, Murli! Can you please give a demo?" requested Karan.

"Yes, once I am done with explaining the complete process, we will do short meditation together."  Saying this, Murli continued with the last step.

## 6. Experience

"In summary, the last step is about surrendering to the experience and allowing your true feelings to emerge. This can lead to a range of emotions, such as joy and comfort. You should appreciate the experience and examine it without getting too attached to it, and this will increase your awareness of your feelings. Take note of any new discoveries or truths in your meditation journal and reflect on them for future meditation sessions.  By doing so, you will gain a deeper understanding of yourself and the world around you."

"I understand, Murli.  While I agree that we must feel the emotions in order to let the affirmations penetrate our subconscious, I don't get the second part you talked about discovering more truths.  What does that mean exactly?" Karan questioned.

"The process of meditation is not only about thinking but also about feeling. Often, people tend to think too quickly and not attentively, leaving little space for their feelings to unfold properly. By practicing this meditation regularly, one can learn to catch the feelings and experience their depth." Murli explained.

He further added "Training one's mind with patience, gentleness, and determination can yield highly impactful results. Eventually, new ideas will naturally become more refined and serene. This is how most scientists find new discoveries, by patiently observing and exploring different possibilities without any preconceptions or biases."

*In conclusion, Murli suggested that one should not rush through the meditation process but rather take time to observe and experience their thoughts and feelings with patience and determination. Through consistent practice, one can develop a better understanding of their own mind and discover new insights that can be applied in different aspects of their life.*

"The whole process is now completely clear to me. If we can get demo of this mediation, that will be icing on the cake." Parth requested.

"Sure, let me show you how to meditate while solving this puzzle game. You two must have visited beaches, so let's use that experience as inspiration for some mind-calming activities. Due to time constraints, we won't be able to do the body-relaxing exercise. Let's get started." Murli allowed a few moments for them to prepare for the demo and then gave the instructions.

*"Please sit in a comfortable position and close your eyes. Take a deep breath in and exhale slowly. Let your body relax as you continue to breathe deeply and slowly.*

*"Now, imagine a beautiful sunny morning. You're at the beach, and you can feel the sand between your toes. Feel the sun on your skin. Hear the sound of the waves crashing against the shore and see the vast ocean before you. Take a moment to fully immerse yourself in this peaceful scene.*

*"As you look up at the sky, you notice the numbers 50 forming*

*in the white clouds. Countdown the numbers in your mind, let your thoughts to drift away as you focus on the numbers. Continue counting down until you reach zero, seeing each number floating in the sky. Now that you've reached zero, allow your mind to enter a deep state of relaxation.*

*"You are now in an alpha state. Anything you believe in this state will become your reality.*

*"Now, imagine yourself on the beach, looking down at your body and surroundings from a distance. Visualize a beam of golden light coming down from the universe, filling your soul with light and power. Feel the light and power of the universe flowing into your soul, filling you with peace and tranquility.*

*"Take a moment to thank God for all the blessings in your life, including the air you breathe, the food you eat, your family, your job, and everything else you can think of. Appreciate everything you have and feel grateful for all of it.*

*"Now, turn your attention to your theme of happiness. Visualize yourself feeling happy and content. Think about the journey you've been on in life, with all its ups and downs, successes and failures. See yourself as a stable being, enjoying every moment of the journey. Every experience, positive or negative, has helped you become a better person.*

*"Give in to the feeling of happiness and enjoy the ride. Feel it fully, experiencing every moment of it. Allow yourself to be fully present in this moment."*

Murli took a long pause and let all of them go through the experience for a while. He then spoke in a softer voice,

*"When you're ready, slowly open your eyes and take a deep breath in. Exhale slowly and bring yourself back to the present moment. Take a moment to appreciate the peace and relaxation you feel before continuing with your day."*

He waited for the boys to return back from this experience. After a few minutes, both Parth and Karan opened their eyes.

"Wow, Murli, I haven't felt this relaxed in years." Parth yelled out in glee.

Karan described his experience, saying, "I was not able to concentrate much as thoughts about the project kept bothering me, but whenever I could focus on the theme, I felt so much calm."

"That's alright, Karan. Something like this happens to everyone. Please keep going and don't give up. That's it, guys, I am done. I gave you all the information you need to live a happy life." Murli took a deep sigh.

"Murli, I can't express how grateful I am for your and Ruchi Didi's kindness towards us. But to be honest, I can't help feeling incredibly ashamed of my initial reaction when you first broke the news of layoffs. I called you selfish, and now I regret my words deeply. I'm sorry for what I said. I can't even look you in the eyes right now." Karan's voice was heavy with guilt and remorse as he spoke.

"Absolutely, Murli! I completely concur with Karan's sentiments. It's disheartening to see many so-called leaders solely prioritizing their own success and treating their team members as mere steppingstones for their own success. However, your remarkable display of empathy towards not just us, but the entire team over the past 12 days has left me utterly speechless with gratitude. Thank you so much for all that you've done." Parth's words were filled with gratitude.

"Please, guys, don't make me emotional!" Murli said with a shaky voice, feeling overwhelmed with gratitude for his team's kind words. He quickly composed himself and continued, "Let's have a cup of coffee, and then I have one last piece of advice for you." Murli quickly walked out of the cabin before Parth and Karan could hear his stumbling words.

As they sipped coffee in the cafeteria, Murli shared his final words of wisdom with Parth and Karan. "In this fast-paced world, we often find meditation to be tedious. Who can close their eyes and sit without thinking? But we must make time in our hectic schedules to meditate and attain inner peace. Whether you sit in a quiet corner of your home or take a few moments at work, sitting quietly with your eyes closed can provide enormous mental comfort. The Bhagavad Gita emphasizes the importance of meditation, as it is a non-physical exercise that offers the best opportunity for inner tranquility and spiritual growth." Murli spoke with a calm and peaceful demeanor, his words resonating with Parth and Karan.

Parth and Karan were paying close attention.

"Let me tell you one last story:

*Sid and Sam were close friends who decided to move away from the city and build identical houses in a peaceful, rural area near a river. After finding the perfect piece of land, they spent a lot of time planning and building their dream homes. Both of their houses had spacious front and backyards, and they each had an hour a day to tend to their gardens.*

*Sid decided to focus all of his attention on his front yard, envisioning a garden full of exotic and beautiful flowers. He put in a lot of effort and turned his front yard into a stunning work of art, which made him proud. However, he neglected his backyard, allowing weeds to take over.*

*Sam, on the other hand, split his time evenly between both yards. His front yard wasn't as impressive as Sid's because he had planted mostly hardy plants that take less time to tend, but it still had some lovely flowers. In his backyard, he planted fruit trees and a vegetable garden that he tended seasonally.*

*When a severe thunderstorm hit the region one day, both friends emerged from their houses to find their gardens decimated. Sid's front yard was completely destroyed, and he was devastated. He had put so much time and effort into it, and it was all gone in an instant. Sam's front yard also suffered damage, but some of the hardier plants survived and could be saved with care.*

*As they surveyed the damage, they realized that the road in front of their houses had been washed away by the flood, leaving them trapped with no way to get food for themselves or their families. They learned from the radio that it would take rescue workers 8 to 10 days to reach them.*

*Sid and his wife were frightened when they realized they had food enough only for couple of days. Sam and his wife, on the other hand, had harvested all of the vegetables from their backyard and picked the fruit from their trees as soon as the rain started. They had enough food to sustain them for the next 8 to 10 days."*

Parth and Karan found the story that was being told to be quite interesting.

"Our existence is much like a lovely house, equipped with a front yard and a backyard yard. The back yard is meant to reflect our spiritual lives which are inside us, whereas the front yard is meant to represent all of the materialistic things in our lives, such as money, a car, clothes, travel, etc. The majority of us are just as focused like Sid on the front yard, which refers to the materialistic things that serve to develop status in the society in order to fulfill our egos. Unfortunately, we don't pay enough attention to the backyard, often known as our spiritual garden.

"I am not suggesting that we shouldn't be concerned with

the material things in our lives. They are necessary for us to continue living in this world, and they bring us comfort; but we must not forget that we also need a spiritual garden in order to keep our souls healthy."

Parth inquired, "So what kind of plants should we put in our spiritual garden?"

"We should cultivate whatever brings joy and stillness to our souls. It is important for us to cultivate the lovely blossoms of gratitude for everything that we have, empathy towards others, harmony, and love. Our spiritual garden is not the place for us to cultivate the weeds of hostility, jealousy, or rage.

"At the moment, you guys and every other member of the team are in the exact same situation as Sid and Sam. The oncoming thunderstorm of the pandemic is poised to wreak havoc on your front yard, i.e., your professional life. You have invested a lot of time and effort into creating your professional success, but there is a possibility that you could be sacked for no reason of your own doing. But if your spiritual garden is filled with beautiful flowers, then it won't matter how many thunderstorms damage your materialistic garden; you will have the strength to develop a brand new and even better front yard!

"The daily practice of reading and reflecting on a few verses from the Bhagavad Gita restores my spirit. I feel refreshed, strengthened, and connected to God." Murli said.

"We have such divine knowledge in our ancient books, and it is so unfortunate that we are never taught these in school." Parth mentioned in disappointment.

"That's true, Parth! Boys, remember one thing, *knowledge without practice is like a bow without an arrow—USELESS!* So, you have received all the knowledge and techniques to use that knowledge, but if you don't practice, it will not yield any transformation in your life. The mind is like a computer - learn to program it with both words and mental pictures so as to get best results." Murli wrapped up his sessions with some final words of wisdom.

After hearing Murli's words of wisdom about the importance of balancing materialism and spirituality, Parth and Karan felt a renewed sense of motivation and purpose. They were determined to cultivate their spiritual garden and attain inner peace and tranquility, while still striving for success in their careers and material possessions.

Parth returned home that day with enormous satisfaction and a fighter's mindset. Murli's wise words had absorbed him and had a profound effect on him. He reflected to himself on how lucky he was to receive such profound wisdom from a man who walks on that path and finds success in every aspect of his life. Parth felt that he had discovered the purpose of his existence: achieving success while adhering to spiritual principles. He pledged to himself that no matter how many obstacles come along the way, he will never deviate from the path outlined by Lord Krishna in the Bhagavad Gita. Before retiring to bed, he began writing in his gratitude journal and set an alarm for 5 o'clock in the morning to begin playing the game of extraordinary life.

The sessions had astounded Karan as well. He had started going to these sessions just as a formality, but over the last 12 days, the phenomenal insights he gained about true happiness had changed his entire perspective about life. He had planned to go straight home from work and ponder on Murli's techniques, but Nidhi invited him to dinner, which he couldn't refuse.

They went to a low-key eatery close to the office for a quiet evening meal.

"Thank God your stupid sessions are finally done!" As her eyes rolled, Nidhi let out a sigh of relief.

"Do not refer to them in such a derogatory manner, Nidhi. Murli and his wife had put in a lot of time and effort to teach us the Bhagavad Gita's profound knowledge. Who goes out of their way to help others these days?" Karan's displeasure at Nidhi was plain to see.

"Given your ardent advocacy, I'm curious to know more about it. So, fill me in on what exactly you have learned over the previous couple of weeks?" Nidhi's question was more sarcastic than inquisitive.

Karan began to enthusiastically impart the wisdom he had learned from Murli.

Nidhi began laughing at him before he could finish, and asked, "Are you serious? In real life, these things do not work. They are only useful in books!"

"But Nidhi..." Karan tried to explain Nidhi further, but she cut him off.

"I like you for who you are, Karan. I'm sorry, but I don't want to be your friend if you start following these idiotic ideas!" She issued a harsh warning to him.

"Please, Nidhi, hear me out first!" Karan tried to calm her down.

"First and foremost, do you like me?" Nidhi openly asked him this question for the first time, but then realized her mistake.

"Yes, Nidhi, I like you more than anything," Karan said, his eyes shining with affection.

"Then listen to me! I don't want to spend any more time with a boring guy who goes on the so-called 'spiritual path' and spends his time and energy. Karan, now is not the time for spirituality. It's time to chase our dreams. I want to live a lavish lifestyle and appreciate every facet of it. I want to be with someone who goes after what he wants, not someone who gives everything away in the name of spirituality. Pay close attention; if you are unable to keep this job, you must forget about me. I don't want to be with someone who is a loser." Nidhi made her case without hesitation. She was also relieved that she had kept doors open for Parth, provided he kept his job.

Karan was taken aback when he heard Nidhi's point of view. He knew Nidhi was ambitious, but he didn't anticipate her to have such an extreme point of view. One part of his mind agreed with Nidhi, but the other yearned for spirituality. Then the repercussions of losing this job flashed before his eyes: financial difficulties, humiliation by friends, and even the loss of Nidhi, who was so dear to him.

"Alright, Nidhi," he said after a moment's thought, his heart pounding. "I shall devote my entire attention to the task at hand. I pledge not to let you down."

"Do you promise?" Nidhi wanted to make sure Karan sticks to his words.

"Yes, I promise," Karan said as he grabbed Nidhi's hand in his.

As Karan was heading back to home, he couldn't help but feel guilty and ashamed that he wasn't able to fully commit to the path of spirituality as preached by Murli. He felt torn between his desire for inner peace and his love for Nidhi, knowing that he couldn't disappoint her by neglecting his career and material aspirations. As he reached home, he couldn't hold his tears back. He buried his head in his hand and felt disgusted with himself for being so weak.

# IV

# THE RIPPLE EFFECT OF SPIRITUAL LIVING

# 21

# THE DIVIDE BETWEEN KNOWLEDGE AND AMBITION

Parth and Karan and their teams had a hectic weekend as usual. Both teams were working hard to achieve their deadlines. Throughout the weekend, Parth's attempts to practice gratitude and meditation were met with mixed results. He appreciated the chance to slow down and reflect on his life. On the other hand, he found it hard to concentrate and stay focused, which left him feeling anxious and uncertain, but he was determined to keep trying.

Karan's mind was constantly racing with ideas and strategies for outpacing Parth's team. He was driven by a fierce ambition to succeed and prove himself, but he couldn't help feeling a sense of emptiness and loneliness beneath the surface. His newfound romance with Nidhi provided a welcome distraction, but he wondered if he was truly ready for a relationship given how much he had on his plate.

It was a new week, but the teams were still fighting to keep up with Aman's aggressive target. There were only two weeks until the teams' fates would be decided.

On Monday morning, Aman was in the conference room, waiting for the team's weekly update meeting. While he waited for them, he talked with Maya. His relationship with Maya had blossomed so quickly that they were exceedingly close in just two weeks. He hung up the call as the entire team, including Murli, entered the conference room while he was talking.

"Good day, gentlemen. Let's get started. You go first, Parth." Aman got right to the point.

Parth and Karan then delivered their presentations. Notwithstanding some initial hiccups in quality and team communication, Parth's team now was functioning as a cohesive unit, as seen by the incredible progress they had made. They were able to deliver 10% more features than Karan's team. Parth was overjoyed with the progress his team had made, and he felt proud of their hard work and dedication. On the other hand, Karan was experiencing a range of emotions, from anger and jealousy to disappointment and self-doubt. He couldn't believe that Parth's team had pulled ahead so quickly, and he wondered if he was doing something wrong. He had tried to maintain a positive attitude and keep his team motivated, but it was becoming harder and harder to stay optimistic.

Nidhi could sense Karan's disappointment and frustration, and she wanted to help him stay motivated and focused. She felt a deep sense of concern for Karan and his team, and she knew that they needed to find a way to catch up with Parth's team.

"You can't give up, Karan! You must take action on this" Nidhi attempted to inspire Karan, when they met in the cafeteria after the review.

Karan was feeling discouraged and defeated, but Nidhi's

words gave him a glimmer of hope. He was grateful for her encouragement and support, and he felt a renewed sense of purpose and determination.

Parth was filled with a sense of longing and sadness as he watched Nidhi and Karan talk. He had been secretly admiring Nidhi from afar but seeing her getting closer to Karan was painful. He was torn between his feelings for Nidhi and his loyalty to his team, and he knew that he had to focus on the latter.

Parth's sense of responsibility towards his team was a powerful motivator for him. He felt a deep sense of duty and obligation to his colleagues, and he knew that he couldn't let them down. He was determined to do everything in his power to help his team succeed, even if it meant setting aside his personal feelings for Nidhi. He then approached his colleagues to discuss the next tasks.

Murli was happy to see such a drastic transformation in Parth - from a self centered individual to a leader working for his team.

Both teams had a busy week, but they were determined to do their best. Nidhi has been drawn to Karan in recent days due to their frequent conversations and discussions. She had resolved to spend the entire week motivating him. She was even secretly assisting his team with a few minor testing activities.

Murli was deeply invested in the success of both teams, and he wanted to see them thrive both professionally and personally. He felt a great sense of responsibility towards them, and he knew that he had an important role to play in their development. Murli's decision to avoid pushing Parth and Karan to practice the techniques was a deliberate one. He felt that true change could only come from within, and he wanted the boys to develop a sense of ownership and commitment to the practices on their own.

The week went by briskly and it was already Friday. Parth was upset over something so went to talk to Murli about it.

"May I enter, Murli?" As he opened Murli's cabin door, Parth inquired.

"Sure, sure. What's going on, Parth?" Murli inquired.

Parth chose to convey his concern as he took his seat. "Murli, I'm trying to employ the strategies you showed us, but I just can't focus," He lamented.

"What exactly is the problem, Parth?" Murli inquired.

"First, while doing meditation, I feel guilty that I am wasting my time doing nothing. Second, I'm having trouble focusing on the theme. All of my work-related thoughts are flooding my mind, and before I know it, 30 minutes pass without me focusing on my theme for even a minute." Parth let out a frustrated sigh.

"Parth, relax! I've already stated that mastering anything requires practice. If you began employing these strategies with the goal of mastering them on the first try, you were off to a bad start. Isn't that right?" Murli inquired, his voice cool.

"Yeah, I understand," Parth said again, "but I should be able to focus for at least a few minutes."

"You've only been applying these strategies for a few days, so don't be too hard on yourself. I have one piece of advice for you: *once you observe your thoughts straying from the theme, consciously bring them back to the theme. It doesn't matter how many times they try to distract you; continually bring them back.*" Murli provided the advice.

"I'll give it a shot, but will I ever be capable of solving the puzzle, Murli?" Parth inquired, slightly concerned.

Murli rose from his seat and approached Parth. He said, with a pat on the back, "I guarantee you will, Parth, if you don't give up! You probably didn't learn Java programming in a week, did you?"

"No, it took me months, and I'm still learning," Parth responded spontaneously.

"That's precisely the point. You are one of the best developers I have seen but you became one with practice and consistency. Continue to practice meditation, and I have no doubt that you will be the finest version of yourself." Murli attempted to instill enthusiasm in Parth.

Parth stood up confidently, filled with energy. "Murli, you are correct. I promise, I will never, ever give up. I won't let you down."

"That's my boy!" Murli was satisfied with Parth's desire to take control of his life.

Parth felt much more driven as he walked out of the cabin, and his body language had entirely changed.

When Karan had observed Parth enter Murli's cabin, he assumed it was about the Bhagavad Gita knowledge, and his hunch was confirmed when he saw Parth exit the cabin beaming with confidence. Karan felt disgusted with himself because, even after receiving such profound knowledge from Murli, he was unable to apply it.

Nidhi was sitting at her desk, watching for all of this. Karan's fury was palpable to her. She approached him to pacify him.

"What's the problem, Karan? Keep going; you're on the correct track. This job is critical for both of us." She did not want Karan to return to his spiritual path.

"True, Nidhi. I see what you're saying. I will prevail in this competition no matter what." Karan's confidence was shaky and uncertain, and he felt like he was putting on a brave face for Nidhi. He knew that he had a lot of work to do if he wanted to catch up to Parth, and he wasn't sure if he had what it took to succeed.

Both teams were organizing their tasks as the weekend approached. This was the last weekend before the results were to be announced. While Karan instructed his team to work overtime even on weekends, Parth advised his team to work only on Saturday and take a day off on Sunday. This astonished his team, but Parth persuaded them to take the break so that they could finish strong in the final week.

Parth utilized Sunday to strengthen his mind and soul. He felt a sense of accomplishment as he reviewed his notes and practiced his meditation. He was proud of himself for sticking with it, even when it was difficult. He was grateful for the wisdom and guidance that Murli had shared with him. He felt like he was starting to understand the deeper meaning behind the Bhagavad Gita, and it was bringing him a sense of peace and clarity. Whenever he felt frustrated or distracted during his meditation, he felt a sense of disappointment in himself. But he didn't let that discourage him - he kept trying and pushing himself to improve.

He went to his parents' house for dinner that evening. Despite the fact that they lived in the same city, he hadn't met them for about a month. Parth felt a mixture of relief and gratitude when he talked to his parents about the layoffs. He had been carrying the weight of that news on his shoulders for weeks, and it felt good to finally share it with someone who cared about him. Their words of support and encouragement lifted his spirits and gave him hope for the future.

At Murli's place, Ruchi inquired about the boys when he and

Ruchi were out in the garden with Radha. The two sat on the grass as Radha began playing with her friends.

"They're doing well, but I have the impression Karan isn't practicing the techniques. He didn't come to me even once last week to ask for advice." Murli expressed his concern.

"How about Parth?" Ruchi inquired.

"The guy is giving it his all. On Friday, he approached me and asked for advice." Murli responded with a twinkle in his eyes.

"At least someone is trying to change his life," Ruchi replied, sighing.

"You know, Ruchi, it appears that I misunderstood these guys."

"What do you mean?" Ruchi inquired.

"When I first started these sessions, I assumed Karan would be the one to see things through. Karan was always more compassionate and seemed to have higher moral ideals, whilst Parth was more concerned with himself. Nonetheless, their responses to this knowledge are diametrically opposed." Murli expressed his surprise.

"Tough situations put a person's character to the test; these can bring out the best or worst in a person."

Murli nodded in accord as Ruchi contributed her perspective.

In the evening, Murli decided to call Aman to check if he had found any new investors to avoid the catastrophe in the making, but there was no response from him.

Aman had been staying with Maya for the past few days. Anita had made it clear that she was disgusted by his presence in the house and that she wanted him away from their child. However, Aman was fighting hard to get custody of his child, though it looked impossible.

To the divorce lawyer who was handling their case, Anita had made it clear that she needed nothing from Aman. None of his properties or financial gains, all she wanted was a quick divorce and to have custody of their child.

Aman was quite troubled and agitated, facing the reality of his actions. He remained quiet, having a drink in the living area, when Maya walked in. She kept her hand on his shoulder and took the glass from his hand. "Aman, you have had enough now. Please come to bed and get some rest."

Aman looked at Maya; he almost had tears in his eyes as he responded, "Maya, am I wrong in wanting to be happy? Am I at fault making a decision that clearly will save my company? Am I being punished for being with you after deciding to end a marriage that had nothing for me in it?"

Maya sat down next to Aman on the couch and placed a hand on his knee, giving it a gentle squeeze. "Aman, you're not wrong for wanting to be happy. Everyone deserves to be happy, and it's not a crime to make a decision that will benefit you and your company. You have to do what's best for yourself and your future."

Aman sighed and leaned his head back against the couch, looking up at the ceiling. "But at what cost, Maya? I've hurt my wife and my child. I've destroyed my family."

Maya took Aman's hand in hers and gave it a reassuring squeeze. "It's not your fault that things turned out this way. Sometimes, relationships just don't work out, and that's okay. You didn't set out to hurt anyone, and you're not responsible for other people's emotions. All you can do is try to make things right and move forward. Believe me, as a lawyer, I am saying all this through experience."

Aman nodded, but his expression remained troubled. "But

what if I can't make things right?"

Maya placed a hand on Aman's cheek and turned his head to face her. "Listen to me, Aman! You're a smart and capable man, and you've worked hard to build your company from the ground up. You won't let it all go to waste just because of this setback. And as for your child, you'll always be his father, no matter what happens. You'll always have a place in his life."

Aman looked into Maya's eyes, and for a moment, all his worries seemed to fade away. She had a way of making him feel better, calming his fears and doubts. He leaned in and pressed his lips to hers, feeling the weight of his guilt lift slightly.

"You're right, Maya. Thank you for being here for me," Aman said, pulling back from the kiss.

"Always, Aman! I'll always be here for you," Maya replied with a smile, and they both settled into the couch, content in each other's company.

The next morning was to mark the beginning of a quite eventful week. It was the last week, a week that would determine the fate of the competition in which both teams had been engaged for the previous three weeks.

On Monday morning, it was time for the weekly status update meeting, but this was not the normal meeting. Considering this was the penultimate status update before the final decision, Aman had invited the entire team, including the support team to attend the meeting. He wanted everyone to know which team was likely to continue working with HealthTech.

He directed Parth to begin his presentation on the status update. Parth began with a confident smile and presented the progress they had made during the previous week. He showed how his team had overcome some major roadblocks and had managed to complete a significant portion of the project. His team members were nodding their heads in agreement, impressed with his presentation.

As Parth wrapped up his presentation, the entire room erupted into applause. Karan felt a sinking feeling in his stomach as he realized that Parth had once again outperformed him, and his team was at least 20% behind Parth's team. He knew that it was unlikely that his team would win the competition. With that, he would lose his job.

Karan tried to put up a brave face as Aman called on him to present his team's progress, but the words stuck in his throat. He struggled to find the right words, and when he finally did, he stumbled over them, unable to articulate the progress his team had made. It was clear to everyone in the room that Karan's team was far behind, and there was little hope of catching up.

Nidhi was disappointed since she knew Karan was very close to losing the competition. No matter how hard she tried, she just couldn't muster any optimism about his ability to recover from this setback.

Aman was thrilled with the progress Parth had made and praised him for his hard work and dedication. He then turned to Karan and said, "Karan, I'm sorry to say this, but it seems like Parth and his team have made much more progress than you and your team. I'll have to discuss this with Murli, but it seems like they will continue working with HealthTech."

Karan remained still, embarrassed in front of the entire team, especially Nidhi.

Murli could feel Karan's pain, so he pitched in to keep him motivated. "Karan, you and your team have done an outstanding job over the last three weeks. To have made this much progress from where you started is incredible, especially given the arbitrary deadline. Don't give up; you still have one week; do your best and leave the rest to destiny!"

Parth was the man of the moment. Nidhi, in particular, found herself drawn to Parth's easy charisma and competence.

As the presentation wrapped up, Nidhi made her way over to Parth with a smile on her face. "Congratulations, Parth," she said, extending her hand. "That was a really impressive presentation."

Parth took her hand, grinning. "Thanks, Nidhi," he said. "I'm really proud of what the team has accomplished."

Karan scowled as he watched the discussion, a tinge of anger in his chest. He'd always been the team's star, the one everyone looked up to. Parth, on the other hand, has suddenly stolen the show.

He approached Nidhi and Parth, trying to mask the venom in his voice. "Excellent job, Parth," he said in a tight tone. "You really know how to work a crowd."

Parth's smile faltered slightly, but he quickly recovered. "Thank you, Karan," he murmured, still smiling. "We all performed an excellent job."

Karan nodded, but he was fuming on the inside. He couldn't bear thinking about being overshadowed by Parth. He was always competitive, but this was different because job and reputation, both were on the line. He felt like his whole identity was tied up in being the best, and he couldn't bear the thought of someone else taking that away from him. Jealousy burned in his chest as he watched Parth receive praise and admiration for his work. The bitterness he felt was all-consuming, and he couldn't shake the feeling that he was being left behind. His thoughts raced as he hung back, stewing in his own frustration and disappointment.

Nidhi, on the other hand, tried to spend time with Parth outside of work. She began to notice that he was totally devoted to the project and taking quick motivational pep talks from Murli. He was always polite and professional, but he didn't seem interested in socializing.

Previously, Nidhi was trying to get closer to Karan in order to keep him motivated, but she now knew it would be Parth who would triumph. She was anxious about asking Parth out because she had witnessed Parth's discomfort when she had been spending more time with Karan. But she eventually worked up the nerve to ask Parth, "Hey, Parth, I was wondering if you'd like to grab a coffee after work sometime." She said, trying to keep her tone casual.

Parth hesitated for a moment, then shook his head. "I'm sorry, Nidhi," he apologized. "You know how much I would love it, but I'm too preoccupied with the project right now. I don't want anything to divert my attention because this isn't just about me, right? It also has to do with my team."

Nidhi was disappointed, but she attempted to brush it off. Somewhere inside she was concerned thinking that Parth would not have liked her spending so much time with Karan over the past week but her worries were put to rest when Parth promised to hold a big party for her after the competition.

She observed as Parth threw all of his energy into the project during the next week. He worked late into the night, continually adjusting and fine-tuning their strategy. Despite his lack of attention towards her, Nidhi couldn't help but admire his determination.

The week passed off. It was the 29th of the month, the last day before the dreadful day, when Aman would decide the destiny of the 40 health tech team members.

Parth called a team meeting to go over the final details. Nidhi sat next to him, watching him firmly lead the discussion. She couldn't help but feel a twinge of admiration for him, even if it wasn't romantic.

Parth exuded confidence. His module had been completed, carefully tested, and was totally working. He and his team sighed as they left the office early. He convinced himself that after so many days of strenuous work, he deserved to sleep peacefully.

Karan and his team were still trying to cover as much ground as possible, but they realized it was futile. The team left the office as usual in the evening, but Karan stayed.

Murli was about to leave the office when he noticed Karan was still working.

"Karan, everyone has left the office. Why are you still working?" He inquired.

"I am just finishing up final testing on our module. I know we will be losing regardless, but I am just attempting to present anything we have generated in usable form," Karan tried to give a justification.

Murli felt sad for Karan and chose to leave the office without saying anything more as Karan worked.

# 22

# A DECEPTIVE VICTORY

Finally, the decisive day arrived, shrouded in a heavy cloud of anxiety and fear. This was the day that everyone dreaded, the day that could make or break their careers. The air in the conference room was thick with tension as the teams nervously awaited the results. Their hearts were pounding with fear as they knew what was at stake. Along with the presentation, both teams were expected to show a demo of their applications to prove that they are fully functional.

Aman could barely contain his excitement, as the meeting would provide him with the clarity he needed to move forward with the team. His eyes gleamed with anticipation as he prepared to collaborate with his colleagues to plan for future releases. Murli, on the other hand, was consumed with worry, as he knew he had to let go of 20 of his team members, with whom he had been working for months. He prayed to Lord Krishna to give everyone the strength they needed to deal with the consequences.

Parth exuded confidence, knowing that he and his team had

done everything they could. But Karan, poor Karan, was a bundle of nerves, his hands shaking as he hoped for some dramatic turn of events that would swing the needle in his favor. Nidhi was a picture of calm and composure as she knew she would be the winner, regardless of who won or lost.

Aman kicked off the meeting, his voice ringing out with an authoritative tone. "Teams, I know it was a stressful month for everyone, but it was unavoidable. I'm sure both teams gave it their all, but there can only be one winner. I'm looking forward to seeing your application demos. Let's get this ball rolling. Let's start with you, Karan and team."

Karan made his way to the front. He was nervous but he had learnt his lesson from the last meeting so this time, he tried to be confident, which surprised his colleagues because they knew they hadn't completed all of their tasks. Karan reported that his team had completed 90% of the tasks allotted to them. His team then demonstrated a number of features that they had developed. These appeared quick and sleek. The coding was also of high quality.

Murli interrupted before Aman could start blasting the team for missing the mark, and heaped praise on Karan's team for their excellent effort. Everyone started clapping, and Karan and his team breathed a sigh of relief. They had come to the meeting anticipating Aman's insults, but instead were commended by Murli.

Aman, sensing a drama, interjected and requested Parth to present the performance of his team.

Parth then began his presentation. He was excited to show the status because he was on track. His team had completed all of the tasks that had been allocated to them. Aman was delighted and praised Parth and his team. Parth's team went ahead with demonstrating their application, but it started behaving weirdly for unknown reasons. Nothing was working properly. The features took an eternity to load.

Parth was terrified. "It appears to be a small problem; please allow me to look into it. I'll have everything sorted out in no time." He spoke nervously.

Aman and others waited for Parth to resolve the issue, but Parth had no idea what was going on. It had been almost 15 minutes.

"What's the matter, Parth?" Aman was visibly agitated. "Couldn't you double-check before coming to such an important meeting?"

"We have checked everything, Aman, but we aren't sure what is happening," Parth said blankly while sitting helplessly. He realized he couldn't fix this code in such a short period of time.

"Can you give me a little more time, Aman? Please allow me to restore this." Parth begged.

"Sorry, Parth, I gave the same amount of time to both teams. I cannot extend the deadline just because you are unable to present a working application. You have seen Karan has, however, presented a workable code, even though it is not 100% complete," Aman raged at Parth.

Parth and his team's hearts began to race after hearing these remarks from Aman. They didn't want to hear any more words from Aman's mouth, but nothing could stop him from delivering his decision.

"Your last day will be tomorrow, Parth. Murli and I shall decide whether any great performers from your team can be retained in the place of Karan's team's poor performers." Aman spoke harshly.

Aman approached Karan's team and patted him on the back as he was exiting the meeting room. "Great effort, team," he gushed. "What you've accomplished has really amazed me. Let us continue to collaborate in order to revolutionize the healthcare sector through innovation."

Karan's team could hardly contain their glee as Aman patted them on the back and gushed about their great effort. But Parth and his team were devastated, knowing that they had given it their all but still failed.

The competition had ended, but the consequences were severe. Karan's team had emerged victorious, while Parth's team was left reeling under the crushing blow of defeat. They were stony faced as they sat in the room. Karan's teammates were ecstatic, but Karan tried to remain calm as he stepped out of the meeting room.

Nidhi dashed behind Karan as soon as he left the room. "Congratulations, Karan!" she said, her face gleaming. "You nailed it!"

Karan nodded hesitantly, accepting her congratulations. "Thank you, Nidhi," he murmured, his voice a little flat.

Parth went out of the conference room, his gut knotted. He couldn't believe what had just happened to him. All of his years of hard work had been rewarded with a pink slip. He pondered how he would inform his parents that he would be out of work soon. He chose not to say a word to Aman but walked out feeling disgusted and angry.

As Parth walked back to his desk with his shoulders dropped, Murli followed him. Murli, being a mentor to Parth, was troubled. Seeing the worry on Parth's face, Murli immediately walked up to Parth and his team members.

"This is bad news, Parth, but you saw it coming, isn't it?"

He tried to console Parth, "But it's not the end of the world. We'll figure something out."

Parth shook his head. "I don't know, Murli. I feel like we did our best as a team."

Murli took a deep breath. "Listen, Parth. Let's connect with our industry counterparts to find suitable jobs for you and your team members."

It wasn't just Parth, but all his team members were agitated and angry.

"We did everything we could, and this is how they repay us?" one team member shouted.

"It's all Aman's fault!" another yelled. "He should have had our backs."

Murli tried to calm them down, but they weren't listening. Karthik, the youngest member of the team, was the most vocal of them all.

"Let's face it, Murli," Karthik said. "Aman is a spineless leader. He has no guts or courage to even face us. He's hiding behind his desk, hoping we'll just quietly leave without a fuss. He doesn't care about us; he only cares about his own reputation."

Murli sighed. "I know it's tough, but we have to keep our heads up for the sake of those who love us back home, those who depend on us each day."

But the team members continued to grumble and complain.

Parth gained his composure and requested Murli to walk with him. He even managed to calm his team down, instilling in them a certain confidence that he would use his network to its full potential to help them all find decent jobs.

Murli and Parth walked up to the common area, which had a soothing plantation all around. They sat in silence, gazing out at the lush green plantation. The sun had just started shining, casting an orange glow across the sky. It was a beautiful sight, but neither Murli nor Parth could appreciate it due to the turn of events.

Parth broke the silence. "Murli, thank you for offering to help me find a job. It means a lot to me. I don't know how I would manage without your support."

Murli nodded. "Don't worry, Parth! I'll do everything I can to help you out. You're like family to me, and I'll always be there for you."

Parth smiled, but Murli could sense that something was bothering him. "Is everything okay, Parth? You seem worried."

Parth hesitated for a moment before speaking. "To be honest, Murli, I'm not sure if I'll be able to find a job in such a short time. And even if I do, it won't be as well-paid as my current job. I don't know how I'll manage to take care of my parents and my loans."

Murli put a reassuring hand on Parth's shoulder. "We'll figure something out, Parth. Don't worry about it. We'll find a way to make things work."

Just then, Aman passed by them, talking on the phone to Maya. Murli was about to approach him for a conversation, but Aman walked past them as if they didn't exist. Murli felt a pang of hurt and frustration. Now, seeing him treat his colleagues with such disdain, Murli had lost all respect for him.

As Aman disappeared from sight, Murli turned to Parth. "Remember how we discussed life's uncertainties during our Bhagavad Gita sessions?"

A hopeful look appeared on Parth's face. "Yes, everything from the sessions is registered in my mind. I know, I do not have all the answers right now about how things will work for me, but a certain unknown assurance is making me feel peaceful within."

Murli shook his head in agreement and had a big smile on his face as he told Parth. "You have truly opened your heart to the teachings. Your hope is resting on a strong foundation, Parth!"

Parth smiled gratefully. "Thank you, Murli. You're a true friend."

Murli smiled back. "Always, Parth. Always," and left for his cabin.

Parth sat in the common area, lost in thoughts, trying to figure out how he was going to pay his bills and make ends meet now that he had lost his job. Aman was now no longer his inspiration. Not because Aman had taken away his job, but because, in the midst of it all, Aman had come across as a shallow man who lacked the courage to look beyond himself. Parth could recall the first time he met Aman and how touched he was to see Aman handle himself as a powerful leader. Aman, today, was looking at the situation through a narrow lens.

Just as Parth was deep in contemplation, Nidhi walked in, and he looked up to see her standing beside him. A smile lit up his face, and she returned it with a warm one of her own.

"Hey, Parth. How are you holding up?" she asked, concern etched on her face.

"I'm doing okay, Nidhi," Parth replied, trying to keep his voice steady.

"I can't believe that this is actually happening, and the company is okay with letting go of someone like you. In my opinion, Aman could have done better." Nidhi said, her voice rising with anger. "How could he just fire you like that?"

Parth shrugged. "It's business, Nidhi! I understand that. I just wish I had seen it coming."

As they continued talking, Karan walked in the common area. Nidhi turned to face him and, in a subtle manner, shared in her joy by congratulating him.

"Congratulations, Karan. You must be so proud of yourself and your team." While she expressed her happiness for Karan, she also made him realize that Parth was right there, and Karan should be mindful of Parth's current state of mind.

Karan tried to console Parth, saying, "Oh, Parth, I'm sorry for what has happened."

"It's okay, Karan," Parth said, trying to be gracious. "I'm happy for you. It's just hard for me right now."

"I understand, Parth. And I'm sorry again," Karan said, his tone apologetic.

As the three of them continued talking, Parth couldn't help but wonder if he would ever find a job that paid as well as the one, he had just lost. He knew he had to start searching, but the uncertainty of it all weighed heavily on him.

Parth tried to focus on the conversation with Karan and Nidhi, but his mind was wandering. He couldn't shake off the thought of his lost job, and the reality of being unemployed was starting to sink in. He hoped Nidhi would give him a shoulder to cry on, but she was too busy congratulating Karan on his success. He knew he needed a break from it all, so he decided to step out and leave for the day.

As he turned to leave, he overheard something that made his heart drop. Nidhi was accepting Karan's proposal as he made it.

He couldn't believe that he had lost his job and the woman he loved in a single day. The weight of his emotions felt like a heavy burden on his chest, and he struggled to catch his breath. He found a quiet corner and sank to the ground, his sobs echoing through the empty hallway.

Parth stayed there for what felt like hours, trying to make sense of the turmoil in his heart. He knew he had to find a way to cope with his emotions and move on, but it felt like an impossible task. The tears kept coming, and he felt like he had no control over his own life.

It felt like his entire world had come crashing down, and he didn't know how to pick up the pieces. The pain of rejection was unbearable, and he felt like he had lost all sense of purpose. He knew he had to face reality and move on, but the thought of starting over felt daunting. He felt lost and alone, with no direction or hope for the future.

Parth tried to compose himself as he walked out of the office building, but he couldn't stop the flood of emotions that had taken hold of him. He felt like the whole universe was set against him. As he sat in his car and was driving back home, he kept sobbing.

While driving home, lost in his thoughts, he came to a stop at a red light. He looked out the window and saw an old, abandoned building with a billboard in front of it. The billboard had a quote that caught his eye: *"Unless the old version fades completely, it won't leave any scope for an amazing new."*

Parth couldn't help but think that the quote was speaking directly to him. He had been so focused on his old job and his feelings for Nidhi that he had forgotten that there were other possibilities out there. The sight of the abandoned building made him realize that he needed to let go of the old version of himself and be open to new opportunities.

Finally, Parth pulled himself up and took a deep breath. He

knew he couldn't let this defeat him. He wiped away his tears and straightened his shoulders, determined to find a new path forward. It wouldn't be easy, but he knew he had to keep going. As he composed himself, he made a promise to himself that he would never give up, no matter how hard the road ahead may be.

With a newfound sense of hope and determination, Parth drove home with a positive attitude. He knew that it wouldn't be easy to find a new job, but he was willing to put in the effort and make a fresh start.

He decided to go to his parents' home so that he could feel like he was in safe hands. He wanted to sleep on his mother's lap, which never fell to provide him unconditional love, and under the umbrella of his father's reassuring words, which always provided him support no matter what. As he pulled into his parents' driveway, he took a deep breath and reminded himself that he was capable of achieving great things.

As he stepped inside, the familiar scent of his childhood home filled his nostrils, and he was greeted by the warm smiles of his parents. Their joyous welcome brought tears to his eyes, and he couldn't help but feel like a little boy again. He hugged his father tightly, desperately seeking comfort and support.

But as he began to recount the details of his job and love loss, the floodgates opened, and he started crying uncontrollably. IIis father's reassuring touch and comforting words slowly eased his pain and filled him with a sense of hope.

"Son, I'm glad to hear that you've lost that stressful job," his dad said with a smile. "You've been working too hard for too long, and it's time for you to take a break."

Parth was taken aback by his father's words. He had always been the one to shoulder the responsibility of the household, and now he felt as though he had let them down.

But his father quickly put his mind at ease. "Don't worry about the home loan installments or other expenses," he said. "We have enough saved up to take care of things for a few months. Use this time to find the right job and collaborate. Find a place that values you more as an individual and respects your talents."

Parth couldn't believe what he was hearing. His father's words gave him a comfort that he had not felt in a long time. He hugged his parents tightly, feeling grateful and relieved.

"Thank you, Dad," Parth said. "I don't know what I would do without your support and encouragement."

His father smiled and patted him on the back. His mother wiped away her son's tears and pacified him. "We're here for you, son," she said. "Always remember that. I will cook your favorite dinner today. Let's enjoy our family time."

As Parth sat at the dinner table, he couldn't help but feel overwhelmed by the uncertainty of his future. Despite his father's reassurance, he still felt a sense of anxiety and fear about what lay ahead.

But as he looked into his mother's eyes, he saw a glimmer of hope and determination that filled him with a sense of motivation again.

"Son, I know it's hard to lose your job, but remember that this is not the end," she said, her voice filled with warmth and encouragement. "You have so much talent and potential, and I know that you will find the right job that will appreciate your skills and abilities."

Her words of encouragement filled Parth with a sense of confidence and determination. He knew that he had the support and love of his family, and that he could take the challenges head on.

That night, despite all the drama at work, Parth had his first peaceful sleep in a long time. He was glad that he had had the courage to talk to his parents openly about his problems.

The evening had been much more dramatic for Karan. Nidhi had decided to celebrate Karan's victory and planned a night out at a nightclub. As they made their way to the nightclub, Nidhi was in high spirits, dancing and laughing with the crowd. Karan, on the other hand, seemed distant and preoccupied.

"What's wrong, Karan?" Nidhi asked, noticing his serious face. "You don't seem so happy about your victory."

Karan took a deep breath, bracing himself to confess something difficult. "Nidhi, there's something I need to tell you. It's about how I won."

Nidhi's expression changed to one of concern. "What do you mean?" she asked.

"You know Rahul, right?" Karan asked.

"Yes, a tester from Parth's team, he was the slowest among them." Nidhi replied.

"I knew he was the weak link in Parth's team, and when I got to know that my team was sure to lose, I approached him."

"For what?" asked Nidhi, surprised.

"I told him that even though his team wins, he will sure to lose his job as he was the weakest of them all, and if he helped me win, I would ensure that he keeps his job."

Nidhi was confused.

Karan continued, "I then took his username and password. Last night, I screwed up their code with his credentials so that nobody doubts me."

As he confessed to cheating to win the competition, Nidhi was stunned and filled with disbelief. She couldn't believe that Karan would resort to such deceitful tactics, especially when he had always been an advocate of fair play and honesty. "Karan, how could you do something like that?" she asked, her voice filled with disbelief.

"I know, Nidhi, I know," Karan said, his eyes filling with tears. "I feel terrible about it now. But at that time, I was so desperate to win. I was afraid of losing my job and disappointing my family and friends. And, at the same time, I didn't want to lose you."

Karan's tears and remorse touched Nidhi's heart, and she felt a mix of emotions - anger, disappointment, and compassion. She knew that Karan had been under a lot of pressure, but she also knew that what he had done was wrong. Nidhi's expression softened. "Karan, I understand that you were under a lot of pressure," she said.

Karan nodded, his head hanging low. "Yes, Nidhi," he said. "I'm filled with remorse. I just hope you can forgive me."

As Karan asked for forgiveness, Nidhi's heart softened, and she reached out to hold his hand. Despite her disappointment, she couldn't bear to see Karan in pain, and she knew that she still liked him. She made a promise to stand by him and support him, no matter what.

Karan felt a weight lifted from his shoulders as Nidhi forgave him. He was grateful for her love and understanding, and he knew that he had a lot to make up for. He took her hand in his and kissed it gently, feeling a renewed sense of hope and determination to be a better person.

23

# FINDING PURPOSE IN DEFEAT

The next day, Aman boldly walked into the office. It appeared to him that a whole office was a divided place between those who managed to keep their jobs and those who lost. He tried to avoid all gossip and whispers and headed straight to his cabin. He called Murli inside his cabin and asked him about the progress on the tasks assigned.

As Murli entered Aman's cabin, Aman could sense something was off. Murli's usual bright smile was replaced with a solemn expression. Aman asked, "What's the matter, Murli? Is everything okay?"

Murli took a deep breath before responding. "Everything is not well, Aman! On the 9th of this month, when you found out about the sessions I was conducting for Karan and Parth, I emailed my resignation to you, but it appears you have forgotten about it. I've given it a lot of thought since you urged me to reconsider, and I've concluded that I no longer wish to work with HealthTech. Over the next week until my notice period ends, I will continue working here."

Aman's expression turned from concerned to furious. "What

are you talking about, Murli? We need all hands on deck during this difficult time. You can't just quit now."

Murli held his ground. "I'm sorry, Aman, but I have to do what's best for my soul. And I don't think staying here is best for me anymore."

Aman couldn't believe what he was hearing. "You're being selfish, Murli! You're abandoning us when we need you the most. You're just like all the others who are jumping ship."

Murli's expression turned from solemn to anger. "I'm not being selfish, Aman! I'm doing what I believe in. And I'm sorry to say this, but you're nothing more than an opportunist. You only care about yourself and your own interests. You don't care about the people who work for you."

Aman felt like he had been slapped in the face. He couldn't believe that Murli would say something like that to him. His anger boiled over, and he shouted, "How dare you say that to me? I've done everything I can to keep this company afloat. I've sacrificed everything for it. And you have the nerve to call me selfish?"

The tension between the two men was palpable, the air thick with unspoken anger and resentment. The argument continued to escalate, with both men raising their voices and accusing each other of selfishness and betrayal. The tension in the room was almost unbearable, as the rest of the team outside the cabin listened in horror to the drama unfolding inside. The entire team was left reeling from the dramatic confrontation, wondering what the future held for HealthTech.

Finally, Murli had had enough. He stormed out of the room, slamming the door behind him with a resounding bang.

Aman was left alone in his cabin, feeling hurt and angry. He knew that he had made tough decisions, but he never expected to be called selfish and an opportunist by one of his own employees.

As he sat alone in his cabin, the guilt of his actions weighed heavily on him. He could feel the weight of the world on his shoulders as he struggled to keep the company afloat. The walls seemed to close in on him, and the air felt thick and suffocating. His mind was racing with thoughts of all the things he could have done differently, all the mistakes he had made. Aman's breathing grew heavier as he felt a wave of panic wash over him. How could he possibly continue to handle the stress and pressure of trying to save the company while dealing with the fallout from his personal life? The burden was simply too much to bear.

Meanwhile, Murli's anger had simmered down as he tried to calm himself down sitting in his cabin. As he sat there, deep in thought, Parth entered the cabin. At first, Murli didn't feel like talking, but Parth's gentle words and soothing voice were like a balm to his troubled soul. They began to talk, and Parth tried to get Murli to see reason, to reconsider his decision to resign from HealthTech.

But as Murli began to speak, it became clear that his decision to leave had more to do with his differing vision for the company than with Aman's recent layoff decision. Murli explained how he had always seen HealthTech as a company that puts the well-being of its employees first, while Aman seemed more interested in the bottom line. He spoke passionately about his beliefs, and Parth listened with rapt attention, nodding in agreement.

As the conversation continued, Parth began to share how his family had been there for him during this crisis, and he thanked Murli for being his guide through the teachings of the

Bhagavad Gita. Murli's face lit up as he recalled the wisdom of the holy book, and the two of them reminisced about the valuable lessons it had taught them. For a moment, it seemed as though their troubles had melted away, and they were two friends sharing a moment of peace amidst the chaos of the world.

It was Parth's and his team's last day of work at HealthTech so a small farewell celebration had been planned by Murli for them in the cafeteria. As the farewell celebration began, the atmosphere in the cafeteria was tense. Parth and his team were visibly emotional, and their faces showed the pain of leaving their jobs behind. Nidhi was too awkward to meet Parth's gaze, so she preoccupied herself with talking to the rest of the team instead. Murli's voice trembled as he tried to keep his emotions in check while addressing the departing team. The silence was deafening as Murli finished his speech. Everyone present knew that this was not just a farewell to a team, but it was a farewell to an era of the company that they had known and loved. It was a farewell to the dreams they had dreamt together, the late nights they had worked, and the success they had achieved together.

As the farewell celebration ended, Parth and his team got up to leave. They hugged each other tightly, tears streaming down their faces. Murli patted Parth's back and gave him a warm smile, and with a heavy heart, they all said their goodbyes.

Aman sat alone in his cabin, watching through the window as a part of his team walked out of the building, and as the door closed behind them. He was left alone with his thoughts about the decisions that led to this moment.

After bidding farewell to his team members and Murli, Parth left for his home with a decision to set out on his own spiritual journey. He had always been curious about the deeper meaning of life, and now he felt ready to explore it on his own. With the teachings of the Bhagavad Gita as his guide, Parth decided to spend a month in seclusion, devoting himself entirely to the study and practice of the sacred text.

He informed his parents that he wouldn't be coming to their home for a month and that he would spend this month in his own flat, learning more about the purpose of life and practicing the techniques Murli had taught them. His parents reluctantly agreed, although they did make him promise that he wouldn't take any extreme measures out of depression.

Parth felt nervous yet excited as he cut himself off from unnecessary information so that he could calm his mind. As he dove deeper into the teachings, he began to see the larger picture of life. He felt inspired and hopeful, realizing that there was more to existence than just the pursuit of material success and fleeting pleasures. The Bhagavad Gita taught him that true fulfillment could only be found by transcending the ego and connecting with the divine. Whenever he felt stuck, he was in touch with Murli for suggestions, and that helped him move forward.

He spent hours reading and meditating on the theme of accepting life as it is and doing your best without expecting anything in return. With each passing day, Parth felt a sense of peace and clarity. He was getting closer to solving the puzzle of an extraordinary life. At times, he felt overwhelmed by emotions, including happiness, contentment, and a sense of connection to something greater than himself.

By the end of the month, Parth had broken free of the beliefs that had kept him bound to the trappings of monetary achievement. He went to meet his parents and was excited to tell them about his journey towards self-realization. When Parth's mother saw him, she immediately gave him a big hug. He felt a warm, comforting feeling wash over him as he hugged his mother back, feeling a sense of love and support from her. With a grin on his face, Parth inquired about the meal she had prepared for him. His mother gave him a reassuring look as she dried her tears and went to prepare his favorite meal.

Parth sat down on the couch with his dad, excited to fill him in on everything he'd done and seen over the past month.

Parth's father was naturally inquisitive about his son's experience: "So how was it, son?"

He felt eager and enthusiastic as he shared his journey with his father, who listened with pride and admiration.

"Through the teachings of the Bhagavad Gita, I have come to understand that there is a greater purpose to life than what I previously believed. I have spent so much time chasing after success, but now I realize that these things are fleeting and ultimately unsatisfying. But the Bhagavad Gita has shown me a path towards true fulfillment. By connecting with the divine, I can transcend the limitations of the ego and find a sense of peace and contentment that goes beyond any material possessions or achievements."

His dad was listening intently, trying to figure out if this was still the same person who cared only about the worldly things. He was pleased to see a change in his son.

"This journey is not easy, and there will be many obstacles along the way. But I am committed to continuing down this path, no matter what hindrances come my way. I am grateful to have had the guidance of Murli and the wisdom of the Bhagavad Gita to help me on this journey, and I know that their teachings will stay with me as I move forward. As I immerse myself in the teachings of the Bhagavad Gita, I am humbled by the realization that my own problems are insignificant compared to the troubles of the world at large. There are people out there who are struggling to survive, to find food and shelter, and to overcome unimaginable hardships. And yet, in the face of all this suffering, there is also hope.

"The Bhagavad Gita has opened up my mind to new possibilities and given me the confidence to look for unorthodox job opportunities. I realize that my previous career aspirations were too narrow and focused solely on my own success. But now, I want to use my skills and knowledge to make a positive impact on the world around me.

"I am excited about the journey ahead, and I know that it will not be easy. But I am willing to take on any challenge that comes my way, knowing that I am not alone in this journey. The wisdom of the Bhagavad Gita will continue to guide me, and I am grateful for the knowledge and insight that it has given me.

"With this newfound perspective, I am ready to embrace a life of purpose and meaning, one that is grounded in compassion and service. I am grateful for the opportunity to embark on this journey, and I know that it will be a life-changing experience." Parth explained his vision with such compassion that his father was awestruck with the clarity his son has gained over the past month.

He hugged Parth tightly and said, "You find the purpose of your life, son; I am always standing behind you like a rock."

At the dinner table, Parth relished his mother's delicious cooking. During the meals, everyone shared some laughs and agreed that this was the most enjoyable time they'd had together in a long while.

"I am very happy to have you back in our lives, son," Parth's mum told him. "We were broken when you left us to start a new life elsewhere. In my opinion, everything that happens is for the best. Even though you lost your job, we have got our family back." Her eyes welled up with tears of joy.

Parth took his mother's hand and apologized, saying, "I was only driven by a desire to succeed back then Ma! But, now I realize it was all shallow and there is nothing more than having your family by your side, I promise, I will never leave you again."

Having had this awakening, rather than plunging himself into job hunting, Parth first supported his entire team in finding a suitable job at other companies. He successfully managed, through his network strength, to get them all decent jobs, which set them back on their career track.

He himself was regularly interacting with his network to find a concept that would be in line with his new-found purpose. This is when, for the first time, Parth heard about Geetika.

One day, while catching up with his friend Varun over coffee, he had shared his enthusiasm for his ongoing search.

Varun took a sip of his coffee and leaned in. "Actually, I just heard about this amazing concept that I think might interest you. It's about women's health, and it's being developed by a woman named Geetika Sachdeva."

Parth's ears perked up at the mention of women's health. "Tell me more," he said.

Varun took a deep breath and launched into an enthusiastic description of Geetika's concept. He spoke of how it was designed to address the unique health needs of women, using cutting-edge technology to track and analyze data. Parth listened intently; his curiosity piqued.

"This sounds incredible," Parth said when Varun had finished. "Do you think you could introduce me to Geetika?"

Varun hesitated. "Well, I don't want to get your hopes up too much. Geetika's idea is still in the early stages, and there's a lot of work to be done. I'm not even sure if it's feasible."

But Parth was undeterred. "I'd still like to meet her," he said. "Who knows, maybe I can help in some way."

With that, Varun agreed to arrange a meeting between Parth and Geetika.

As the two sat in the contemporary cafe, sipping coffee, Geetika launched a detailed explanation of her concept, her eyes shining with excitement. She was a confident and passionate woman, and Parth was immediately drawn to her energy and enthusiasm.

He listened carefully, nodding in understanding as Geetika spoke. He was impressed by the depth of her knowledge and her commitment to improving women's health.

"That sounds like a really innovative approach," he said when she had finished. "But have you thought about how you're going to develop and launch the application and software?"

Geetika's face fell a little. "To be honest, that's where I've been struggling. I have some basic knowledge of technology, but I don't know enough to make this a reality."

Parth leaned forward. "Well, I think I might be able to help with that. I have experience in software development, and I think I could help you create a roadmap for development and launch. We could work together to make your vision a reality."

Geetika's eyes widened in surprise and gratitude. "That would be amazing," she said. "I've been searching for someone who could help me with this, but I wasn't sure where to start."

As they continued to talk, Parth found himself becoming more and more intrigued by Geetika. Her passion for women's healthcare was contagious, and he found himself feeling inspired by her commitment to making a difference.

At the same time, he couldn't help but notice how strikingly attractive she was, in a simple and unassuming way. Her natural beauty was enhanced by her confidence and intelligence, and Parth found himself wanting to get to know her better.

As they finished their coffee, Parth felt a sense of excitement and anticipation. As they stood up to leave, he smiled at her, and said, "I think this could be the start of something great."

Geetika grinned back at him. "I couldn't agree more. I'm so excited to see where this goes."

He walked her to her car, and as she got in, she turned to him. "I just want to be upfront with you, Parth," she said. "I don't have much to offer in terms of salary right now, but I'm willing to offer you a stake in the company. I believe that with your technical expertise and my vision, we could really make this work."

Parth nodded thoughtfully. "I appreciate your honesty, Geetika. I do have financial liabilities to consider, but I'm definitely interested in being a part of this project. Let me evaluate my options, and we can discuss this further."

Geetika smiled gratefully. "That's all I can ask for. I'm just glad that we can work together on this."

As they parted ways, both of them felt a sense of enthusiasm and eagerness. They had managed to impress each other with their talents and personalities, and they both felt that this could be the start of something truly special. They agreed to stay in touch and set up another meeting to discuss the project further.

Parth walked away from the cafe feeling invigorated and inspired. He had been searching for a purpose, and he felt that he had finally found it. Working with Geetika on this project could be the start of a new chapter in his life, one filled with purpose and meaning. He couldn't wait to see where this journey would take him.

24

# THE POWER OF PURPOSE AND LOVE

Parth returned home with a sense of excitement and purpose. He immediately went to his father and told him all about his meeting with Geetika.

"I'm really excited about this project, Dad," he said. "Geetika has an incredible vision for women's healthcare, and I think I could really make a difference with my technical skills."

His father smiled encouragingly. "That's great, son. I think this is a perfect opportunity for you."

Parth nodded, feeling grateful for his father's support. "But what about freelancing opportunities?" he asked. "You've always encouraged me to explore different avenues for income."

His father nodded thoughtfully. "That's true. I still think it's important to have multiple streams of income, especially when you're just starting out. But this project with Geetika could be a great opportunity for you to really make a difference in the world. And who knows, it could lead to even more opportunities down the line."

Parth considered his father's words, realizing that he was right. He said, "You're right, Dad. I think I should take this opportunity and see where it goes. And of course, I'll continue to look for freelancing opportunities as well."

His father smiled proudly. "That's my boy! I'm proud of you, Parth. You're taking control of your future and making things happen."

"I don't want to put any additional financial burden on you, Dad. I know you agreed to pay my home loan installments, but it would be quite selfish of me to utilize your retirement funds to save my home." Parth attempted to confess.

"Don't be concerned, Parth. This is only a temporary situation in which you require my financial assistance, but I am convinced that you will find the proper opportunity shortly."

Parth was relieved to hear his father's words of assurance, but he didn't want them to bear any financial hardship as a result of his obligations, so he expressed his thoughts, "Thank you for your trust in me, Dad, but I think I should sell my flat and put the funds into this new venture with Geetika."

Parth's father was taken aback by this proposition, " Are you sure, Parth? This is a significant decision."

"Dad, I am quite confident about this new venture. I believe I should take this risk." Parth responded with assurance.

Parth's father said after some thought, "All right, Parth. If you are certain of what you are doing, then go ahead".

"Dad, thank you so much! But what about social pressure? Will you be embarrassed if your son needs to sell his flat, which he purchased with great fanfare?" Parth inquired, embarrassed.

"Don't be worried. Our friends and family is already mocking us because our 27-year-old son is unemployed. Now they'll add another taunt to it," Parth's father burst into laughter, "*but jokes aside, people will always say things. If we start paying attention to whatever they say, we'll never be able to take responsibility for our life.*"

Parth felt a sense of gratitude for his father's support and encouragement. He knew that with his father by his side, he could accomplish anything he set his mind to.

"Thank you, Dad. I promise, one day I will make you proud!" He thanked his father and made a mental note to continue to seek his father's advice and guidance as he embarked on this new journey with Geetika.

Parth started working with Geetika on the project. With his experience at HealthTech he was able to bring new insights into the concept Geetika had about the project and its complexities. As they worked together on the project, their online meetings turned into daily conversations. As they continued to talk, Parth found himself drawn to Geetika's energy and enthusiasm. She spoke passionately about the work she was doing and the impact it was having on the lives of women in her community. Parth admired her dedication and felt a growing sense of respect for her.

He found that he was enjoying his conversations with Geetika more and more with each passing day. He admired her intelligence, her sense of humor, and her unwavering commitment to helping others. He found himself feeling a sense of connection with her that he had never felt before. He felt a rush of excitement as he thought about the possibility of exploring a relationship with Geetika. However, he also felt a sense of hesitation. He didn't want to jeopardize the friendship they had just started to build, but at the same time, he didn't want to miss out on a chance to get to know her on a deeper level.

They discussed the project's progress and brainstormed new ideas, but they also found themselves talking about their personal lives. Despite their growing connection and chemistry, they both knew that their focus needed to be on the project. They didn't want to complicate things by acknowledging their feelings for each other, so they kept it professional.

Six months later, they were able to assemble a tiny team of 3 developers working out of shared office space. They had a plan sketched out for how to build their application. With Parth's leadership, the first version of app's development was completed in a lightning-fast six months. As the launch date approached, they both felt a sense of excitement and anticipation. They had poured their hearts and souls into this project, and they couldn't wait to see it come to fruition.

Finally, the day arrived. The application was launched successfully, and it was an instant hit. Users loved the user-friendly interface and the innovative features. Parth and Geetika celebrated their success together, feeling a sense of pride and accomplishment.

Sitting in a restaurant having dinner together, Geetika opened a discussion.

She smiled at Parth, feeling a rush of emotions. "You know, Parth, I've always appreciated your company and found it very intriguing. I've always been drawn to your simplicity and how grounded you are," she said.

Parth couldn't believe what he was hearing. He had always hoped that Geetika felt the same way he did. "I feel the same way about you, Geetika! I admire your passion and determination towards your work. And I feel like we connect on so many levels," he said, his heart racing.

Geetika looked down at her plate, a shy smile forming on her lips. "I know this might sound cliché, but I never thought I'd find someone who understands me the way you do. It's like we're on the same wavelength," she said.

There was a pause and silence after that, with Geetika hoping that Parth would speak up and add more to what she had just said.

Parth mustered up the courage and said, "Geetika, I know this might be sudden, but would you be interested in exploring our relationship beyond friendship? I've always felt a strong connection between us, and I don't want to miss out on the possibility of us being together."

Geetika blushed as Parth took her hand in his, feeling a warm and comforting sensation spread through her body. Her heart was beating faster as she gazed into Parth's eyes. She couldn't believe that they were finally having this conversation, and that Parth felt the same way she did. She felt a wave of tenderness wash over her as she listened to him pour out his heart, his voice filled with emotion.

As the night wore on, Geetika knew that this was just the beginning of a beautiful journey with Parth. She felt a sense of excitement and anticipation for what was to come, and she knew that no matter what, she would always cherish the memory of this special moment between them.

As they had finally let out their feelings for each other, Parth felt the need to discuss more about their personal lives. He told Geetika, "Geetika, you know what?"

With a certain excitement, Geetika inquired, "Yes, tell me!"

"It's been about twelve months now, but we hardly know each other apart from our work. I think there is a need to break the ice; let me be the first one to do that."

Parth then went on and shared with Geetika about his parents. How they meant the world to him, and in this conversation, he even opened up about his devotion towards the Bhagavad Gita. Geetika looked deeply into his eyes as he spoke about his family and his values. She was intrigued by his vision of life and felt herself drawn further closer to him with each passing moment.

"I think it's amazing how you put your family at the center of your life," she said, smiling warmly. "It's so important to have that kind of support system."

Parth nodded, a hint of pride in his voice, as he spoke about his parents. "They've always been my rock," he said. "And Murli, he's been such an important mentor to me. He taught me so much about the Bhagavad Gita and how to apply its principles to everyday life."

Geetika heard Parth talk about Murli with a lot of respect, so she asked, "Are you still in touch with Murli?"

"I kept in touch with him for the first six months, but then I lost contact with him owing to our rigorous project work. He is also not active on social media, and the only way to contact him is by phone," Parth answered, a little disappointed.

Parth's voice was upset, but Geetika tried to reassure him, "That's how it works. We become so preoccupied that we lose connection with people who were once very important to us. Yet, his teachings will always be with you".

Parth felt reassured and decided to contact Murli first thing the next morning. He said, "Yes Geetika, that's true. He has explained the principles of the Bhagavad Gita in such simple and practically implementable way that I have been able to benefit from many of them during the development and launch of our also project."

Geetika leaned forward in her chair, intent on hearing more. "What kind of principles are we discussing?" she inquired.

"Well, one of the main ideas is the importance of selfless action," Parth explained. "It's all about focusing on the greater good and not just our own desires or needs. When we act selflessly, we become more connected to others and to the universe as a whole."

Geetika listened intently, feeling a sense of wonder at the depth of Parth's beliefs. "That's really beautiful," she said. "And it makes a lot of sense, too. I feel like we could all benefit from putting ourselves in other people's shoes more often."

Parth smiled, feeling a deep sense of connection with Geetika. "Exactly! And that's why I'm so passionate about our project," he said. "It's going to make a real difference in people's lives, and I think we have the potential to do some really amazing things together."

Geetika's heart fluttered at Parth's words. She had always admired his dedication and intelligence, but now she felt herself drawn to him in a way that went beyond mere admiration.

"I feel the same way," she said softly. "I can't wait to see where this takes us."

Parth's eyes sparkled with excitement as he gazed back at her. "Me neither," he said. "I think we're going to do some truly incredible things together, Geetika."

He then confidently inquired in a courteous tone about Geetika's life. He had no clue that Geetika's life had a pretty dark past attached to it. As they continued to talk, Geetika found herself opening up to him in ways she never had before. She felt a sense of trust that she had never experienced with anyone else, and it made her heart swell with affection. Parth was surprised when he heard about the challenges that Geetika had faced in her life. He had always admired her strength and resilience, but he had never imagined that she had gone through something as difficult as an abusive relationship.

"I had no idea, Geetika," he said, his voice filled with concern. "I'm so sorry that you had to go through all that."

Geetika nodded, her eyes filled with a mix of sadness and determination. "It was a really tough time, but as your mentor Murli has said, everything occurs for a reason. That appears to be the case for me as well," she said, smiling. "That abusive relationship is what sparked the idea for this project. I wanted to create something that would help other women like me who face similar challenges."

Parth felt a sense of admiration for Geetika's strength and her commitment to making a positive impact on the world. "That's amazing," he said. "I had no idea that our project was so personal for you. It makes me even more excited to be working on it."

Geetika smiled, feeling a sense of connection with Parth that went beyond their shared passion for the project. "I'm really grateful to be working with you," she said. "It feels like we're both bringing our own unique experiences and perspectives to the table, and that's going to make our work even more powerful."

Parth nodded, he knew that working with her was going to be a transformative experience, both personally and professionally.

"As hard as it was to go through that experience, yet I'm grateful for it," Geetika said. "It taught me a lot about resilience and determination, and it gave me the strength to pursue my dreams."

"I believe there is nothing we can't accomplish together with you at my side." Parth stated as he took Geetika's hand in his.

As they talked about their personal lives, Parth couldn't help but feel a sense of contentment and happiness. He knew that he had found someone special, someone who he could spend the rest of his life with.

Geetika too felt the same way, as she listened to Parth talk about his hopes and dreams for the future. She realized that she had found someone who shared her values and beliefs, someone who she could trust and rely on. Parth's words had touched something deep inside her, and Geetika felt herself falling even more in love with him. She couldn't help but smile at the thought of exploring their relationship further, of getting to know Parth on an even deeper level.

Finally, the date night had come to an end. Parth and Geetika called for an Uber, both feeling a sense of excitement and nervousness. As they got into the cab, they couldn't help but feel a rush of emotions. They knew that the connection between them was strong, but they had never expected to confess their feelings to each other that night.

Parth, without saying a word, reached for Geetika's hand, their fingers intertwining. Geetika's heart skipped a beat as she felt a tingling sensation run through her body. She looked at him with deep emotion, unable to express what she was feeling in words. In that moment, she knew that Parth was the one she had been waiting for all her life.

As the cab drove through the quiet streets of Pune, Parth wished that the ride would never end. He savored every moment with Geetika, wanting to make it last forever. Finally, they arrived at Geetika's place. She leaned in to kiss Parth on the cheek, and without turning back, she quickly rushed towards her house, but before she could make it to the door, Parth called out her name.

Geetika turned around, wondering what Parth wanted to say, and she was constantly blushing, thinking about the special moment between her and Parth. To her surprise, he had gotten out of the car and was walking towards her. As he approached her, he grabbed her in his arms and kissed her passionately. Geetika was caught off guard, but she didn't resist. She wrapped her arms around him, feeling like she was on top of the world.

The Uber driver watched in amusement as the couple shared a romantic moment. He couldn't help but whistle, congratulating them.

Parth laughed as he walked back to the car, feeling like he was on cloud nine. Geetika was equally amused and excited about what had just happened.

As the car drove away, Geetika couldn't stop thinking about the moment Parth held her in his arms.

After that magical night, Parth and Geetika couldn't seem to get enough of each other. They worked together on their project, bouncing ideas off each other and inspiring each other to be the best they could be. As their project flourished, so did their relationship. They became inseparable, spending long hours together at the office and then going out for dinner or a movie.

Over the course of two years, their business flourished as their relationship. Their product became the market leader in the women's healthcare segment. The team had grown from 3 to more than 100 in just two years. They took care of their employees like family, and everybody was doing their bit to sustain the number one spot.

On a quite Sunday morning, Parth decided to go for a walk in the neighboring garden after finishing his meditation. In spite of the cold, the early sun in Pune casts a lovely glow over the city. Strolling through the garden, Parth's thoughts turned to the three years he had spent going from a struggling employee at HealthTech to the CEO of one of the most promising startup businesses. It had been nearly six months since he had last spoken with Murli, so he decided to give him a call.

"Good morning! Murli, how are you?" Murli was greeted enthusiastically by Parth.

"Hello there, Parth! I'm fine. How are you doing?" Murli shared Parth's enthusiasm.

Parth told Murli about his company's efforts to improve the lives of women all around the world, as well as how successful his start-up had become.

"Parth, I am happy for you. Keep up the fantastic effort, no matter what!" Murli's voice was as encouraging as ever.

"Yes, Murli! Whenever I feel stuck, your teachings serve as a beacon for me." Parth said with gratitude in his voice. He then reiterated his relationship with Geetika.

"I'm delighted to hear your relationship with her is flourishing with each passing day. If you're certain she's the one you want to spend the rest of your life with, don't waste any time, my friend!" Murli smiled as he encouraged Parth as they kept talking about it for a few more minutes.

"I wasn't sure whether I should ask her to marry me, Murli, but as we talked, I have realized she's the one I want to be with for the rest of my life. Thank you, Murli! You continue to guide me on my life's journey." Parth thanked Murli as he hung up the phone.

Parth knew that he had found his soulmate in Geetika, and

he couldn't wait to spend the rest of his life with her. So, one day, he decided to take her out for a romantic dinner to a special place that held a lot of significance for them. As they sat there, enjoying each other's company, Parth could feel his heart racing with anticipation.

He took a deep breath, reached across the table to take Geetika's hand, and looked deeply into her eyes. "Geetika, you know that you are the most important person in my life. I love you more than words can express, and I can't imagine spending a single day without you by my side. So, what I'm trying to say is...will you marry me?" he asked, his voice trembling with emotion.

Geetika's eyes widened in surprise and delight as she heard his words. She felt a wave of happiness wash over her as she looked into his eyes, and without hesitation, she said yes. Parth gazed deeply into Geetika's eyes, his heart pounding with joy and excitement. He had always known that there was something special about her, but he never imagined that she would also be willing to spend the rest of her life with him.

They spent the rest of the evening talking about their future together, dreaming of all the adventures they would have and the memories they would make. And soon enough, the day arrived when they exchanged their vows in a beautiful ceremony surrounded by their parents and friends.

As they stood there, hand in hand, gazing into each other's eyes, Parth knew that he had made the best decision of his life. He knew that he would always cherish this moment, and the love that they shared would only continue to grow stronger with each passing day.

25

# THE DAWN OF SECOND CHANCES

N ow, a year later, Parth and Geetika were celebrating their first wedding anniversary in Goa. To keep the spark alive in their marriage, they intended to take annual anniversary trips. They had taken a whole week off from their hectic schedules to spend time with each other. The sun was shining brightly, and the beach was calling out to them. They walked hand in hand along the shore, enjoying the sound of the waves crashing against the shore and the salty smell of the sea. As they strolled down the path, they couldn't help but reminisce about the journey they had shared together. Their steps were light and carefree.

They were staying at a luxurious beachfront resort. Parth observed a Mercedes arrive at the resort's lobby and a chubby man in suit get out of the car while he and his wife waited for their chauffeur to deliver their car so they could go shopping. Parth was staring at him, puzzled, as he tried to recall the man's face.

Geetika was curious: "Who is he, Parth? Do you know him?"

Parth was frustrated: "I don't know, love. I feel like I've

seen him before, but I can't recall —where?"

The man finally caught up to them and enveloped Parth in a bear hug, much to his surprise. "Parth, my friend! You've erased me from your memory, haven't you?"

Parth was bewildered. "I'm sorry, but I can't seem to remember you."

The man chuckled, "It's Karan, buddy. Karan Malhotra from HealthTech!"

Parth's jaw dropped. "Karan? What happened to you?" Karan's metamorphosis from dashing boy to pudgy middle-aged man with a ghostly appearance shocked Parth.

Karan laughed, "Oh, so it's that bad, huh?"

Parth was mortified. "I didn't mean it like that, Karan. I'm sorry."

Karan waved his hand dismissively and said, "No worries, man. It happens all the time. But to my surprise, Parth, you appear even younger than you were four years ago."

Parth accepted the compliment with a smile and said, "Hey, let me introduce you to my lovely wife, Geetika."

Geetika smiled and said, "Hi, I'm Geetika. It's nice to meet you."

Karan smirked, "Ah, so you're the one who finally managed to get Parth to settle down. I used to work with him, you know. But now, I've gained some weight."

Parth interjected, "Enough with the jokes, Karan. What have you been up to these past four years? Do you still work with HealthTech? How is Aman doing?" Parth threw a barrage of probing questions to Karan.

Karan's face darkened as he recounted Aman's grave mis-judgment in laying off some of his finest employees and letting go of Murli. HealthTech lost its edge and was unable to retain clients, while new sales became a distant dream.

Parth was stunned to hear about Aman's downfall, and he probed further about what happened to the company.

With a hint of bitterness, Karan divulged that Aman sold the company in a hasty deal and fled Pune for good. He had lost his dynamism and was influenced by Maya, whom he had married after his divorce with Anita.

Parth listened with rapt attention as Karan unleashed his anger, expressing his fondness for Anita and her kindness in divorcing Aman without taking a single penny from him.

Parth interrupted, "Is Maya still with Aman?"

Karan's response was scathing. "No, she was only attached to his wealth and success. After his career downfall, she left him, taking most of his wealth in a divorce settlement. She made his life a living hell. Now, Aman is working as a project manager for an IT company."

Parth was left speechless, his hand instinctively covering his mouth as he took in the information. In his heart, he silently prayed for Aman, wishing him well despite everything that had happened. He thought to himself that maybe it was Karma, for everything that Aman had done to them had come back to him. Nonetheless, Parth couldn't help but remember the time when Aman was his role model.

"Where are you working these days?" Parth inquired of Karan.

As Karan continued speaking, his tone turned boastful and condescending. He wanted to showcase his success to Parth and make him feel inferior. His words carried a hint of arrogance and a desire to one-up his former colleague. Karan went on to talk about his current position as Chief Technology Officer at a Bangalore startup, with 10% ownership of the company. His words were filled with a sense of achievement and satisfaction, highlighting his success and superiority. Karan's boastful tone and desire to belittle Parth indicated a sense of insecurity and the need for validation. Despite his achievements, it seemed he still felt the need to prove himself and gain recognition from others.

"I am really happy for your Karan," Parth said with genuine joy in his voice." What brings you to Goa?"

"I'm here to meet with some of our customers." As Karan was speaking, a red Ferrari came up to the resort's porch, drawing everyone's attention.  The chauffeur approached Parth and Geetika.

"If you wish to go, Ma'am, we're ready." He asked Geetika.

"I'm sorry, Karan, I would have loved to spend more time with you, but I have promised Geetika that I would take her shopping," Parth remarked, a trace of regret in his voice.

Parth was interrupted by Geetika. "It's all right, honey. After four years, you finally saw your friend. You two continue your conversation. I'll go ahead regardless; your clothing choices are anyway terrible," she exclaimed, laughing.

"Very funny!" Parth responded with a grin and questioned, "Are you sure?"

"Absolutely, you guys enjoy it," Geetika said as she approached the car.

"Is this your car?" Karan was astonished.

Parth, still looking after Geetika as she sped away, said, "Yeah, Geetika enjoys sports cars, so we decided to buy one last year."

Karan was stumped. "What do you do, Parth?" he inquired. "What do you do for a living?"

"Since we have the rest of the evening to ourselves, let's grab a bite and have a chat over coffee at the restaurant." Parth put his hand around Karan's shoulders as they walked into the restaurant in the resort.

As they were sipping their coffee, Parth launched into an animated story about his life after HealthTech. He told Karan all about Geetika, the incredible woman he'd met, and the success they'd found with their latest project. But what really caught Karan's attention was the enthusiasm with which Parth spoke about the transformation he'd undergone after diving deep into the teachings of the Bhagavad Gita.

Karan then understood, with a sinking feeling in his stomach, that Parth had surpassed him in every respect. Despite Karan's dishonest victory in the competition, Parth had managed to outshine him. Karan felt a mix of envy, regret, and shame as he realized this. There was no use in trying to impress Parth with his supposed accomplishments, he told himself, feeling defeated and humiliated.

As Parth asked Karan, "Where did you get lost, Karan?" he snapped out of his reverie.

After taking a deep breath to calm himself, Karan began telling his story to Parth, who listened attentively, his eyes fixed on Karan with empathy and concern. As Karan shared his struggles and despair over his current situation, he felt a wave of vulnerability wash over him. He spoke openly and honestly, revealing a deep sense of emptiness and dissatisfaction, despite his material success.

Parth straightaway inquired about Nidhi. He knew that Nidhi and Karan were dating during his exit from HealthTech and were even planning to get married soon. Karan's face changed when Nidhi's name was mentioned. His smile turned sarcastic, and his tone became sombre. "Oh, Nidhi," he said. "Yeah, we got married right after I got promoted. Things were good for a while, but then she changed so much. We had to part ways."

Parth was shocked. "What? You guys got divorced?" he exclaimed.

Karan nodded. "Yeah, it wasn't easy," he said. "But sometimes things just don't work out, you know?"

Parth could feel the weight of the situation settling in. He wanted to express his condolences, but he wasn't sure what to say. "I'm so sorry, man," he said finally, and then Karan took over the conversation, telling them about the struggles he faced with Nidhi's erratic behavior and the depression he got into during the process of getting a divorce.

He paused, gathering his thoughts, before continuing. "Nidhi and I had a lot of good times together, but things started to change after we got married. She became more and more distant, and I couldn't figure out what was going on. Eventually, I found out she'd been seeing someone else."

Karan's voice grew quiet, and Parth could sense the pain in his words. "It was like my whole world had come crashing down," Karan continued. "I didn't know what to do. I tried to make things work, but she just wasn't interested. We fought all the time, and it just got worse and worse."

He looked up at Parth, his eyes haunted. "It was the lowest point in my life," he said. "I didn't want to get out of bed; I couldn't eat, and I couldn't sleep. I felt like a failure. I'd put everything into that relationship, and it had all fallen apart."

"But you got through it," Parth said, trying to offer some comfort.

Parth's understanding nod and gentle touch on Karan's shoulder made him feel heard and validated. "Yeah, eventually," he said. "It took a lot of time and a lot of therapy, but I came out the other side. I realized that I couldn't keep blaming myself for what happened. It was a two-way street, and Nidhi made choices too. I had to learn to forgive both of us and move on."

There was a moment of silence as both men let the weight of the conversation settle in. Parth's mind was reeling from the shock of Karan's divorce announcement, but he pulled himself together.

As they kept discussing their old days at HealthTech, Karan realized that he had to go out for dinner with his customers.

"Sorry, Parth, I have to leave now for dinner with my customers, but it would be great if we could catch up for breakfast tomorrow morning," Karan asked.

"Sure man, 8 o'clock?" Parth replied.

"You got it," Karan got up from his chair, thanking Parth for an interesting talk.

As Karan was leaving the restaurant, he turned back and said, "I want to confess something, Parth," with guilt in his eyes.

"What is it, Karan?" Parth inquired, intrigued.

With hesitation, Karan eventually gathered up the nerve to confess the truth. "I was the one who had screwed up your code with the help of Rahul."

Parth was taken aback with Karan's confession, feeling a mix of surprise and betrayal.

"Yes, Parth, and I sincerely apologize. For the past four years, this guilt has been eating me from within." Karan admitted, his voice shaking.

Parth was lost for words as he sat there frozen. But as Karan continued to speak, Parth saw the guilt and remorse in his friend's eyes, and he began to feel a sense of empathy towards him. Parth could see the pain that his friend was going through and felt a sense of compassion towards him. He knew that holding onto this guilt would only hurt Karan in the long run, and he wanted to help him find a way to move forward.

Gradually gathering himself together, Parth said, "I would have been furious if I had known this a few years ago, but looking back, losing my job at HealthTech was the best thing that ever happened to me. Otherwise, I would have been a frog in the pond, trying to make the best of whatever was available in that pond itself. But, after losing my job, I was able to reflect and find purpose in my life, which widened my perspective about career options. I was able to reunite with my parents, meet Geetika, and create such a fantastic business. I now firmly believe what Murli used to tell us: *Accept situations as they are; whatever happens is for the best if you are willing to look on the bright side of things.*"

He then stood up, touched Karan on his shoulder, and pacified him, saying, "It's OK, Karan; I forgive you. You no longer have to live with this guilt."

Karan felt like the weight on his shoulder had been removed after years. He hugged Parth and complimented him for having a great heart that could forgive him even after such a dreadful act. In the end, Karan left the restaurant feeling a sense of closure and renewed hope for the future. He knew that he still had a lot of work to do to overcome his guilt, but he was willing to put in the effort and make things right.

Parth reflected on how Aman and Karan had gone from promising young men to ordinary guys just trying to make it through life. He felt terrible for Karan because he had the same opportunity to be happy that he had by putting into practice the wisdom they had gained from Murli. In the midst of his internal monologue, Geetika returned from her shopping spree, and the two set out for a stroll along the beach.

Next morning, as the first rays of dawn seeped through the curtains, Parth stirred from his peaceful slumber, while Geetika still slept soundly. Rising from his bed, he embarked on his customary morning routine of meditation and yoga, seeking a serene state of mind. His mind wandered to his conversation with Karan the previous day, filled with empathy for what Karan had to go through. Gazing out of the window, the breath-taking view of the beach and the clear blue sky provided a soothing balm for his thoughts.

Later in the morning, Parth and Geetika were waiting for Karan's arrival for breakfast. "Hey guys, nice to see you again." Karan greeted them cheerfully.

Parth greeted Karan warmly and invited him to join them for breakfast. For a while, they all chatted cheerfully, catching up on old times and exchanging news.

"Karan, you should have listened to Murli. Life would have turned out differently." Parth expressed his disappointment.

Karan sat there listening intently, his eyes wide with wonder. "Yes, Parth! I remember those sessions with Murli," he reflected wistfully. "But I never took it seriously. I was too preoccupied with my own ambitions."

Parth reached out to console his friend. "Hey, it's never too late to make a change," he stated emphatically. "You still have a lot of potential, Karan. Never give up on yourself."

Karan's face softened, and hope glowed in his eyes. "Do you really believe that?" he inquired eagerly.

Parth gave a warm smile. "Certainly," he replied. "And you know what else? Geetika and I will be with you every step of the way."

Geetika nodded, her eyes twinkling with compassion. "We're all in it together," she explained. "And we'll make certain you find the happiness and success you deserve."

Karan felt a newfound warmth spread through his chest, and he felt a glimmer of hope for his future for the first time in a long time. Maybe, just maybe, he can change his ways and find a new sense of purpose.

He inquired about Murli's well-being after Parth mentioned him. "I owe Murli a debt of gratitude for introducing me to the Bhagavad Gita, Parth. However, I am ashamed of myself for not having the courage to walk the path. What is he doing now?"

"After leaving HealthTech, he and Ruchi Didi moved to their hometown near Coimbatore," Parth responded. "They run a one-of-a-kind school there."

"Really? What's so special about it?" Geetika inquired, surprised.

"Murli was always disappointed that the divine wisdom of the Bhagavad Gita and the power of our minds were never taught in schools. Beside regular academics, this school focuses on training young children's minds to achieve great success."

"That's incredible!" Karan exclaimed.

"But wait, there's more! He also runs an orphanage where he offers the same high-quality education to underprivileged children." Parth informed further.

"Hat's off to him and his wife!" Geetika couldn't stop herself from admiring Murli and Ruchi. "You didn't tell me about it, Parth. We should help them through our CSR programs."

"That's a fantastic idea." Parth took Geetika's hand in his and said, "I was about to ask you about this."

Karan couldn't help but admire Parth and Geetika's respect for one another.

Parth gave Karan a friendly smile. "What's stopping you from connecting with Murli for guidance?" he asked after a brief pause. "I can assure you that his teachings changed my life."

"You're right," Karan said, reflecting on Parth's words. "I was so stupid that I didn't seek assistance from such a remarkable person." He, then, congratulated Geetika on her achievements and wished them both the best.

Geetika thought Karan was a wonderful person who had learned a lot about life after going through a difficult time. "Remember now that you're starting over, there's more to life," she advised.

"Thank you both for your amazing support. I'll leave you guys now to enjoy the rest of this romantic vacation," Karan said, bidding them farewell with a mischievous grin.

The conversation between the three friends was heartwarming, with Parth and Geetika showing their kindness and support for Karan. Parth's disappointment at Karan's lack of progress in life was evident, but he didn't judge him for it. Instead, he offered encouragement and support, showing that he believed in Karan's potential. The conversation highlighted the importance of having a support system and the impact it can have on one's life. They said their goodbyes while laughing heartily.

Parth couldn't help but take Geetika's delicate hands into his own as they found themselves alone. "I am so grateful to have met you," he said solemnly, gazing deeply into her eyes.

Geetika, on the other hand, couldn't help but tease him. "Hmm, really?" she inquired, a sly grin playing across her lips.

Parth, taken aback, quickly responded, "Why? Do you have any doubts about how much I adore you, my love?"

Geetika simply laughed at his reaction, reveling in their playful banter. She then revealed what had piqued her interest earlier. She mentioned how Parth's face lit up when Nidhi's name had come up in conversation with Karan.

Parth was taken aback by her observation and struggled to find the right words to explain his reaction. He finally mustered the courage to admit, "Yes, I had a crush on her back then. But she ended up going with Karan over me."

Even though Geetika was aware of this, she was curious about Parth's past. Parth, on the other hand, was eager to move on from the subject, claiming that Nidhi was just a forgotten memory.

Geetika's curiosity took an unexpected turn when she inquired, "Was she pretty?"

Parth paused, not wanting to offend Geetika, but he knew he couldn't avoid the question. "Yes, she was a very beautiful girl," he admitted.

For a brief moment, silence fell between them, but Geetika quickly hugged Parth, declaring, "You are mine, only mine." It was a tender moment between them, reaffirming their feelings for one another.

When Karan bid farewell to Parth and Geetika, he was filled with excitement for the road ahead, eagerly anticipating his meeting with Murli, but at the same time he was worried if Murli would like to meet him at all after he had blatantly ignored all his teachings. As he was walking towards his hotel room filled with dilemmas, he saw a quote from the Bhagavad Gita framed on a wall:

उद्धरेदात्मनात्मानं नात्मानमवसादयेत् ।
आत्मैव ह्यात्मनो बन्धुरात्मैव रिपुरात्मन:

**Elevate yourself through the power of your mind, and not degrade yourself, for the mind can be the friend and also the enemy of the self.**

Reading the quote from the Bhagavad Gita, he felt a sense of clarity wash over him. He realized that his worries and doubts were only holding him back, and that he needed to focus on elevating himself and his thoughts. He took a deep breath to let go of his concerns thus choosing to trust in his own abilities and in the journey ahead.

He had always been a believer in the power of the mind, and he knew that he needed to harness that power now more than ever. He repeated the words of the quote to himself, determined to make them his mantra for the road ahead.

As he walked down the alley, Karan felt a renewed sense of purpose and determination. He knew that meeting Murli would not be easy, but he was ready to face whatever challenges lay ahead. He would keep his mind as a friend and not an enemy, and he would stay focused on his goals.

With this newfound resolve, Karan opened the door to his room, ready to begin his *journey from crisis to clarity.*